F

Praise for
A HEART TO SERVE

"Few men have lived a life as remarkable as this! Bill Frist's story—from crude operating rooms in the Sudan to the highest post in the U.S. Senate—provides unique perspectives on many of the major issues of our times."
— Frederick W. Smith, chairman and CEO, FedEx Corporation

"Dr. Frist is an extraordinary individual. Nurtured in a family that modeled the values of common sense, hard work, love for country, and compassion for those who are hurting, [he] has resisted being intoxicated by his great success—first, in the operating room as a heart transplant surgeon, then more recently in the halls of power in Washington. Instead, he has consistently chosen to serve others. . . . A HEART TO SERVE will inspire you to . . . become—like Dr. Frist—a force for the good of others. I heartily recommend this book."
— Franklin Graham, president,
Billy Graham Evangelistic Association, Samaritan's Purse

"Doctor Frist's message is simple: Discover your passions, then use them to serve. Part insider's account of the Senate, part captivating storytelling, part personal revelation of how values color leadership, this compelling book is a clarion call to action to figure out how we can best serve. From the accounts of anonymous mission work in Sudan, the dramatic emergency response to the shooting of General David Petraeus and Capitol police officers, to a mother's quiet gifts and a brother's dream of serving millions through health care, the reader is inspired by the potential and power of service."
— Senator Orrin G. Hatch

"Dr. Frist leads us on an engaging journey of principled action through a life of leadership grounded in family and community values. Thank God that we have humanitarians like Bill Frist to lead and bring awareness to worldwide poverty."
— Jerry West, former NBA all-star and executive

more . . .

"As a heart surgeon colleague, I have profound insights into Senator Frist's expertise inside your chest, yet I am even more impressed by the passion burning inside his. Learn about leadership from one of this nation's great public servants."   —Mehmet C. Oz, MD

"Bill Frist reminds us all in this compelling book that politics and public service are about far more than winning elections. They're about the commitment, compassion, and courage that good leaders bring to the noble causes they pursue. Bill Frist had those qualities in abundance, and the United States Senate was a better place because of him."   —Senator Edward M. Kennedy

"A wonderful collection of inspirational examples of leadership, public service, and compassion for others."
                                        —General David H. Petraeus

"Whether he's in his surgeon's mask in a hospital in Uganda, or in cuff links in the marbled halls of DC, Bill Frist is working hard to save and improve the lives of the poorest people on the planet. He's an inspiration."
            —Bono, lead singer of U2 and co-founder of the anti-poverty
                                        advocacy organization, ONE

"In A HEART TO SERVE, Bill Frist draws upon his family legacy, his personal faith, and his experiences as both a cardiothoracic surgeon and a United States Senator, offering readers a sincere self-portrait of one of our nation's most dedicated leaders in health care policy."
—President Bill Clinton, founder, William J. Clinton Foundation,
                                        42nd President of the United States

A HEART TO
SERVE

The Passion to Bring Health, Hope, and Healing

FORMER U.S. SENATE MAJORITY LEADER
WILLIAM H. FRIST, MD

CENTER
STREET®

NEW YORK   BOSTON   NASHVILLE

Center Street
Hachette Book Group
237 Park Avenue
New York, NY 10017

www.centerstreet.com

Center Street is a division of Hachette Book Group, Inc.
The Center Street name and logo are trademarks of Hachette Book Group, Inc.

Printed in the United States of America

First Edition: October 2009
10 9 8 7 6 5 4 3 2 1

Library of Congress Cataloging-in-Publication Data

Frist, William H.
  A heart to serve : the passion to bring health, hope, and healing / Bill Frist.—1st ed.
    p. cm.
  Includes index.
  ISBN 978-1-59995-016-7
  1. Frist, William H. 2. Legislators—United States—Biography. 3. United States. Congress. Senate—Biography. 4. United States. Congress. Senate—Majority leaders—Biography. 5. Surgeons—United States—Biography. 6. Physicians—Tennessee—Biography. I. Title.

  E840.8.F75A3 2009
  328.73'092—dc22
  [B]
                                  2009012397

Book design by Charles Sutherland

CONTENTS

1

Mission of Mercy

The single-engine ten-passenger Cessna Caravan dipped dangerously low, a mere four hundred feet above the large trees and sparse brush dotting the sands of southern Sudan. I could feel the African heat rising from the earth below. I was flying under the radar to avoid detection by the Sudanese government's high-flying bombers and the fourteen ominous helicopter gunships they had stationed at nearby Juba.

Our circuitous journey had begun more than six hours earlier, just before sunrise, in Nairobi, Kenya. There we had filed an ambiguous flight plan so no one could track our plane. We were flying into Sudan clandestinely, without permission and decidedly against the will of the regime in Khartoum, which the United States had formally designated as a supporter of terrorism. Since the United States had no diplomatic relations with the huge African country, we had no passports, no visas, and no official documentation. Nobody in the U.S. government knew our whereabouts or our intentions. Though our plane was full of medical supplies and we were on a mission of mercy, we were sneaking into the Islamic Republic of Sudan at our own risk.

We flew first to Entebbe, Uganda, landing just in front of the old, bullet-pocked terminal—the scene, some twenty-two years earlier, of the famous 1976 Israeli commando raid that liberated nearly one hundred Air France passengers and crew members who'd been taken hostage by Palestinian terrorists. We quickly refueled the Caravan and headed northwest to Bunia in the Democratic Republic of Congo. Then we veered north and dropped to barely above tree level, surreptitiously entering southern Sudan.

We were on our way to the remote region called Lui (pronounced *Louie*), about a thousand miles south of Khartoum, Sudan's capital city, and five hundred miles west of the Nile. There, a makeshift medical clinic had been opened a few months earlier by Samaritan's Purse, the Christian-based humanitarian relief organization headed by Reverend Franklin Graham. No more than an old schoolhouse with one doctor and a few Sudanese assistants—brave and willing, but with no formal medical training— the clinic at Lui was the only medical facility for half a million residents in that part of Sudan.

For the six of us in the Caravan, it had already been an arduous trip, and the element of risk loomed larger as we approached our destination. We were flying into the midst of an ongoing civil war between northern and southern Sudan. The National Islamic Front that controlled the Government of Sudan (GOS)—the same government that harbored Osama bin Laden for five years—was conducting a scorched-earth policy in an effort to wipe out the black African Christians, animists, and non-Arab Muslims living in southern Sudan. In response, a rebel movement known as the Sudan People's Liberation Army (SPLA) had emerged in the early 1980s.

It wasn't easy to distinguish the good guys from the bad guys in this war. They were fighting over water, potentially massive oil reserves, and political clout, their battles fueled by racial and religious resentments. But story after horrible story bore witness to atrocities by the Khartoum regime. The GOS tortured and killed indiscriminately, raping women and young girls repeatedly, and forcing men, women, and children into slavery. Although I couldn't condone everything the SPLA had done, I sympathized with the people of southern Sudan and their plight under the persecution by the regime in Khartoum, and I had come to know their popular and charismatic leader, John Garang (who subsequently became a close friend), and his ragtag rebels who opposed the forces of the GOS and its terrorist-sponsoring president, Omar al-Bashir. Nevertheless, the medical team of which I was a part was committed to providing medical care to anyone who needed it.

At the time of my first trip to Lui, in early 1998, the civil war had dragged on for more than fourteen years. War had pushed the population into areas where food and water were sparse, leading to widespread famine and disease. More than two million people had already died. A recently intensified aerial bombing campaign by the GOS had forced millions more to flee their homes, abandoning their small patches of farmland or traditional cattle grazing areas.

In Lui, the primitive hospital and a tiny church were practically the only permanent structures, and both buildings were frequent targets of GOS bombardment. This was especially galling, since some of the government's own Islamic troops, captured by the rebels, had been treated by doctors at the facility.

Although I was a sitting United States senator, I was traveling to Sudan as a private citizen—a physician by trade—on a medical mission sponsored by Samaritan's Purse. I'd been invited by Dr. Dick Furman, a general and thoracic surgeon from Boone, North Carolina. He and his brother Lowell for years had taken a month off each year to volunteer their services to fill in for full-time medical missionaries in the developing world. Soon they were recruiting other surgeons to do the same, then medical doctors, nurses, and technicians. Their idea grew and grew, becoming World Medical Mission, a faith-based organization committed to sending hundreds of doctors each year to Third World countries, including some in the most dangerous parts of Africa.

I'd met Dick through my older brother, Bobby, who'd trained with Dick during surgical residency at the University of Kentucky in Lexington. Later, Dick and his wife, Harriet, would visit Bobby and his wife, Carol. During my medical school years, I would join them and listen to the fascinating stories about Dick's mission trips around the world. The stories reminded me of the time when our dad had taken a medical mission trip to Mexico, using it as a springboard to found a Presbyterian-based medical mission foundation. *Maybe someday*, I thought, *I'll be able to help people around the world, too.*

As for Franklin Graham, I'd met him only once before my first trip with World Medical Mission. I was coming off a plane in Nashville during my 1994 campaign for the U.S. Senate, and we recognized each other. Both of us are pilots, so we talked planes for a while. He told me that he'd just received the gift of a plane for Samaritan's Purse from the head of the Tennessee Democratic Party. Since I was working night and day to unseat a Tennessee Democrat at the time, the last thing I wanted to hear about was the kind deeds my opponents were doing! But then again, Democrats and Republicans are in this world together trying to make it a better place—though with different approaches, for sure.

Now Dick and I were making our way across sub-Saharan Africa on a mission sponsored by Franklin's organization. At the time, few had taken up the cause of the people of Sudan. The major media had barely mentioned their plight, and nobody dared risk flights into southern Sudan—nobody except gutsy, devoted pilots like the man sitting next to me, Jim Streit of AIM AIR, a church-supported group flying out of Nairobi and other mission bases around the world. Jim and his fellow pilots are a rare breed. They could easily be earning six-figure salaries flying commercially in the United States, but instead they choose to serve for paltry wages in some of the most dangerous areas of the world.

Accompanying us to Sudan were Robert Bell, an executive with Samaritan's Purse; Scott Hughett, Samaritan's Purse special projects coordinator and Dick's son-in-law; and Kenny Isaacs, who'd pioneered Samaritan's Purse's efforts in Sudan. And in a passenger seat behind me was David Charles, a young neurologist from Nashville. David had recently completed his residency at Vanderbilt University Medical Center and joined me as a policy fellow for a year in my Senate office in Washington. As I glanced back at him during the flight to Lui, I wondered whether David was questioning the wisdom of his decision. Little had he known when he'd come to Washington to study policy that two months later he would be flying with me into the bush country of war-torn Sudan!

Now the plane dipped still lower. Up ahead, just beyond a clearing, we saw a makeshift airstrip—little more than a stretch of graded dirt, just long enough to bring the Caravan to a stop. A battered jeep sat next to the landing strip, and a lone fellow stood nearby, holding a cane pole with a plastic bag tied to one end—our wind sock.

I circled the field to make sure the runway was clear of animals, then quickly brought the Caravan down for a short-field landing. No sooner had we hit the ground than I turned around and saw David's face. He was pale as a sheet yet dripping with perspiration, his eyes wide with anguish.

Thinking the bumpy ride (the last hour had been at 400 feet above the treetops to avoid detection from the air) and heat had gotten the best of David, I called back to him over the noise of the plane's engine, "David, are you doing okay?"

"No!" he shouted, pointing out the plane's window. "We're all going to die!"

I followed David's stare and saw a stream of ragtag camouflage-uniformed soldiers running out of the bushes and directly toward the plane from every direction. They looked young, almost like teenagers, but they were all brandishing Russian-made AK-47s, many raising their rifles high in the air as they approached. Regardless of their age, these boys were obviously not to be trifled with.

What did they want? Did they plan to attack us and destroy the airplane? Were they members of the Sudanese government-sponsored militia, about whom we'd been emphatically warned? We had no idea. Worse yet, we had no recourse but to watch and wait. If we tried to turn around, taxi back down the airstrip, and take off again, we'd be an easy target. With so many guns, one of them was bound to bring down our plane.

I looked back at Dick and Kenny. "Are we in the right place?" I asked.

"I sure hope so," Dick deadpanned, before cracking a hint of a smile.

For a few long seconds, we simply sat there, watching the throng of dirty, disheveled soldiers drawing ever closer to us. None of us was armed, and even if we had been, any attempt at a firefight would have been futile. David bowed his head.

A few more seconds passed; large drops of perspiration dotted our foreheads, and only partly from the intense African heat. Finally, Kenny, who was the only one of us who had been to the Sudan before, broke the silence with a joyful yelp. "Yeah, yeah," he said, his face pressed against one of the plane's windows. "These guys are on our side!"

"What?" someone gasped.

"Yeah, they're friends," Dick agreed. "I think they are here to protect us, not to hurt us."

Despite Kenny's and Dick's reassurances, we took our time opening the plane's doors. Sure enough, as we climbed out, we were greeted by the warm smiles and friendly faces for which Africa is famous. We tried not to notice the arsenal of AK-47s.

We quickly set to work unloading the food, water, and medical supplies we had brought along—bandages, surgical instruments, medicines, cots, tape, syringes, anything we'd thought we might need. Time was of the essence. Our protectors pitched in, stacking as much as possible in the jeep or on their backs, while Jim Streit refilled the fuel tanks from a fifty-five-gallon drum that we had brought with us. In a few moments, Jim was back in the cockpit, and the Caravan's propeller cranked up again. Before we'd finished loading the jeep, the plane was already taxiing down the bumpy airstrip. To remain any longer would be to invite a visit from the GOS's roving Antonov bombers.

Surrounded by the teenage soldiers, we watched as the plane lifted into the sky and headed back toward Nairobi, whence we'd come. I thought, *There goes our lifeline to safety.* No cell phones, no radio, no communication. We were on our own.

*   *   *

OUR ARMED HOSTS ESCORTED US A BUMPY FIVE MILES TO WHAT HAD once been the village of Lui. The dirt road was laced with land-mines, and occasionally our driver took a wide sweep around a warning marker in the middle of the road. We passed the old hospital, a one-story structure that had been bombed out and deserted for more than a decade, with landmines placed all around it during the recent war just to make sure that no one tried to resurrect it.

A little farther on, we saw the new "hospital," actually an abandoned schoolhouse with the roof blown off. Since the war had started nearly fourteen years ago, it had been far too dangerous for children to attend school. Consequently, an entire generation of young people had grown up with little or no education.

The school, the original hospital, and the town's first church had all been built by a remarkable and still-revered missionary doctor, Dr. Kenneth Fraser, who'd arrived in Lui in 1920. In the mid-1800s, Lui had served as a regional slave-trading center, and Dr. Fraser and his wife launched their mission work under the very tree where slaves had once been sold. Dr. Fraser's writings describe how, shortly after arriving in Lui, he performed emergency surgery on a tribal leader's son who had been attacked by a lion. By saving the boy's life, Dr. Fraser won the respect and acceptance of the formerly distrustful villagers. In time, he grew his mission to include a medical facility, then a church, then a school, and eventually a prospering village. Dr. Fraser, whose gravesite behind the church is still respectfully visited today, saw healing built trust, something we would experience in a similar way eighty years later.

From the late 1980s and through the mid-1990s, war decimated the village. Those who were not killed were driven off or were living in the bush. Through arbitrary bombings and surprise ground attacks, the GOS prevented the displaced villagers from mounting any resistance or resuming normal life. What remained of the village had been under government control until about two years before our arrival, when the SPLA finally drove out the government troops. As mentioned, the entire area around the old hospital was still laced with landmines, buried there either by the GOS troops or by local SPLA rebels. The landmines killed so many that the former residents feared returning. Lui was a ghost village.

Samaritan's Purse had established a reputation of integrity as a humanitarian, Christian relief organization, so Kenny Isaacs and his team were asked to consider providing medical help to the region. They began working in Lui in late 1997, just months before our surgical mission team landed. By that time, the village's population barely topped 250 people. There was no commerce, no stores—just a church, the abandoned hospital, and the deserted schoolhouse.

Samaritan's Purse transported metal sheets all the way from Nairobi, Kenya, to make a new roof for the school. Inside, they set up an examining room and a makeshift operating area and cordoned off a couple of wards, crowded with about twenty beds—all this in what had been a two-room schoolhouse.

After a lot of grunt work, the facility was finally ready for patients. But the people were still scattered in the bush. Nevertheless, as soon as Samaritan's Purse brought in a surgeon, word traveled quickly, and people began to come out of the bush. When a family brought a sick relative, they quickly threw up a *tukul*—a mud-walled, thatched-roof hut—to stay in. By the time we arrived, the *tukuls* surrounded the abandoned school, and Samaritan's Purse had put up a fence made of cane, sticks, tree limbs, and twigs to define the hospital compound.

Our hosts led us to the *tukuls* where we would be staying. We noted the sign posted above the entrance gate: "No spears, daggers, guns." Pulling aside the cloth that served as a door, I ducked inside the *tukul* and glanced around. It was a space about ten feet in diameter, with a mat on the hardened ground and a fire pit in the center in case the weather turned cool at night, as it often does under the clear African skies. I dropped my backpack and headed immediately to the hospital. Dick, David Charles, and I were curious to see the place we'd be working for the next week.

We were walking toward the schoolhouse when somebody called out, "Stop! Don't move!"

We froze as the voice continued to call out. "Stay on the path! There are landmines everywhere."

One of the Sudanese staff members walked up to us and deliberately explained, "If you hear an airplane, run for the outcropping of rocks over there," pointing behind the building. "Or dive into one of the bomb shelters you see dug in the ground near the *tukuls*," he pointed. The "bomb shelter" was nothing more than a pit, five feet deep and three feet wide. "Seek cover immediately," our host said. "Our protectors don't have any planes, so if you hear one, you can be fairly sure it is not a friend. The bombers usually loop around the hospital, getting their marks, and then it takes about two minutes for them to circle back to drop their bombs. So you have two minutes to reach safety—no more! But whatever you do," he added, "stay on the path! Landmines can be anywhere. We've had many people killed and a number of people badly maimed by shrapnel."

Dick, David, and I proceeded, walking gingerly toward the hospital, our eyes now glued to the narrow, well-worn dirt path. Once inside the schoolhouse, with the old, large black chalkboards still hanging on the far wall, we met with the Samaritan's Purse doctor at the hospital, who informed us about several of the patients on whom he wanted us to operate the following morning. As I listened to the doctor present the patients to us in the dark room (of course, there was no electricity), I wondered how in the world we would be able to operate in these primitive conditions. There was no anesthesiologist, no trained nurse, no electricity (except what we could produce with the small generator we'd brought with us), no array of surgical instruments to choose from, no gloves or gowns. It was a long way from the modern facilities I'd grown accustomed to at hospitals like Boston's Mass General or Nashville's Vanderbilt.

And then there were the cases. I was trained as a general surgeon and specialized further in chest and heart surgery. But the cases being described were way beyond what I'd read about in my modern surgical books—pathologies that I didn't think could exist in the twenty-first century. But they do, not just in Sudan, but all over the developing world.

That night, as I lay my head on the mat in the *tukul*, searching for some much-needed sleep, I thought, *This is going way beyond anything I have ever done.* Talk about being out of my comfort zone.

The following morning, I awakened long before dawn. Dick and I took a run, being careful to stay on the beaten paths. Then I took a cold shower under a bucket tied to a tree before heading over to the hospital. At the makeshift operating room, we boiled some water in a tin coffee pot, then let it cool enough to wash our hands with a bar of soap, trying to maintain as sterile an operating environment as possible. With no electricity or running water, and with windows open to counter the sweltering heat, the buzz of mosquitoes in our ears, and occasional animals wandering by just outside the room in which we were operating, true sanitation was simply not possible, but we did our best.

We had no shortage of patients, not just from the surrounding bush but from all over southern Sudan. Word spread fast that you could be cured in Lui by some American doctors. Patients arrived with diseases and medical conditions that had been neglected for years, as well as with newfound hope for treatment and possible cures. The clinic built trust.

A typical case we encountered was a man with a massive hydrocele—a testicular mass as large as a football. The young man could not work in the fields or even walk without the aid of a wheelbarrow-type contraption that he'd made to carry the mass as he stumbled along. You simply don't see that sort of extreme pathology in America, but such cases were not at all unusual in Africa. We worked for several hours to remove the mass and fix the hydrocele, allowing the young man to function normally, work in the fields, and provide for his family once again.

As Dick and I were operating, the assistant who'd helped prepare the patient for surgery told us of her seventeen-year-old son who had died because of an obstruction in his intestines due to a hernia of the abdominal wall. No treatment for the boy's malady had been available anywhere in the region. We soon learned that throughout southern Sudan, especially among certain tribes, there seemed to be a congenital weakness of the abdominal wall that led to a proliferation of inguinal, or groin, hernias. Incarceration of these hernias, whereby intestines get trapped in the narrow opening of the hernia and lose their blood supply, was the leading cause of non-war-related deaths among young Sudanese males. A hernia repair is one of the simplest operations I know—yet such basic life-saving medical treatments were largely unavailable here.

We operated in the tiny schoolroom all day alongside the local Sudanese assistants who were learning the procedures. We were astonished by their indefatigable energy. When the sun went down, we worked by flashlight. One person held a pair of flashlights over the patient while the rest of us hurried to complete the operation before the batteries went dead.

Such was the week: long days of work followed by quiet nights around the outdoor dinner table, talking with the faith-based mission team who provided support for the clinic—an amazing group from around America who were spending their lives in service to others.

During our last case on our final day before departure, a message came to the operating theater that a patient in the recovery room wanted to see "the American doctor." By that time, all I wanted to do was to go back to my *tukul*, wash up, tumble onto the mat, and fall asleep. But I couldn't refuse this last request. Dick, David, and I walked next door to the one-room hut that we were using as a recovery room. In the darkness, I could vaguely make out the silhouette of a man lying on a bed in the corner. Drawing closer, I saw white bandages covering the stump of what had been his left leg; a similar dressing covered his right hand.

But what drew my attention was not the man's injuries, but his bright smile, a smile that, even in the darkness, seemed to illuminate the man's dark brown face. I noticed a Bible beside his bed, not an unusual sight at a Samaritan's Purse clinic. I leaned over, put my hand on the man's shoulder, and through an interpreter, I asked why he wanted to see the American doctor.

The man told me his story. Two years earlier, his wife and children had been murdered during the war. Even as he spoke of the atrocity, he continued to smile, and his eyes remained bright. I nodded as I listened, my own heart breaking at the thought of losing my wife, Karyn, and our three boys in a senseless, seemingly endless war. I knew there was no way I would be smiling.

"Then eight days ago," he said, "I stepped on a landmine. I lost my leg and my fingers." He raised his hand slightly, so I could see that most of his hand was gone. And yet he continued to smile.

I nodded again, trying desperately to understand. I listened as he told how he had been brought to the hospital at Lui from about twenty kilometers away, and how the American doctor had saved his life.

Finally, I couldn't resist the obvious question. "Why are you smiling?" I asked. "Or should I say, how can you possibly be smiling?"

"Two reasons," he said through the interpreter. "One, because you come to us in the spirit of Jesus. And two, because you are an *American* doctor."

"What do you mean?" I asked.

The man rose up on the bed as best he could on his mutilated limbs and uttered words that would remain indelibly impressed in my heart. "Everything I have lost," he said, his eyes bright in the darkness, "my family, my leg, my hand—will be worth the sacrifice if my people can someday have what *you have* . . . in America." He paused, then spoke as if uttering a prayer: "Freedom. Freedom to live and worship as we please. The freedom that America represents."

I swallowed hard. I looked up at Dick and David, and I could tell that they, too, had been moved by the man's statement about the values that so strongly characterize the United States.

Over the years, I've been back to Africa many times. I've made medical mission trips to the Congo, Uganda, Kenya, Sudan, Tanzania, and Mozambique. I've never seen that man again, and I probably never will. But I've never forgotten his smile and his heart.

Moreover, in recent years, I have become increasingly convinced that medicine can truly be a currency for peace in our world—a way for America to reach out in friendship and compassion, creating lasting partnerships with people on every continent. Looking back, the awareness of that truth may have begun in that dark room, fostered by a man who had lost nearly everything but his faith in God and his hope for freedom.

Long after Dick, David, and I boarded a plane and flew back to America, Samaritan's Purse continued working in Lui. I would go back there regularly every year or two on mission trips to do surgery. In 1999, the hospital moved from the schoolhouse back over to the original hospital, the area around it finally cleared of mines. And then, after locals could fully assume all of the responsibilities of running and staffing the hospital—ten years after our original trip—Samaritan's Purse transferred control of the hospital to the local community.

That first trip to the Sudan opened doors of personal and spiritual growth for me. I've discovered that serving other people who have no means to pay you back is addictive in a strange, almost incomprehensible way. I've also made a point of bringing one of my three sons each time I go to Africa. I want them to see the raw humanity, the resilience of the human spirit, the poverty, the squalor, and the disease up close, firsthand—so they'll understand how much we Americans take for granted, and, more important, so their hearts will be moved with compassion and recognition of the joy one gets in serving others.

Several years later, Franklin Graham met personally with Sudan's president, Omar al-Bashir. "Mr. President, as you know, Samaritan's Purse has been helping the people of Sudan in many ways," Franklin reminded him, "not the least of which is the hospital in Lui."

Al-Bashir looked at his aides and caustically asked, "Didn't we bomb that hospital?" The president and his aides burst out laughing.

Franklin's response was ready. "Yes, Mr. President, you did," he said. "But Mr. President . . . you missed!"

In fact, after my first trip, the area around the hospital was bombed seven more times, and many lives were lost and much property was destroyed, but the local survivors—with the help of Samaritan's Purse—made repairs and carried on. And as the hospital grew, so did the community.

Over time, the village of Lui has grown to more than fifty thousand permanent residents. Samaritan's Purse constructed a new ward in the hospital, a tuberculosis treatment facility a few kilometers away, a chapel, a nursing school (the first in southern Sudan), and an extremely active outpatient treatment center—an open-air, thatched-roof sort of veranda that is constantly crowded with patients. They drilled three wells to ensure the supply of clean water. By 2009, the hospital had expanded from a twenty-bed facility to nearly one hundred beds.

Today, the hospital at Lui is one of the best-equipped medical facilities in southern Sudan; almost three thousand patients from all over southern Sudan are cared for every month at the facility. Each month, more than a hundred patients have their tumors taken out, burns excised, spears removed, bones set, and hernias repaired in one of the two operating room theaters. In the process, Samaritan's Purse has trained local men and women in management and the prevention of HIV/AIDS, as well as modeling compassionate care for those already afflicted. Interestingly, except for tribal conflicts, the fighting in that area has stopped. *Medicine breeds understanding, hope, and peace.*

When we first started going to Lui, no market or commercial activity existed there. Then, as the hospital proved that it was in Lui to stay, families set up a few tables in front of the facility, from which they sold a bit of tobacco or maize. Sometimes, patients' family members conducted their business outside the hospital as they waited for their loved ones to recover. Over time, the few tables increased to more than twenty. The following year when we returned, I noticed people at a series of stalls selling not just maize and tobacco, but produce as well as homemade apparel and sandals. Eventually, the local merchants expanded to peddle many other items. It was a return to civilization, to commerce, and to normal, hopeful living. And it all began with a dream and a deserted schoolhouse.

I'm convinced that the growth in Lui is a model of what can be done to build trust on a larger scale around the world when medicine is used as a currency for peace. Since this trip to Lui, I have made annual medical mission trips to the developing world. I go as a doctor . . . as a volunteer. I don't go with security. I don't go with press. I've had the opportunity of operating on the complications of tuberculosis in Mozambique, treating patients for extreme dehydration in a cholera hospital in Bangladesh, giving vaccinations to children in Darfur, and repairing life-threatening hernias in southern Sudan. And in Botswana and South Africa, I witnessed how a single virus HIV could hollow out society—an observation that I would soon take directly to the floor of the U.S. Senate and to the president of the United States. In the Congo and in Sudan I've learned a useful lesson: People don't usually go to war against people who helped save their children. While the world often sees America's tougher side—our military might and our economic prowess—when people around the world see America's more compassionate, humanitarian side, the barriers come down, and peace becomes possible.

America's humanitarianism and the innumerable volunteers from organizations like Samaritan's Purse rarely make the headlines or the evening news. Yet this is one of those things that makes America great—the fact that we are a country filled with people who care for those who are less fortunate, people who will give of themselves not only monetarily, but with their very lives, people who actively demonstrate a heart to serve.

2

A Legacy of Caring

Everyone is shaped by their family, and I suspect that in my case, it's truer than in most. So to help understand what makes the Frist family tick, let me take you back to Meridian, Mississippi, a railroad town of about fifteen thousand residents, where in 1914 my grandfather, Jake Frist, was the stationmaster at the local railroad yard.

Around 1906, my grandparents, Jacob and Jennie Frist, had moved from Tennessee to Meridian, located midway down the state, fifteen miles west of the Alabama line. Grandfather—an average but likable fellow, ambitious, and industrious—had struggled to work his way up from conductor to become the new stationmaster for the New Orleans & North Eastern Railroad.

February 3, 1914, dawned cold and overcast, but typical of most busy winter days at the Meridian terminal. By 2:45 in the afternoon, boxcars and passenger cars from earlier runs had backed up on tracks one and two, where they sat waiting to be connected to other trains. Shortly before 3:00 P.M., an Alabama Great Southern passenger train clamored into the station on track four. Grandfather realized that track three, the track in between the idle cars and the Great Southern train, was obscured from the view of people leaving the station waiting rooms. He walked out to the platform between tracks three and four to keep an eye on the main concourse, where the Great Southern train was now boarding. While he was standing there, he heard the whistle of the Mobile & Ohio, bound for St. Louis, approaching the station on track three.

Grandfather headed up the platform to warn those passengers walking in both directions along the boardwalk about the incoming train. That was when he realized the Mobile & Ohio was coming in fast, too fast, possibly as much as eighteen to twenty miles per hour, a fine cruising speed, but far too fast for entering the train station. Worse yet, Grandfather knew that the passengers streaming out of the waiting rooms had not seen it—and could not see it because of the train blocking their view—or heard it above the noise of the other trains already in front of the station. He broke into a run alongside the incoming train, shouting ahead and waving at the crowd to clear the track. Most of the waiting passengers noticed him and stepped back—all except one, an elderly woman carrying a baby bundled in her arms.

Frail and aging, Emma Wood, of Electric Mills, Mississippi, was not accustomed to train travel. In fact, she would never have been in Meridian that day if her three-year-old grandson, Harlan Scoggins, hadn't badly injured his back. The family doctor had wrapped the child in a stiff plaster cast and encouraged Emma's daughter and son-in-law to see a specialist at a hospital just outside New Orleans. Of modest means, the young parents could not afford the time to make the trip, so Grandma Emma volunteered.

Shortly before 3:00 P.M., Emma Wood heard her train called. She carefully picked up young Harlan and made her way out of the station, through the passengers' entrance gate, and down the main concourse, right onto track three. Perhaps she was frightened or confused by the sight of the stationmaster rushing up the platform and waving his arms at her; possibly it was the awful screeching noise that puzzled her and prevented her from hearing his shouts, or perhaps she was distracted in her struggle to carry her grandson in his awkward cast. Whatever it was, Emma turned slowly, only to see the huge black engine billowing smoke and bearing down on her.

Stark terror flashed across her face, and she froze in place.

Sprinting along the platform, shouting and waving his arms, Grandfather barely nudged ahead of the train. He saw Emma's dilemma and recognized she had no further chance to escape. At the last second, he hurled himself off the platform right in front of the locomotive and slammed into the transfixed woman on the tracks, the impact shoving Emma and her grandson off the track and out of the way of danger. But Grandfather wasn't so lucky. The locomotive smacked into Jake Frist, tossing him more than twenty feet in the air, his side crushed by the front of the engine, his leg snapped in two when it caught in the locomotive's sill. Grandfather landed on the boardwalk next to the tracks, his head scraping along the planks and cement, shredding his face.

C. C. Redwood, the train's engineer, could only watch in horror. He later said that in that instant, he knew for certain the stationmaster at the Meridian terminal would be killed. In fact, as the train slowly came to a stop, everyone who saw my grandfather lying crumpled and motionless on the station's wooden planks knew he was dead.

A crowd quickly gathered around Emma and her young grandchild. Except for a few scrapes and bruises, and shaking with fear, they seemed okay. Still lying on the wooden planks, Grandfather was cut and bleeding, but breathing, still talking, amazingly still alive.

A Mobile & Ohio physician, Dr. Gully, ran from the station and attended to my grandfather, still slumped on the sidewalk next to the tracks. Somehow, after the hullabaloo at the tracks calmed down, Dr. Gully arranged to transfer all three of the victims, Emma Wood and three-year-old Harlan as well as my grandfather, to Meridian's Turner Hospital.

Someone must have informed Grandmother Frist, because she headed off for the hospital to find him, bringing the family doctor, S. H. Hairston, with her. Dr. Hairston later said that he found Jake alive, but he was "in a poor state and in much pain."

The doctor described Granddaddy Jake's condition in his medical journal, noting that Jake's left leg was fractured between the knee and ankle; he had a huge contusion along the left hip and deep lacerations around the skull. Whether he said so or not, Dr. Hairston knew his patient would be a long time recovering.

Granddaddy Jake stayed at the hospital for two weeks, then was confined to his home for nine months. For the better part of a year, he was completely disabled. When he finally returned to work at the station, he could walk only with the aid of a cane. The limp, as Dr. Hairston described it, was slight, but it belied the true depth of Jake's pain and injury.

"At the present time," wrote Hairston on February 6, 1915, "he attends to his duties with great difficulty, and I feel that he has not recovered and will not for some time fully recover." Dr. Hairston was right.

Back then, in the heyday of the railroads, two coveted awards existed for acts of extreme bravery in connection with the industry. One was the Andrew Carnegie "Hero Award," which came with a medal and a thousand-dollar stipend for the education of the recipient's children. Only sixteen of the medals had been awarded in the decade since the act had gone into effect. The Carnegie Hero Fund Commission awarded the seventeenth to my grandfather.

The second coveted honor was the Medal of Honor for Lifesaving on Railroads, which Congress had established in 1905. In March 1915, the White House awarded this medal to Granddaddy Jake. The letter, signed by Woodrow Wilson, stated, "You have been awarded a medal for extreme daring whereby on February 3, 1914, you imperiled your life in saving the lives of others. I am pleased to convey to you herewith this medal as a testimonial of the nation's appreciation of your courageous and praiseworthy act."

Grandfather's medal was passed down as one of our family's most cherished treasures. Years later, I would borrow it from my cousin Johnny Frist to keep in my office when I became majority leader of the United States Senate—a reminder of the intergen-

erational responsibility we have as parents and families to pass
on our values.

Meanwhile, by November 1914, my grandfather had gone back
to work, much sooner than he should have. Partly, I like to think,
he did so from a common Frist family trait—the absolute abhor-
rence of inactivity. (My wife, Karyn, teases that all Frist males
hate sleep! And she's probably right.) But the next four years
were increasingly difficult for Grandfather, as his physical condition grew worse. In 1919, having never fully recovered from the
events of the railway accident, my grandfather suffered a stroke
and died, his death most probably connected with the physical
complications that stemmed from the injuries he received when
he was struck by the locomotive. He was only fifty-six years of
age, and he left behind a widow, four children, and a massive
debt.

My father was a mere eight years old when Granddaddy Jake
died. He experienced a deep sense of loss, which I'm not certain
he ever got over. Years later, when I'd ask my dad how he developed such genuine humility, he'd always refer to the loss of his
dad.

The heroic tale that my father and his siblings heard as they
grew up engendered an absolute devotion to family. Moreover,
the story instilled in those of us in future generations the will,
the urge, to respond instinctively with action, the drive to make
one's mark, and the need to do so somehow by helping others
live better and more fulfilling lives; better yet, if possible, by saving lives.

My grandfather's death cast a long shadow over the life
of the family he left behind, especially over his youngest son,
Tommy, my father. Without a pension, a life insurance policy
payout, or the income from the railroad, the family was forced
to turn their home into a boardinghouse, just to make do. Grandmother revamped the original ten rooms of the house into fourteen to ensure adequate rent. Mindful of her young children,

Jennie looked for what she called "quality" guests, and ran a strict, upright establishment. Years later, Dad told me, "Mother was very careful to select people with education and who were cultured," hinting I'm sure that throughout life, in good times and bad, I should choose my friends wisely. He never defined *cultured* for me, but over the years I learned that his definition had very little to do with fine manners, the arts, or formal education, but more with honesty, character, and respect for others.

The eclectic group who rented rooms from my grandmother could easily have been the cast of a Broadway musical. Among those living there at various times were the Reverend Pennyman, an Episcopal minister; a young Jewish bank teller named Mose Gaston, who eventually became president of a Meridian bank, and his gentile wife; a sophisticated lumberman named Mahlon Floyd Parker, who was married to a stylish English woman and drove an expensive Marmon, one of the premier vehicles of the time; two pretty Meridian schoolteachers; a professional golfer—a young Scotsman—who ran the local course; a demure woman who could neither hear nor speak; and Jerry Hairston, a retired minor league baseball player who now worked for the railroad.

A nurse and at least two doctors also boarded at Grandmother's. One of the doctors was Dr. Franklin Gail Reilly, a University of Tennessee graduate who fought in World War I, and then went on to get specialized training in pediatrics. Dr. Reilly settled in Meridian in 1922 as Mississippi's first residency-trained pediatrician. He lived at Jennie's boardinghouse with his wife, Harriet, and baby son, Billy. During my dad's childhood, "Dr. Gail" often took the young Tommy Frist along with him on house calls. Dr. Reilly later founded a hospital in Meridian that is still thriving. His son, Billy, grew up to be a prominent pediatrician like his dad, and today runs the hospital his father founded.

The other doctor living at the boardinghouse was Jerry Hairston's brother, Dr. S. H. Hairston, the physician who had cared for my grandfather after his accident. Hairston, a man who would have a profound influence on my father's life, developed a solid surgical practice and eventually founded another Meridian hospital.

Peering into the past from my vantage point today, it is easy to see that while Dad learned much from the various renters at the boardinghouse, he was most intrigued by the medical doctors. Through them, he enjoyed stories about all kinds of patients; he listened carefully to the doctors' diagnoses and grew fascinated by their treatments. Dad's early interest in medicine was piqued as he listened to the conversations around the dinner table each evening. Dr. Hairston, especially, became a mentor, tutoring Dad in his studies and encouraging his budding interest in medicine. Eventually, Dr. Hairston hired young Tommy Frist at his fifty-five-bed Meridian hospital, where Dad worked after school every day.

Equally influential in my dad's early years was his hero worship of older brother John Chester—Chet, as everyone but Grandmother called him. Because of their age difference, it's not surprising that a fatherless boy like my dad should turn to his elder brother as a substitute, a role model; indeed, Chet was like a surrogate father to my dad. They were practically inseparable. Chet loved his younger brother with intensity and served throughout their years in grammar and high school as Dad's champion and protector. On the other hand, Dad's hero worship of his brother exacerbated his own shyness and would lead him to question his "inferiority," and why he never did anything as well as Chet.

Grandmother recognized Dad's need for approval and provided him with additional emotional support; Dad reciprocated with an unalloyed love for her. Dad made certain that he never disappointed his mom; he always treated her with the utmost respect, willingly obeyed her commands, and lived as straight as an arrow. He never smoked, never drank, never cursed; he was a model of integrity reflecting the Christian values his mother taught him. When he started earning a meager amount of spending money, he always gave his mother a portion of what he'd made. When he went off to college, he continued that practice, and wrote to her almost daily.

Dad later told me, "My mother never raised her voice or scolded me one time in her life. Likewise, because of her influence, I have never raised my voice or spanked any of my children. I have never really been angry at one of my children."

I can't vouch for the "being angry" part, but I can attest to the fact that Dad never punished my four siblings or me by spanking or scolding. Nor did our mother. They expected us to do the "right thing" and make wise decisions and always used affirmation and positive reinforcement or quiet expressions of disappointment if we stepped out of line and needed to be reprimanded. It seems almost hard to imagine, nowadays, that Mom and Dad could raise a family of five children with such a positive philosophy and value system—but they did. Clearly, Dad emulated his mom in the parenting of his own children.

After two years at Southwestern College (now Rhodes College) in Memphis, Dad transferred to Ole Miss, where he enrolled in the premed certificate program. Besides intriguing him, medicine offered what he wanted most: a way to provide a good living for the family he hoped to have one day and a profession that would validate his father's selfless, impulsive sacrifice. He loved people, and he wanted to touch them just as Dr. Hairston had done.

Unfortunately, Dad didn't have the funds to attend medical school. Undaunted, he went to Ole Miss two weeks early to earn a little money. He picked up the trunks and baggage of the more affluent students as they arrived at the railroad station in Oxford and then lugged them by mule-drawn wagon to the dormitories. He set about earning his tuition at Mississippi by publishing a football calendar, on which he sold space to local stores and other advertisers. Dad also ran a concession stand at the home basketball games, where he earned a whopping fifteen dollars one night—a lot of money in those days. He was an entrepreneur—by instinct and by necessity.

In 1928 and 1929, there were no play-by-play radio or televi-

sion sports broadcasts, so, capitalizing on Ole Miss's great football tradition, Dad came up with an idea to provide "play by play"
reports to the Oxford students who could not travel to the away
games. Using Western Union, Dad had the details of the game
transmitted to him at Ole Miss, where he charged fans a dollar to
sit in the gymnasium and listen to his account of the game, announced through a megaphone.

Dad relished mixing hard work with creativity. Years later,
he told me that he always found it easy to create a job when he
needed money, even during the Great Depression. "It was easy
for me to get a job," Dad recalled, "because I was willing to work.
And, I guess I was innovative."

Dad was a little lucky as well. For instance, one of Dad's jobs
was babysitting for the dean of the two-year medical school, Dr.
Billy S. Guyton, a prominent ear, nose, and throat specialist. Dr.
Guyton took a liking to the hardworking Tommy Frist. When it
came time for the tall, redheaded student to apply for the final
two years of his medical training, Dr. Guyton called the dean at
Vanderbilt in Nashville. When Dad told Dr. Guyton that he had
no money, not even enough to get to Nashville, Dean Guyton
loaded his family and their babysitter into his car and drove Dad
from Oxford all the way up to Nashville.

Fifty years later, the Guyton and Frist families crossed paths
once again. Dean Guyton's son Arthur later wrote the most widely
read physiology textbook in the world. When I was a surgical
resident at Massachusetts General Hospital in Boston, for two
years I worked side by side with Robert Guyton and Steve Guyton, two of Arthur's ten children—all of whom, quite remarkably, became physicians.

In 1931, upon graduating from Ole Miss with his "Preclini-
cal Medical Certificate," Dad entered Vanderbilt Medical School
with ten dollars in his pocket and his heart set on becoming a
surgeon. He didn't know another person on campus, but as he'd
done for his undergraduate studies, Dad once again earned the
money for his own education by working at odd jobs and exercis-
ing his entrepreneurial flair. In exchange for room and board, he

recruited medical-student boarders for a Mrs. Compton, whose house became affectionately known around campus as "Pauper's Paradise."

Dad completed his studies at Vanderbilt Medical School in two years, although he hinted that constantly working may have caused him not to do as well as he had hoped. "I graduated, not with very good grades," he said. "I had a high B average, but not an A, because I didn't have time to study." Nevertheless, he launched out on the final leg of his lifelong dream to become a surgeon—the all-encompassing residency training at a university hospital.

Dad went to Iowa City for a rotating internship at the various University of Iowa hospitals, but near the end of his first year of residency, he suffered a collapsed lung. At the time, his condition was diagnosed as tuberculosis, and he was forced to drop out of the program—on doctor's orders—for about six months. During that time, he was cared for by his mother, who had moved farther south to Fort Lauderdale, Florida.

Dad returned to Iowa to finish the remaining eighteen months of his training, but he soon encountered a stumbling block he couldn't get around. Despite his best efforts, he ran out of money during the second year of his doctor's residency program at the University of Iowa. Dad was out of options. It was time to apply what he had learned and try to make a living.

Although Dad was disappointed about leaving his residency, squelching his dream of becoming a surgeon, he was excited to get back to Nashville to see Dorothy Harrison Cate, a vibrant young teacher originally from Hopkinsville, Kentucky, with whom he had fallen in love while at Vanderbilt. Dorothy was the sister of a prominent Nashville physician, Dr. William R. Cate Sr., who had developed a thriving private practice as a general medical doctor.

Dad set up his medical practice in downtown Nashville in 1935, teaching Vanderbilt residents and medical students on the side. Dr. Cate and Dad had become good friends, so when the established doctor invited Dad to join his medical practice as a junior partner in 1937, my father readily agreed. Dad and Dr. Cate worked together for five years.

Dad threw himself into the practice with Dr. Cate, courting Dorothy after work, and succeeded at both endeavors. He and Dorothy married and set up housekeeping in Nashville, where Dad continued to partner with his brother-in-law. Times were tough, and it took a lot of hard work for a new, young doctor to build a practice, but Dad never shied away from hard work; in fact, he embraced it. He supplemented his income by conducting routine physicals for a local insurance company and by treating patients at the state penitentiary, where he earned fifty dollars per month.

When America entered World War II, Dad did, too, starting as a first lieutenant and working his way up to major in the Army Medical Corps. He served as chief of internal medicine for three years at Maxwell Field Air Force Base in Montgomery, Alabama. After the war, Dad returned to Nashville, set up his own medical practice, and started from scratch again. Two years later, he became partners in a new clinic with Dr. Addison Scoville, with whom he would practice for the next half century.

Dad loved practicing medicine and he devoted himself to it. Soon, he became the busiest and most sought-after doctor in Nashville, with patients sometimes waiting months for an appointment to see him. He never turned patients away, welcoming rich and poor alike. Over time, he became the personal physician to the governor of Tennessee, then later to six other governors, as well as Grand Ole Opry stars such as Sarah Cannon (better known as Minnie Pearl), and many other celebrities. He never lost his humility.

"Dr. Tommy," as Dad was affectionately known by his patients, had a marvelous gift for making his patients feel comfortable and special, as though each individual was the most important person on his busy schedule that day. Dad was as much counselor as he was physician, although he had no professional degree in the realm of psychology; he simply had compassion and common sense. He was comforting and reassuring; he gave people hope. He treated the whole patient and the whole family. When a young patient was to be married, it was usually Dad who brought the couple in for marriage counseling.

When Dad began his practice, the specialty of cardiology did not really exist. But Dad gravitated to the study of the heart, attending courses taught by the famous Boston heart specialist Dr. Paul Dudley White. He soon developed a reputation as the doctor to see when patients experienced heart ailments.

At the same time, Dad was quick to embrace new and better technology, constantly seeking to improve care to his patients. When the electrocardiograph (EKG) proved reliable, he became the first doctor in Nashville to have the new machine, outside of the teaching hospital at Vanderbilt. At the time, the EKG machine was the size of a large wheelchair, cumbersome and not easily transported. But Dad didn't merely use the machine in his office for patients referred to him. Quite the contrary, he took the machine to patients all over the region. Furthermore, he began reading EKG strips for doctors from rural areas all around Nashville, and eventually for hospitals across Tennessee. Runners brought a fresh batch of EKGs each day. Dad would read the tests and send back the results the following morning.

A few years later, in the early 1960s, the technology evolved so a newfangled listening device allowed instantaneous, real-time diagnosis over the telephone line. It was revolutionary. At the bedside a hundred miles away, a doctor could hook a patient up to an EKG machine, then attach the machine to a telephone that in turn would transmit the signal to a special printer in Dad's office in Nashville. Dad could read the strip and immediately tell the doctor the diagnosis and recommend treatment. Still later, Dad was the first in town to get a machine that translated the blips over the telephone into a readable EKG strip printed out in his bedroom in our home on Bowling Avenue. That way, Dad could read EKGs any time of the night if a doctor needed his help. I remember hearing that telephone ring regularly through the night during my boyhood.

Forty years later, these vivid memories of Dad's willingness to leverage new technology as a means to improve health care led me to join forces with then-Senator Hillary Clinton in drafting a major health information technology bill taken to the floor of the Senate in 2005. And today, that same spirit moves me to support President Obama's leadership in modernizing information technology as a way to reduce medical errors, improve quality, and lower the costs of health care in America.

With the U.S. economy booming after World War II, Dad's practice grew as well. He and Mom were also slowly growing more financially stable, so Dad developed an interest in real estate investing—a natural sidelight for the doctor with entrepreneurial instincts. He gradually acquired and renovated most of the small houses surrounding his medical office across from Vanderbilt on West End Avenue.

In the early 1970s, successful Nashville businessman and entrepreneur Jack Massey and some other investors felt it was time for Nashville to have a luxury hotel just outside of downtown. They approached Dad to join their group in part because of friendship but also because, by then, he owned most of the properties in the block they considered the perfect location for their hotel. Dad got in on the investment with almost no cash, instead putting up the land he had put together over the years. Today, Loews Vanderbilt Plaza Hotel stands on that property. Dad was proud of the contribution he and his friends had made to the expanding midtown of Nashville by building the hotel, which still remains as one of the best hotels in town.

IN 1952, THE YEAR I WAS BORN, OUR FAMILY MOVED INTO A COMFORTable five-bedroom house on four acres on Bowling Avenue just outside the city limits—a handsome place Dad had long dreamed of owning. Karyn and I live in that very house almost six decades later in part to honor and preserve the fond memories of a close family of seven, meaningful traditions, and the enduring legacy of Mother's and Dad's simple values.

During the 1950s, Dad scrambled constantly to make the

mortgage payments. He did whatever was necessary to keep his family's home. The home and the land around it were important to Dad, not merely as property, but for what they represented— love, security for the family, and memories and values for the next generation. The home saw the family grow. A white barn out back soon housed three horses, and the field enclosed a pen with white turkeys and even a billy goat for a while.

Dad always said that his interest in hospitals originated with him being an orderly when he was twelve years old. But his more contemporary interest in hospital operations and construction began as two trends merged in his life. The first was a growing interest in the demographics of America's aging population and the impact they were having on society. The second trend was the increasingly wasteful way in which hospitals were run at a time when technology was advancing and costs were continually escalating.

In 1959, Dad was appointed to the American Medical Association's (AMA) Committee on Aging and was subsequently named to the President's National Commission on Aging. He went to his first AMA committee meeting, which included five former presidents of the organization. At the conclusion of the gathering, Dad, a humble family doctor from the southern town of Nashville, rose from his chair and boldly said, "We should do something tangible about aging, instead of just talking about it." Dad liked action.

Taking his own advice, he returned to Nashville and almost immediately opened a retirement home affiliated with our Presbyterian church, a few miles from our home. As his interest in helping the aging grew, Dad later founded the American Retirement Corporation, which ultimately grew to become one of the largest retirement-living chains in the United States. (Today it's part of Brookdale Senior Living.)

About that same time, he and a group of doctors were experiencing difficulty finding beds for their patients in Nashville hospitals. Although the city boasted several large hospitals, all the beds were full. Moreover, having worked at all the local hospitals, even serving as chairman of the board for most of them,

Dad knew firsthand that most hospitals were not well run. One Nashville hospital at the time was run by a retiree with no management experience at all—the director was simply a political appointee. Many of the employees received subpar pay and worked in crowded, antiquated, and unappealing facilities. Much of the equipment was outdated, and the hospitals had no access to capital to modernize.

Dad envisioned a different kind of hospital for his patients: a well-managed facility, with well-trained and appropriately paid staff who looked forward to reporting for work each day, a hospital where the patients received excellent care and good, nutritious food and were embraced by a sense of warmth, compassion, and hope. He wanted the patients'—and employees'—immediate environment to be uplifting and conducive to healing, believing that attitude plays a vital role in health. Dad's initial idea was to combine a single fifty-bed hospital facility with a one-hundred-bed nursing home. He originally wanted to create a nonprofit hospital, but he could not interest the local government or any organizations in putting up the money for it. Finally, Dad found seven doctors willing to sign for a loan jointly to finance the facility. When it came time to name the hospital, Mother suggested, "It's right across from Centennial Park. Why don't you call it Park View?"

Park View hospital opened in 1961, marrying two of my father's great passions—serving the aged, through the nursing home side of the facility, and serving the sick, through the acute care medical hospital side of the facility. Unfortunately, Dad's seemingly great idea failed. The reason was understandable: Those in the nursing home side ultimately wanted the same level and intensity of care as what they saw on the hospital side. And that was financially impossible to do because of the high intensity of care that was demanded on the acute medical side.

Others would have thrown in the towel and given up. Not Dr. Frist. Dad simply said, "My initial idea was a bad one; I was wrong. So let's make the necessary adjustment, now, quickly, and convert all the beds in the facility to be a hospital only." Within six months, Park View was a thriving, bustling, acute-care hospital, meeting the high standards of quality and efficiency that Dad set out in his initial dream. It still thrives today, now renamed Centennial Hospital. Dad understood how to learn from his mistakes.

Although it was not yet apparent to anyone at the time, Dad and his partners had planted the seed for a revolution in health-care services that would be felt all over America and indeed around the world.

WHILE DAD WAS BUSY DEVELOPING PARK VIEW HOSPITAL, MY brother Tommy attended college at Vanderbilt, followed by med school, first at the University of Tennessee in Memphis, then at Washington University in St. Louis. I was a young teenager and as yet, no one in our family had done anything significant in business. We lived comfortably as a middle-class family of seven, Dad making ends meet on his medical practice income and beginning to save for the future.

Tommy had the entrepreneurial instinct in the family, influenced I'm sure by all the odd jobs that Dad had created during his years in school. To my father's great chagrin, Tommy left college for a while, long before that became the fashionable thing to do (now called a "gap" year, but then called "dropping out") to expand his tiny college desk blotter advertising business—the same concept that Dad had proved successful thirty years before at Ole Miss. Now, Tommy dreamed of selling blotters not just at Vanderbilt, but at a hundred colleges around the country. He dreamed big. He formed a company called Collegiate Advertising, had some business cards printed, mixed in his own love for flying, and bought an old cloth-covered, wooden-propeller Stinson airplane to fly around the country setting up his franchises. Dad made it work, first at Ole Miss, then at Vanderbilt. Tommy dreamed to take it nationwide. The venture was a success for the twenty-one-year-old, because it brought him a fair income. And he surpassed his goal, putting out blotters at 112 colleges. It was a success to me, because Tommy brought me home a college pennant from each institution he served. Every night I'd fall asleep as an eight-year-old kid under the shadows of thirty college pennants pinned to the wall at the foot of my bed.

Selling desk blotters, however, was a seasonal business, so Tommy turned to catch the wave of the latest craze around the country—outdoor trampolines—setting up two outdoor trampoline centers in communities just outside Nashville. I spent many a summer afternoon and evening with Trisha, at the time Tommy's steady girlfriend (and now wife of almost fifty years), collecting fifty cents from boys and girls for each thirty minutes of jumping on the trampolines in two nearby towns, Donelson and Madison. Trisha and I would be manning one trampoline center, Tommy the other. A year later, as happens with all fads, the trampoline business folded, and our ever-supportive and always patient mother inherited the responsibility of selling Tommy's thirty, used, green nylon trampolines, stacked for months behind the home on Bowling, through the newspaper classified ads.

Tommy watched from afar with great interest as the fledgling hospital that Dad had put together took hold and flourished in Nashville. Franchises and chains of businesses were much in the air in those days, and following his surgical internship in Nashville, Tommy ruminated on the possibility of creating a chain of hospitals like the one Dad had created. Most hospitals at that time were nonprofit entities operated by religious organizations or local governments. Doctor-owned hospitals of the past had a poor image generally because they were typically underfinanced, and thus had to cut corners wherever they could. But Tommy's dream was different. And it, too, was big.

One of Tommy's fraternity brothers at Vanderbilt just happened to be Spence Wilson, son of Kemmons Wilson, founder of the Memphis-based Holiday Inn hotel group, a relatively new and thriving hotel chain, the first of its kind. Holiday Inn had mastered the concept of a chain of facilities across the country, standardized to a level of dependable quality and service, all at a reasonable price. Tommy wondered why similar principles had not been applied to health care, especially when quality of care for patients in hospitals was so uneven and service so variable from one facility to the next.

In talking with Spence about the launching and growth of Holiday Inns, Tommy began to dream of developing a company that could spawn a group of hospitals, owned not by doctors but by investors, similar in quality and standards to Park View: new, privately financed, clean, and well-equipped facilities. The investor-owned concept, using the marketplace through a public stock offering, would guarantee the capital to provide high-quality, modern, consistent service. Tommy imagined how those hospitals might join together for mass purchasing of medical supplies and equipment, creating bargaining power that simply could not exist with unaffiliated, free-standing facilities. Tommy saw it all so clearly, yet it had never been done before. It required thinking out of the box.

Although Dad's passion was caring for patients and not hospital administration, with the success of Park View he became regarded as an expert on the development of high-quality, for-profit hospitals responsive to doctors and centering on patients' needs. Tommy knew his dream could only be accomplished with the help and experience and reputation of his father.

Tommy had also always admired the entrepreneur Jack Massey, a close friend and patient of Dad's. Mr. Massey was a pharmacist and had owned a pharmacy and surgical supply company back in the 1930s. Dad bought all of his medical supplies from his company over the years. Mr. Massey was also the marketing genius behind Kentucky Fried Chicken, which he had purchased from Colonel Sanders for $2 million, then grew into a chain known worldwide, wisely keeping Colonel Sanders as the figurehead and primary pitch man. Mr. Massey also had an understanding of hospital management and was serving as chairman of the board of the large, highly respected Baptist Hospital in Nashville. Tommy knew neither he nor Dad had the necessary business experience; that role could only be filled by Mr. Massey, who could provide the franchising expertise, while Dad could be the physician in charge who was the master of building a hospital that focused on the quality of care for the patient.

After his surgical internship at Vandy, Tommy and Trisha entered the Air Force, where they were stationed at Robbins Air Force Base in Macon, Georgia. With his vision still being formulated, he approached a hospital near Macon and discussed the potential for a private, for-profit hospital partnered with a chain of other investor-owned hospitals. He discovered a surprisingly receptive audience. Buoyed by the encouraging response in Georgia, Tommy knew his next step was to broach the subject with Dad.

Returning to Nashville one weekend and sitting around the kitchen table at the home on Bowling, Tommy explained his ideas to Mother and Dad. Much to my brother's dismay, Dad didn't want to listen to the idea. Not that he couldn't grasp the concept; he simply didn't want it to be his son who would make the dream a reality. "Doing surgery is the best job in the world," Dad declared. "It's something I always wanted to do. You've worked hard to be a doctor. It's the greatest privilege in the world. Why would you want to give that up?"

I would hear these same words thirty years later.

This was a tense time for both Dad and Tommy. But Tommy was determined. He approached Mr. Massey directly about the possibility of launching a chain of hospitals. A disciple of private enterprise and the advantages that the market brought to bear, Mr. Massey responded better than Tommy imagined, not only with ideas and suggestions, but with the sort of enthusiastic support Tommy had hoped to find in Dad.

It moved Mother, and she brought her oldest son's case to Dad. "Tommy wants to do this. He feels it is the right thing to do. It's his dream. He believes in it. He believes he can care for more people by serving this way than being a surgeon. And if it doesn't work out, he can always go back and take care of patients. Tommy, I think we should help him do it."

And that's all it took. The initially reluctant father would follow his son's dreams.

Mr. Massey provided the business acumen and the financial backing; Dad had the medical expertise and embodied the values; Tommy had the crystal clear vision and provided the driving energy. They turned to a patient of Dad's, Nashville lawyer Henry Hooker, to handle the legal matters. They needed a name. Tommy simply imitated the name Holiday Inns of America and called it Hospital Corporation of America (HCA). Together they laid the foundation for what was to become a new multi-billion-dollar industry that would forever change the health services sector.

Dad became president of the nascent organization. He made it clear, however, that his involvement was contingent upon the company's maintaining high-quality care as inexpensively as possible, in pleasant and patient-friendly surroundings—precisely what Tommy hoped to do. Forever the patient's doctor, Dad would continue his busy clinical practice, but he would serve as president of HCA at the same time.

Dad was good for HCA. In addition to his experience of working with hospitals and his skill in managing their medical staffs, he possessed the intangible appeal of a genuine, humble, hometown doctor whose sole motivation was to heal. People trusted him, and he always kept their best interests at heart. He worked indefatigably to make HCA successful, calling on his physician colleagues around the country, many of whom he had taught at Vanderbilt or known in military service, and bringing one hospital after another into the fold. Dad especially loved the small hospitals, the ones in which it was possible to really get to know the people working there. His favorite was among the first, a forty-bed hospital built in Erin, Tennessee, in a community that previously had no regional care. Using the private market to build hospitals in regions where there was no care—it made so much sense, yet was so revolutionary.

Dad made a practice of entering the hospitals through the

kitchen, greeting each worker as he passed as if he or she was
the person most instrumental to the operation of the hospital.
He always ate lunch in the hospital cafeterias alongside the employees, avoiding boardrooms and executive dining rooms. Such
was Dad's commonsense, simple approach to life and work, the
same one he'd followed since growing up as a kid brother without a father, listening respectfully to everyone else at the dinner
table sharing their life stories. It was pretty basic. And pretty
powerful.

HCA grew rapidly, revolutionizing the way hospitals operated—
nonprofit and for-profit facilities alike. It was listed on the
New York Stock Exchange in 1970 and became the first NYSE
business to achieve $1 billion in revenues in its first decade of
operation.

For more than twenty years, with Tommy guiding the company, HCA experienced phenomenal growth and became the
largest and most respected hospital management company in
the world, with over three hundred hospitals in ten countries.
Tommy instinctively knew how to engage change; he believed
that successful companies needed to transform—actually radically reinvent—themselves every decade or so. When the hospital company grew too large and unwieldy in the late 1980s,
Tommy and the company's management took it private, paying
all the public shareholders for their shares, so they could retool
and prepare the company for the challenges and opportunities
that they would face over the next twenty years. They went
back to basics. They sold assets of the company that were not
in their core expertise of acute, domestic hospital care, refo-
cused the company on their original long-standing mission, and
then after a few years went back to the marketplace to take the
company public again. Dad, throughout these years, remained
the icon of company values. The consistency of his integrity,
compassion, and caring permeated the company. He stood for
quality and caring.

The motto of HCA, which is repeated on a plaque in the
lobby of every HCA hospital in the country, is captured in the

founding words of Dr. Thomas Frist Sr.: "It's not bricks and mortar and equipment that make a hospital. It is the warmth and compassion and attitude of good employees that leads to quality care." He knew that the bottom line would take care of itself.

In 1994, it seemed the time came to pass the baton to the next generation of leaders. Tommy and the board thought they had found the perfect new leadership, and Tommy stepped back from day-to-day operations with the expectation that the same principles and values would be continued. The company changed names and became Columbia Hospitals system. Profits, not patients, became the guiding mantra.

Unfortunately, in changing generations, the company lost its founding values and vision. The new leadership didn't have the same heart as Dad and Tommy, and before long, it began to show. The company stumbled; legal problems ensued. The company that Jack Massey, Dr. Frist Sr., and Dr. Frist Jr. had started, cultivated, and carefully nurtured over almost three decades had lost sight of the principles and values that had made it great.

By 1997, my brother Tommy could no longer stomach the downward direction the company was taking. He had written the CEO of his seven concerns about the direction of the company and never received a response. Through a series of events that could fill a separate book, Tommy was asked by the board of directors to resume active leadership. Acting with board support, he engineered a broad coup and brought back his old, trusted management team. HCA was taken back to its former self, and over the next decade it continued to grow and prosper. Dad died in 1998, having seen the values of HCA flourish once again under the stewardship of his son.

I never worked for HCA or in an HCA hospital, nor did I ever serve on the company's board. However, I'm humbled and honored to have been an active observer of the company's proud history. I've learned a lot over the years by watching what Tommy and Dad were able to build at HCA. They combined private enterprise with public service and, most important, true concern for patients and their well-being, creating in the process one of the finest organizations in American health care. They knew how to serve. They invented a new industry, built on service and on values of heart. It all started with a young man's dream, a pursuit of his passions, a father-and-son relationship, a commitment to hard work and basic values, and a refusal to ever accept defeat.

3

A Family Like No Other

If Dad was the heart of our family, Mom was its soul. Dorothy Cate Frist was a strongly opinionated, brilliant woman who in a different time would have made a tremendous political candidate. Well-read and articulate, she loved debating controversial ideas. My sister Mary, six years older than me, went to Vanderbilt, so her college friends often stopped by our house, sometimes to see Mary, but just as often to converse with my always welcoming mother. The friends felt free to drop in at our home on Bowling day or night, and Mom loved sitting around our large yellow linoleum-topped kitchen table bandying about ideas with them. In the process, she taught me early on to see both sides of an issue before making a decision.

Mom was politically liberal, to the left of everyone else in the family. In the earliest days of the civil rights movement, it was Mom who was the outspoken advocate for racial integration. Later, in the sixties, she just as adamantly opposed the Vietnam War, outraging many of the prominent conservative businessmen and women in Nashville with her strong, vocal arguments against our country's involvement in the war.

With Dad maintaining office hours all day long, even on Saturdays, and making house calls and late rounds at the hospital seven days a week, he had little time for keeping up with current events. Mother read both newspapers from cover to cover daily, the more liberal morning *Tennessean* and the more conservative afternoon *Nashville Banner*. She devoured *Time* and *Newsweek* and then each evening passed along the information and ideas to Dad regarding the stories she deemed important. Dad laughed heartily whenever he felt Mom's not-so-subtle attempts to influence his thinking. Though he always listened to her and respected her views highly, Dad remained staunchly conservative throughout his life. Perhaps not surprisingly, Mom and Dad rarely discussed politics unless in the presence of others.

Mom's social activism was more than mere rhetoric. She modeled a genuine compassion, caring especially deeply for the needy people of our community. Her numerous gestures of generosity to people who did not have the wherewithal to repay her were legendary in Nashville. Almost always in obscurity, with as little fanfare as possible, Mom moved to meet needs wherever she found them. I never knew her once to go to a charity gala, but I've heard hundreds of stories about her helping individuals who were down and out and had no one speaking on their behalf. If she saw someone on the street begging for money, Mom never passed by without making a contribution. Around the time of the annual Girl Scouts' cookie sales, a steady stream of green-uniformed Scouts would visit the Bowling home for a week or more.

My wife, Karyn, inadvertently discovered one of my mother's exceptional acts of charity when she went to H. H. Gregg, an appliance store then on Thompson Lane, to purchase a television during a stretch of unusually hot summer weather our first year back in Nashville. While she presented her credit card to pay for the television, the clerk recognized the name and said, "Oh, Mrs. Frist. We're so glad to see you. And by the way, we just wanted you to know that we delivered those eighty air conditioners to the orphanage yesterday."

Karyn looked back at the salesman quizzically. "Eighty air conditioners?"

"Aren't you the Mrs. Frist who ordered . . . ?" The salesman's face dropped as he realized his mistake. Had it not been for the salesman's gaffe, we would never have known about Mom's anonymous, simple, yet generous act of charity, especially since Mom had specifically instructed the salesman, "Deliver the air conditioners, but don't tell anybody that I'm doing this—and especially not my husband!" Dad, the spendthrift, believed in helping people, too, but Mom had raised giving to an art form. Mom didn't make a fuss about her benevolence. Quietly and out of sight, she just did it.

We almost never went out to dinner, and I can't remember going to a really fine restaurant as my siblings and I were growing up. For the most part we ate every meal at home. Occasionally on a Sunday afternoon, we'd go to lunch as a family; Mother and Dad's favorite was Morrison's Cafeteria in the local strip shopping center. If we were not at Morrison's, we might be at the B&W, another family-style cafeteria in the neighborhood, or over at Allen's Hotel, a modest family-run hotel off West End Avenue where the treat for the family was peppermint ice cream with hot fudge sauce. It was simple dining, certainly not fancy, and it was inexpensive for feeding five kids. My parents did not drink alcohol (though Dad would prescribe a glass of red wine to all patients who had heart disease); Dad even avoided coffee, though Mother would usually have a cup after she got him off to work every morning.

Nor did they actively participate in the Nashville social networking scene, though they were always invited because of the positions of respect that both had earned in their own ways, Dad in taking care of so many within the Middle Tennessee community and Mother in personally helping the underserved in so many charitable ways.

Mom's number-one priority was her five children. Nothing was more important to her, and I think that is why, in part, that she did not take formal leadership roles in social events. She had taught school after she and Dad were married, but when Tommy was born, Dad insisted she not work so she could focus on raising their child. Tommy, the eldest of my four siblings, was born in 1938, fourteen years before me; Dottie was eleven years older than me, Bobby ten, and Mary six.

As I was growing up, the broad age span of my siblings meant that my impressionable early years around the house were spent primarily with Mary, and to a lesser extent Bobby and Dottie. Being the "baby" of the family afforded me the opportunity to sit back and listen and learn through the experiences of others.

Our home in Nashville was the place where all the kids in the neighborhood would come to play. Part of the reason was that Mom's kitchen was always filled with tantalizing smells of delicious homemade food. Another inviting factor was that we had a big yard and an assortment of animals and pets—not merely dogs and cats, but, over the years, rabbits, white turkeys, a billy goat, occasional chickens, and even horses. As a young child, and until I was about ten (when the city limits were moved to include our house and there was an ordinance: "No horses in the city"), we had three horses on the two acres behind our house. The white barn and hayloft was the site of many Halloween parties, seemingly a world away from the realities of the main house.

Sunday afternoons the front side yard would be the site of an all-family touch football game. The teams would grow as people driving by stopped in, soon to be recruited to the team most desperate for able players. Both Bobby and Tommy had quarterbacked their high school football teams, so they were relegated to being receivers, just to keep the game more fair. Dad and my siblings always made a position for the youngest, making sure I wasn't left out of the fun.

Today, Dad would be considered a workaholic. He would be home for dinner every night, but afterward, without exception, he went back to the hospital to make rounds, or he'd make house calls. But we never felt neglected, realizing that he was helping other people every second he was not with us. And I think the Ping-Pong game squeezed in after dinner and before Dad's rounds almost every night made his separation a little less noticeable. And the fact that it was hard to walk around town without someone pulling you aside to confide how thankful he or she was that Dad had taken care of him or her through the night left little room for us to complain about his absences.

Mom wasn't actively involved in Dad's medical practice, at least not in a traditional sense. But it was Dorothy Frist whom patients would call at home, knowing that "Dr. Tommy" would be busy, to solicit medical advice on how to treat their upset stomach, heartburn, headache, or aggravated arthritis. Mom was so loved and trusted, and had such a good relationship with the pharmacist Dr. Moon over at Moon's Drug Store, that she'd quite frequently call in prescriptions for patients, and the pharmacist would fill them! "I'll let Tommy know tonight," she'd reassure Dr. Moon. She was the ultimate doctor's wife—patient, tolerant, empathetic, and frequently physician in absentia!

Mom allowed me enormous freedom as a boy growing up in Nashville. For instance, before I was eight years old, to the astonishment of other parents, Mom permitted me to take the city bus downtown to go to the YMCA every day with my neighborhood buddies, John Gibson and Tommy Nesbitt, without parents or other adult supervision. Of course, Nashville was a much smaller city then, but Mom just didn't want me to be afraid to do anything. She figured that's the best way to learn your way in the world. And, of course, I was the last child of five, so she'd seen it all anyway.

Like most mothers, Mom's goal was my success; she wanted her children to learn the value of contributing and being successful and winning. She went out of her way to see that each of her children developed a positive self-image and approached life with confidence. When Woodmont Grammar School, my elementary school, held its annual paper drive to raise funds, Mom not only encouraged us to participate but spurred us on to help our class win the contest. It was my mother who drove her blue and white station wagon, afternoon after afternoon, from house to house, so we could run in and pick up discarded newspapers. If we were selling raffle tickets for the annual school carnival, she helped make lists of people we could go see, and yes, if we hadn't sold the last two dollars of our raffle book, she would buy them herself.

But self-initiative can occasionally get you in a bind. One day in the fourth grade, when the teachers were recruiting students for the school talent show, I inadvertently (and probably wishfully) gave the impression to my teacher that I could play the banjo.

"Wonderful, Billy," the teacher said. "We'll put you on the program."

The only problem was that I didn't even own a banjo, much less know how to play one. But I was too embarrassed to confess in front of the class. That afternoon, I ashamedly explained my predicament to Mother. Without missing a beat, she saw another lesson to be learned. "It looks like you are going to have to learn to play the banjo!"

For the next three weeks, Mother sat me down every day and taught me how to play a single song on the newly purchased banjo. I got through one rendition of "Home on the Range" in the school talent show, having learned my lesson about not overstating one's abilities in the exuberance of the moment—or else. Having a mother who would step up and support her son, even when he made a mistake, was a blessing.

Was I spoiled? Oh, probably (my siblings would say most definitely). But Mom had a different method of building my self-esteem. While she knew the value of learning from mistakes and recognized how important it was for me to know how to lose as well as win, and how to overcome failure and other pressures, she built my self-confidence by helping me to succeed more often than not.

Dad's genuine love for people, his deep interest in getting to know them as individuals, and his natural ability to listen intently to what folks said left an indelible impression on my heart and mind. Within minutes of meeting someone, he made them feel significant; he affirmed their dignity. And it was real. Dad was an experienced and, probably more important, an instinctive diagnostician, but he never confined his fascination with folks to his medical practice or his business dealings. At dinners, at social events, at church, when we ran down to the store, when we took a trip, he was always taking time to talk to someone, usually someone others might not notice, much less recognize—the boy working at the gas station, waitresses and road construction workers, the receptionist behind the desk, and even vaguely familiar faces.

The Frist family members were spiritual people and attended church regularly. As a boy, Dad had a string of Sunday school pins for perfect attendance. As a family we attended Westminster Presbyterian Church on West End Avenue. Dad was a deacon and then elder in the church. He never preached at anyone, nor did he wear his religion on his sleeve; he simply lived out his faith on a daily basis. When my siblings and I were younger and Dad had come in early from his nightly rounds, he'd come into our rooms and have us get out of bed for evening prayers. When we balked at kneeling beside our beds or questioned why we couldn't pray from our pillows, Dad replied, "The Lord doesn't answer a lazy man's prayers." So we dutifully pulled out of bed and got down on our knees to pray along with Dad.

Mom's faith ran deep as well. Whereas Dad's was based on action and service to others and thanksgiving, Mother's was rooted in a strict Methodist upbringing, with deeply religious parents who made her memorize Bible verses and taught her that frivolous activities such as dancing were sinful. (When I was a very young boy, my out-of-town cousins were discouraged by my grandmother from spending the night with us because we played music and had a pool table.) Young Dorothy Cate had a mischievous side to her that left her a little suspicious of those who held such rigid beliefs. But all of the Sundays and Wednesdays she spent growing up in church left her with a complete repertoire of great old hymns that she loved singing with the family, especially in her later years.

Throughout my childhood, the telephone was a constant reminder of Dad's instinctive response to human need and his accessibility to his patients. Often as I was growing up, I'd awaken in the middle of the night to the telephone's ring, followed by the sound of Dad's car pulling out of the driveway in response to someone's call for help. It was hard on the family at times, but we children never felt cheated. We knew Dad was busy helping other people to get well, often saving lives with his knowledge and skills. And he prevented us from feeling hostile toward his career by making life around our home so complete. He never missed one of our baseball, basketball, or football games. When Dad was at home, he gave us his undivided attention . . . until the telephone rang again.

I occasionally went along with Dad on his after-dinner house calls, and accompanying him was an education in itself. Dad always toted a black leather medical bag with him, in which he carried his stethoscope, a few thermometers, an assortment of medicines and bandages, syringes, and other basic medical paraphernalia. In those days, a doctor could carry just about everything he could use in that single doctor's bag. Dad also carried a notebook in his shirt pocket to help him remember names and details about his patients. Before going in to see a patient, he would review his notes, which included tidbits of information about the patient's family members, personal struggles, sometimes even photos of the children attached to the back of the notebook page. Dad wanted those he treated to know that he genuinely cared about them and their families as people, not simply as "patients."

Dad's bedside manner in people's homes was not much different than it was in the hospital. He always sat down in a chair, or next to the patient's bed, laid his hand on the arm or shoulder of the patient, and looked the person in the eye as he or she talked. More than anything, Dad listened; he never gave the impression that he was in a hurry. Although he did not normally spend an inordinate amount of time with any one patient, they all felt that he had given them huge amounts of undivided attention. It was a lesson that would serve me well later in my life.

Although Dad's real interest always came back to his patients in Middle Tennessee, he also invested in initiatives that he felt could better the world community. In the late 1950s, he traveled to Mexico on a short-term medical mission trip on behalf of the Presbyterian Church—his first-ever international trip. I do remember going out to the airport as a seven-year-old to welcome Dad home. He'd brought back a stack of black-and-white Polaroid photographs depicting patients lying three people to a medical cot. Another photo showed a missionary surgeon gowned in white, holding lovingly in his arms a young child he had just operated on, a primitive medical clinic in the background. These images stuck with me.

Dad was profoundly moved by his medical missionary experience. Within weeks, he helped found the Medical Benevolence Foundation (MBF) for medical missionaries, an organization associated with the Presbyterian Church. MBF grew in time to a huge global organization, today sending medical personnel on short-term mission trips, as well as providing medical supplies and equipment to needy people all over the globe, with more than one hundred hospitals and clinics serving hundreds of communities. The seeds Dad planted always seemed to grow magnificently.

Dad always said he was not smart enough on his own, so he had to rely on others. Often when his patients brought him good ideas, good things happened. For example, there's the story of Cumberland Heights, a 170-acre recovery and rehabilitation center for those with alcohol and chemical addictions, located about twelve miles from our home. It is worth sharing because it is a typical example of an individual's single, simple idea blossoming into something larger than ever imagined, with a legacy that will affect thousands and thousands of people for generations to come.

It all started in early 1964, when Nashville entrepreneur and our neighbor Bob Crichton sought Dad's professional help in finding the best treatment possible for his alcoholism. After careful research, Dad said, "If you really want the best in the country, you need to go to the Hazelden Clinic in Center City, Minnesota." Mr. Crichton, then a prominent and well-loved insurance executive in Nashville, thought it terrible that Tennessee, indeed the whole South, did not have an affordable, residential treatment facility the caliber of Hazelden. The need was huge. At the time there were an estimated 6.5 million alcoholics in the United States; the dark stigma attached to being an alcoholic in those days meant that only 10 percent were receiving treatment. Could Dr. Frist, who seemed to be able to fix everything else medical, help him start such a facility in Nashville?

Dad, as was his manner, listened carefully when Bob came by to discuss the problem, but he told him that it would simply be impossible for him to take on this new project. "Bob, I cannot give it the attention it deserves," Dad responded.

That night, however, as he did every night, Dad reviewed the day in detail with Mother as they lay in bed. He told her of the dire need for a drug and alcohol treatment center in Tennessee and how effective the facility in Minnesota was. Mother's natural sensitivities were affected; she asked a number of probing questions. Just before she and Dad drifted off to sleep, Mom said, "I really pray that someone will step up to make Bob's vision happen. It could make a lot of people's lives better."

Dad tossed and turned all night, troubled by Mother's comment.

By morning, he had totally reversed course.

At 7:00 A.M., he called Bob Crichton to say he had changed his mind. Crichton was ecstatic. "Where do we start?"

"We have to get good people who know what they are doing," Dad replied, already thinking about some prospects. "If we do that, they can go out and hire the sort of people we need."

A week later, Crichton called Lon Jacobsen, chief counselor at none other than Hazelden itself. Crichton and Dad asked him to design the Nashville facility, and then to come down to run it. Jacobsen agreed.

Dad helped lead a fundraising drive, and by the year's end, more than $284,000 was raised; the groundbreaking ceremony took place on January 13, 1966—a mere six months after the foundation's chartering paperwork was filed. The doors opened seven months later, and by the end of the year, the facility that Dad had at first said he simply didn't have time to deal with had treated ninety-seven patients from sixteen states and one foreign country.

The campus is still thriving today, more than forty-two years later, treating more than ten thousand patients annually and indirectly touching the lives of more than 127,000 family members and friends of the patients. Patients range from the indigent and unemployed, to small business owners and corporate managers, to nationally recognized personalities from the sports and entertainment fields. The initial one-hundred-thousand-dollar commitments that Dad and Mr. Crichton secured have grown today into an annual operating budget of over $26 million.

The Robert Wood Johnson Foundation still characterizes chemical abuse as "the nation's number-one health problem," costing over $144 billion annually. But because of Dad's willingness to listen to the "yes" of his heart (an epiphany precipitated by Mother), in spite of an initial "no" from his mind, more than two hundred thousand patients have benefited from remarkable rehabilitative programs at Cumberland Heights. In October 2007, the five Frist children and our spouses proudly participated at Cumberland Heights in the dedication of the Dorothy Cate and Thomas F. Frist Family Life Center, given in honor of our parents' past contributions.

Dad was part of many stories like that, all originating in the seed of an idea, the recognition of a need, and the follow-through to what it takes to make dreams come true. He had a passion to bring health, hope, and healing to others.

AFTER GOING TO PUBLIC ELEMENTARY SCHOOL AT WOODMONT, I attended the same private boys' school, Montgomery Bell Academy (MBA), to which both of my brothers had gone. I was a good student, but I had to work hard. Never the athlete that my brothers were, I lost myself in extracurricular activities, which I loved. My classmates voted me as their president three years in a row.

Part of that, no doubt, was because I constantly sought to include people. Cliques rubbed me the wrong way; I reflected my dad's belief that every individual had something good to offer, so everybody should be included. I couldn't stand it if I saw someone ostracized because he wasn't smart enough, wasn't cool enough, or didn't live in the "right" neighborhood. It was natural for me to befriend the unpopular guys, and I tried to look for the good in every person, just as I'd seen my mother do when she provided a refuge for our childhood friends when they had gotten into some kind of trouble.

I loved to write. For a summer job, while still in high school, I worked at the afternoon newspaper, the *Nashville Banner*, and my senior year I was the editor of the yearbook. I followed in my brothers' footsteps and played quarterback on the football team, though I was never very good.

Looking back, life was going along well. I was having a good high school experience, my siblings had all gone to college, gotten married, and started their families, both of my older brothers were now on their way to becoming doctors, my sisters were thriving, and Mother and Dad were healthy.

But for me, everything was about to change.

I was coasting through my early teenage years, when one summer morning I came out of our house and spied my brother Bobby's red motor scooter, parked in the garage behind our house. I knew Bobby wouldn't mind if I borrowed it to take a spin.

Just before I hopped on, Mattie Belle, a dear woman who lived with us for twenty years working as a housekeeper, saw me and gave me a reprimanding look. "If you're gonna ride that dangerous thing, you better put a helmet on your head," she said, nodding toward Bobby's motor scooter. Mattie led the way down into the basement, where she found an old motorcycle helmet that cousin Johnny had left behind years before. To placate Mattie Belle, I put the dusty helmet on, fastened the chinstrap, and took off on the scooter.

I was about a block from my house on Bowling Avenue when I spotted a good friend, Phil Brodnax, and his sister

Shelly. Honking the horn with my left hand, I started waving enthusiastically—and maybe a bit too energetically—with my right. The last thing I remember was the crunching sound of metal and a heavy thump as the scooter slammed into the back of a stopped car. I don't remember ducking my head, but luckily the brunt of the impact was absorbed first by my left leg ripping off the handlebars, and then my helmet as I smashed through the rear window. I fell off the back of the car into the ditch on the right side of the road.

Lying limply in the gutter, I was still conscious, aware of the bright sun and the still-deafening whirring of the scooter's engine with the throttle stuck wide open. I looked down at my left leg, and a deep twelve-inch flap of skin and flesh, muscle, and blood was my first clue that I was in trouble. I saw the bone protruding through my right ring finger, and when I tried to touch it, it was apparent that my left arm had been completely broken, with my wrist hanging at a right angle to my forearm. *Man,* I thought, *I should have listened to the advice of my parents and never ridden a motorcycle.*

It took the ambulance awhile to get to the scene. An orthopedic trauma surgeon, Dr. Dewey Thomas, fortunately just happened to be driving by and came to my rescue, stopping the immediate hemorrhage. It was Dr. Thomas who spent all night putting me back together. Being just a block from home, Mother arrived on the scene before the ambulance. I recall her calm, reassuring voice telling me that everything would be okay.

And it was, but before all was said and done, my list of injuries included a shattered right kneecap, multiple broken bones in my hand, arm, and nose, a concussion, and the leg laceration. I had glass embedded in my back that I was still picking out six months later. But I was alive.

I spent two weeks in the hospital. The accident changed my life. It gave me at a relatively young age my first sense of mortality; I realized that had Mattie Belle not chided me into wearing that helmet, I would have died. Listen to wise counsel. The accident ignited a flame within me, a desire to live every day to the max, to make every day count. That sense of mortality has haunted me ever since. A day that passes is a day gone forever.

For the next year, I worked on physical therapy, most of which centered on my right leg, since the right kneecap had to be totally removed. I resented having to waste so much time day after day doing leg lifts while sitting on the bathroom counter with weights strapped around my right ankle. *Why me?*

During my junior year, I was sufficiently rehabilitated to play football with a knee brace as the second-string quarterback. I was slow and really couldn't throw the ball very well, but since both of my brothers had been stellar quarterbacks, that seemed to be the natural position for me to play. I rarely got into a game my junior year, but we did go on to win the state championship under the legendary coach Tommy Owen (who claimed more state champions than any coach in Tennessee history). And during my senior year, I got to play behind the "greatest quarterback ever to play at MBA," according to Coach Owen (though contested by my quarterback brothers). If I ever need to, I can always proudly boast to having played in the state championship game, even though I took only three snaps during the last two minutes, when the game was already well in hand.

What do you do if you grow up loving sports but suddenly suffer a disabling injury? You find a sport in which the disability can be minimized, and that's exactly what I did. My cousin Johnny, fourteen years my senior, had learned martial arts during his service in Vietnam. I was fascinated by karate, especially the mystical mind-body interplay. I drove my family members bonkers as I kicked my leg up to the top of the kitchen door archway and then stood in the doorway practicing my stretches, with one leg firmly against the doorway and my other leg stretched to the top of the woodwork. While my friends mastered the conventional sports, I earned a brown belt in karate.

Another pursuit I came to love was flying.

When Tommy was gallivanting across the country in his Stinson plane the year he took off from college, he would fly back to Nashville for weekends. He loved flying, and always looked for excuses just to soar through the air for a few hours. It was (and still is, last year flying a single-engine plane from Nashville to Italy) an addiction for him. One Saturday when I was about six, he took me out to the general aviation side of Nashville's airport (then-called) Berry Field and proudly showed me his cloth-covered plane. The next thing I knew, Tommy was hand-cranking the wooden propeller, and minutes later we were taking off, his excuse this time being that he wanted to try out a new roadside barbecue pit for lunch over in tiny Bolivar, Tennessee. Within minutes, I was hooked. I felt the sense of freedom in being aloft for the first time, the opportunities of being able to fly for just thirty minutes and then be so far away, landing in a tiny town I'd never heard of, borrowing someone's car at the rural airport, eating a freshly smoked pulled-pork barbecue sandwich for lunch. I dreamed that flying could open worlds for me. Going to bed at night, I'd look up at the pennants from schools all over the country and think to myself, "Now I know how he does it—flying!"

During the summer before my sixteenth birthday, Tommy and Trisha invited me to come visit them during his military service, when Tommy served as a flight surgeon at Warner Robbins Air Force Base in Macon, Georgia. He and I agreed that my visit would be the perfect opportunity to begin my flying lessons—a detail we didn't mention at home, so as not to needlessly worry Mother and Dad. It was our secret. I soloed in Piper Cherokee 1969Z a few weeks later, cutting off my shirttail as a memento, as most student pilots do to celebrate their first major milestone in flying. That white shirttail, now framed, has accompanied me everywhere I have moved since. At that young age, flying instilled in me a sense of freedom. I loved the sense of adventure, and I loved that edge of danger. It was skill-driven and it was knowledge-based. Flying also fit my personality. It put me squarely in control of my destiny. It taught me to trust my instruments, a lesson with broad applications, since sometimes in life you need to rely on more than your own instincts. It meant making no mistakes— mistakes meant death, literally. It meant judgment . . . misjudging the weather had devastating consequences. Most of all, flying gave me a tool that I would use, and enjoy, for the next forty years.

Like Tommy, I looked for every excuse to fly. While others were playing team sports at MBA, I was running out to the air-field every afternoon to earn my multiengine rating, my commer-cial license, and my instrument rating.

Flying has come in handy over the years. I went on during my years at Princeton to run the "country's oldest collegiate flying club" (which entitled me to a substantial discount of being able to fly for twelve dollars an hour), flew throughout medical school in Boston to go to board meetings as a young alumni trustee at Princeton, bought old and very inexpensive airplanes and then refurbished them to sell, and in my medical years, used general aviation to pick up hearts and lungs to transplant back at Van-derbilt. When I entered politics, flying allowed me to cover the state and meet with people in ways that would have otherwise been impossible. In a single day, I could fly myself across our five-hundred-mile-long state, being with constituents in as many as six events in all three Grand Divisions of the state. Tennesseans want to see and talk directly to their senator in their hometown. Flying made that possible for me. Visiting all ninety-five counties during a session of Congress was made a lot easier by flying. And it all started with an older brother taking his kid brother to get a barbecue sandwich on a serendipitous journey one Saturday afternoon.

IN THE FRIST FAMILY, PROBABLY BECAUSE I WAS THE LAST OF FIVE, I was always the adventurer, seeking to do things in a different way. All my brothers and sisters had gone to college in Nashville, but I wanted to get away from home, to spread my wings, and to see what life was like where no one knew I was one of the Frist kids, or cared.

Few students from MBA had gone to Ivy League schools—almost all stayed in the South—but the year before graduation, a good friend of mine in high school whom I looked up to, Gordon

Peerman, had toured Princeton and the University of Virginia. He told me how enthralled he was with the gothic structures on the Princeton campus and the teaching strategy of very small classes called "precepts." Gordon ultimately got a scholarship to the University of Virginia, but his magical description of the faraway campus up north remained vivid in my naïve mind. I'd never known anyone who'd gone north to school.

When it came time to apply to college, I put Princeton as my first choice, much to the wonderment of Mother and Dad. I'm sure they feared I'd lose all of the solid Southern values that so characterized our growing up. Why go to Princeton, they asked, when right here in the South you have the University of Tennessee, Ole Miss, and Vanderbilt?

The decision to list Princeton first was heavily influenced by the quiet counsel of Tommy, who was always the one in the family to shoot for the stars. Tommy and his wife, Trisha, were like a younger set of parents to me. They began dating when I was an infant and patiently allowed me to tag along everywhere they went. When they married, I even went along on part of their honeymoon, sitting between them on the front seat of their car, all the way to Florida. So a few years later, when Tommy nudged me toward Princeton, I was quick to consider it.

Upon graduation from high school, rather than working to make a little extra money for college, I wanted to take a few weeks of the summer and see the country. One day after school, I suggested to my closest neighborhood friend, John Gibson, "Let's do some traveling. Let's take a cross-country trip to California before we have to split up and head for college."

"My parents would never allow me to do something like that on my own," John said. "But since it's your idea, they might let me. Let's have your mother call my parents and make the suggestion." Mother was always the one in the neighborhood who could grease the wheels for something a little out of the ordinary or the expected. John's parents, probably reluctantly, said okay, so that summer John and I, untraveled and inexperienced, set off on our own across America, with no real destination in mind.

We were simply two eighteen-year-old kids, going from place to place, camping along the way, trying to see what we could discover.

We were amazed at how vast and how diverse America really is. We traveled all the way to the Grand Canyon, where we hiked down to touch the Colorado River at the base of the canyon (arriving with bleeding feet because of poor preparation). We drove on to Palo Alto, home of Stanford University, where we stayed with a family friend (and wondered, How can students spend so much time playing tennis?). We drove the length of Pacific Highway Number One, awed at the beauty of the California coastline (and equally amazed—though not necessarily as impressed—by the hippies of the time). For three and a half weeks, John and I ambled across the country and back, stopping to explore big cities and tiny towns, experiencing firsthand the highlights of each area. We grew up a bit, as well; I will never forget that fast-talking car repairman in Arizona who successfully convinced me to buy four new "special for the desert" tires that would better withstand the heat on our long drives!

All too soon, it was time to say good-bye to friends and family and head off to college. I'd been accepted at Princeton.

4

Breaking Away

Princeton was a long way from Middle Tennessee and from the values and family that I so cherished. My brothers and sisters had all gone to college in Nashville, not far from home. I was breaking the mold. On the other hand, I was free, out from being the little brother of the Frist siblings in Nashville, free to make my own decisions, good or bad; free to choose what I'd eat, when to get up or to go to bed, or even if I wanted to go to bed at all!

Originally chartered in 1746 as the College of New Jersey, Princeton is rich in history. Most of its early presidents were preachers (Presbyterian, as was I, which gave me some subtle, intangible affinity to the place) as well as educators, including Jonathan Dickerson, Aaron Burr Sr., and Jonathan Edwards, whose sermon "Sinners in the Hands of an Angry God" remains one of the most famous ever preached in America.

Another early Princeton president, a favorite of mine, was the great preacher John Witherspoon, the only college president and the only clergyman to sign the Declaration of Independence. Benign in appearance, Witherspoon was an indefatigable ball of energy. Besides preaching twice on Sunday and handling other pastoral duties, Witherspoon carried a heavy teaching load. He saw no conflict between faith and reason, and encouraged

Princeton students to test their faith against a commonsense philosophy, which he felt would strengthen their Christian commitment, rather than erode it.

Nor did Witherspoon have any qualms about teaching religion and politics. In fact, his faith compelled him to be a strong proponent of liberty. Under Witherspoon's leadership, Princeton became known as a "seedbed of the American Revolution." Many of Witherspoon's students entered public service. Eventually, the pastor/educator taught at least one president and one vice president of the United States, as well as nine cabinet members, twenty-one senators, thirty-nine congressmen, three Supreme Court justices, and twelve state governors. Witherspoon himself was a member of the Continental Congress, and in 1783, members of the Continental Congress met at Nassau Hall, the large stone building that once housed the entire college, still the dominant building on campus where I arrived in the fall of 1970.

I went to Princeton University knowing no one. It seemed like another world to this southern boy. It seemed as if every person I met there had gone to some elite eastern boarding school, reinforcing my feeling of inadequacy. I met a group of freshmen (some of whom reminded me of how "backward" they'd heard the South to be) in my dorm, Holder Hall, and quickly got drawn into one of the traditional capers at Princeton—the stealing of the bell clapper from atop Nassau Hall. Tradition said that if students could remove the clapper from the large bell in the stately bell tower before the first day of classes, the administration would call off classes until the following week. Whether the administration ever actually agreed to such shenanigans is rather dubious. Regardless, each year, some freshmen valiantly attempted to scale the high bell tower and remove the heavy metal bell clapper. Almost always, they would get caught, and classes commenced as scheduled. The problem was, of course, that everyone knew about the tradition, and there were relatively few ways to ascend to the top of the tower without being seen. Making matters worse, the proctors—as the campus police were called—kept a wary eye on the tower, lest some wild-eyed freshman should get too close.

Nevertheless, three of my newfound friends and I waited until about 2:00 A.M., then launched our assault on the bell. A couple of guys staged a distraction near where we knew the proctors stood guard, while my buddies and I scaled the back side of Nassau Hall like a group of commandos, taking advantage of a lightning ground wire that ran from the roof to the ground. Rather than traverse the roof where we certainly could be seen, our idea was to ascend within. We got in a window on the third floor, somehow found the trap door in the ceiling to the bell tower in the darkness, pried it open, and scurried through, closing it securely behind us. We climbed an old wooden ladder up through the dark musty tower, shadows playing on the walls, carrying the wrenches and hacksaw necessary to cut the clapper from its base in the huge cast-iron bell. We'd been successful at being admitted to Princeton, so surely we would be successful in our first caper there! We were almost there, just a couple of minutes to go. Just as I began to saw through the clapper, I heard rustling from below, penetrating flashlights flooded the area, and a proctor grasped my ankle. "You're busted, boys," he called with feigned anger.

We'd been on campus two days, and we were already in trouble.

We didn't get punished, perhaps because the prank was such a part of the Princeton tradition. And although I hate to admit it, another group of students succeeded two nights later; to this day, they remind me with gentle ribbing that they were successful where we had failed! The tradition of trying to steal the bell clapper has since been outlawed at Princeton for liability reasons.

As anyone who lived through the late 1960s and early 1970s can tell you, the mood on campuses across the nation was anything but tranquil. The campus unrest that accompanied the anti-Vietnam War movement had died down a bit by the time I arrived. Then in May 1970, President Nixon announced the

United States would expand the war into Cambodia, and renewed protests erupted, the most infamous resulting in four students' deaths and nine others' being wounded during a confrontation with the Ohio National Guard serving as riot police on the campus of Kent State University in Kent, Ohio. In the aftermath, students staged sit-ins on campuses around the nation; millions of others went on strike, refusing to attend classes; more than nine hundred colleges and universities shut down for a cooling-off period as protests continued.

The pastoral campus of Princeton was not immune to campus protests. We had our share of campus radicals, but I was not one of them. My only concessions to the radicalism of the times were my long hair and jeans, consistent with the times. Of course, being a southerner, in the minds of the more liberal elements at Princeton, I was suspect already. We talked differently in the South; we had mistakenly tolerated racial divisions much longer than other areas of the country; we remained the bastion of conservatism, a not-so-popular image often evoked by mention of President Richard Nixon's term, "the silent majority."

For all these reasons and more, I felt slightly out of sync when I began my academic career. While no one ever expressed anti-southern prejudice toward me, snubbed me, or denigrated my cultural roots, I felt different. I hailed from a strong, conservative Christian family; I avoided the drug culture that was popular at the time and was not drawn into the party scene. I didn't feel I needed to do those things to get along. What's more, although I lamented the Vietnam War and the turmoil it had caused, I was not alienated from my country. I loved America and I respected our flag and all the values for which it stands.

The inevitable result, I suppose, was that I shunned social involvement in campus life those first few months, all of which led to a terrible case of freshman loneliness. As an autumn chill wrapped around Princeton, painting the campus with a spectacular palette of colors, deadness seemed to wrap around my spirit. I vividly recall listening wistfully to the clanging Nassau Hall bell as I walked through the grand arches of old East Pyne Hall, shuffling through the fallen leaves at eleven o'clock at night on my way back from the library to my tiny dorm room across campus in Holder. The loneliness was almost palpable. *Maybe my parents were right. Why hadn't I just stayed at home for college?*

Feeling inferior academically to my fellow students who had gone to the elite prep schools of Andover and Choate and St. Paul's ("What does MBA stand for?" they'd ask), I threw myself into my studies, primarily out of fear that I wouldn't keep up with my fellow students, pursuing both a premed curriculum and a full course load of political science and economics courses. Part of the reason I'd decided to attend Princeton was that I was interested in policy issues and public affairs, a field in which Princeton was preeminent, as suggested by the school's famous motto, "In the Nation's Service." All along, I knew I would become a doctor, just like my brothers Bobby and Tommy, cousin Johnny, and of course my father, but I was also attracted to how public policy just might be used as a means to better the lives of others.

There was also the world of writing. Toward the end of my freshman year, I became more acclimated to the Princeton culture and began writing for the student newspaper, the *Daily Princetonian*. To this day, I remember the lessons shared with me by my senior editors—what to get in the first two paragraphs as a hook, the importance of anecdote, just one memorable statistic, the expansive final paragraph. Working on the newspaper also gave me a ready outlet to express my opinions, which caught the attention of the few like-minded students and were excoriated by those of other persuasions.

In those days, we had to write our articles and then physically set the type by hand. At least one night each week it was my responsibility to go to the printing press office off Nassau Street around 10:00 P.M. to do the layout and help set the hot metal type, stacked line by line, column by column in well-worn small wooden boxes for the next morning's paper. I'd leave about three or four o'clock in the morning, the oily-smelling black ink heavily staining the old T-shirt that I had purposely worn for the task. During the fall of my sophomore year, I was an assistant editor—

one of about ten sophomores given this lofty title as a reward for all of the T-shirt-stained nights of hard work—which entailed more late nights at the newspaper office.

You never know in life when something you invested yourself in and worked hard to be good at might suddenly come in handy years later for an entirely different reason. One night I was covering a story down at the newly named Forbes College, an old hotel on the edge of campus recently converted to a dorm to handle the expansion for women who just two years before had been admitted to Princeton for the first time. I was on the brick patio just back of the college building when three young men, clearly not Princeton students, aggressively approached me as I was writing on a pad, beneath a lamppost on the otherwise dark porch.

"How about your wallet, fella?" the one standing just in front of me said, as his two friends positioned themselves behind me.

From hanging around the news desk, I knew that there had been reports of small gangs from nearby Trenton coming onto campus and robbing students. It didn't take me long to put two and two together.

"My wallet is mine," I said a lot more confidently than I probably should have. But I did know that I was just thirty feet from the open door to the dorms, and that I had spent three years training and practicing karate after I'd lost my kneecap in the accident.

One of the thugs behind me pushed my back as he reached for my wallet, just as the one in front of me thrust forward to grab my arms. In karate, the real secret is simply the repetition that makes moves become reflex. The reflex here was striking the assailant's outreached arm behind me forcefully with a right arm sweep, and almost simultaneously doing a side kick forward to the other assailant's chest. One down and one hurting. But as I looked to the left and behind me, I saw a tall shadow lifting a heavy black iron chair above his head. Another reflex—a roundhouse kick to his head. The iron chair tumbled to the side, and this assailant did not get up.

The police came, and indeed these three were young punks

from the Trenton area who had come to Princeton to prey on the easy targets, especially unassuming southern boys like me. It ended there, or so I thought.

About a week later, I got a call in the middle of the day from Frances Carter, the revered traditional headmaster back at my Nashville high school MBA.

"Bill, you did everything right while you were at MBA. But someone just sent me the report that you are getting in fights at Princeton. That is not what we taught you here. Our motto is 'Gentleman, Scholar, Athlete.' Remember that."

To this day, I don't know if he was chiding me in a friendly or a scolding way. What I do know is that to make his point he read the report in front of the daily MBA assembly, and from there the word traveled to my mother, who called the next day to say, "Stay out of trouble! That is not why we let you go to Princeton; that would not have happened if you'd stayed in Nashville to go to school." But before she finished her admonition, she, in her always supportive and optimistic and sunny way, said, "I'm sure glad you took all that karate stuff in high school when everyone thought you were a nut for choosing such an offbeat sport!" Even in the negative she would stress the bright spot—and find humor where others didn't.

At the end of my sophomore year, I had to choose a major. Most students in that day planning a medical career majored in a science. But consistent with a pattern that I would follow through life, I wanted to follow a road less traveled—a major in public policy. Princeton had developed a unique institution called the Woodrow Wilson School (WWS) of Public Policy and International Affairs. Founded with an endowment by Charles and Marie Robertson in 1961, the school's purpose was to train students to enter government service. The WWS is predominantly a graduate school, but sophomores could apply to the program, which provided a two-year multidisciplinary undergraduate curriculum in politics, economics, history, and public policy.

I was admitted to the WWS, where I would be a lone premed student in a sea of future lawyers and policymakers for the next two years. It was a glimpse of the world I would enter in earnest twenty-five years later, when I became the only medical doctor among a sea of lawyers in the U.S. Senate.

For the rest of my undergraduate career, I was living in two very different worlds. After a full day of studying basic economics and politics at the distinctive "Woody Woo" building (which critics say looks like a giant bicycle rack), I'd walk across the stone patio for a three-hour wet chemistry lab in the Frick Chemistry Building. These disparate groups of students and faculty rarely interacted—the prelaw set discussing and debating the great political issues of yesteryear and today, and the premed set intently and competitively focused on pure basic science and how to elevate their class rank in order to get into a top med school. I loved them both and enjoyed shifting gears each day, shuffling back and forth. Being equally comfortable in these contrasting worlds required a lot of work on my part—but I thrived on it.

While most people saw me on campus as a conservative, probably because of my traditional southern values, I was not among the most conservative students at Princeton. The more hard-line conservative group of about thirty students on campus was led by Andy Napolitano, who later became a New Jersey judge and is best known today as an articulate and amiable judicial analyst on Fox News. Although I was sympathetic with their conservative philosophies, my views were more centrist; many would characterize me as more of a bleeding heart. I'd rather spend my late afternoons with my ten-year-old "little brother" in the community Big Brother volunteer program than attend an organizational meeting for the hardcore Conservative Alumni of Princeton (CAP).

Nevertheless, at the end of my second year, members of Andy's group asked me to represent them in a debate on the issue of whether Army Reserve Officers Training Corps (ROTC) should remain on the Princeton campus or be told to leave. Unquestionably, had the issue been voted upon by the more left-leaning student population, typical of this tense Vietnam era, ROTC would have been voted off campus. And the faculty was even more strident and vocal in their anti–United States government and anti-ROTC biases. The debate would be held in the historic board room of Nassau Hall in front of none other than the board of trustees of the university. Never in recent history had two students been asked to debate in front of the trustees on such a controversial issue, so it was considered a pretty big deal.

My opponent and I were given ten minutes each to present our cases. I was terribly nervous. I'd debated in high school, but never in college. Though the board included a few former military types and business leaders, on the whole it, too, was relatively liberal in thinking. But I did my best to make a convincing case, using logic and arguments that seemed pretty clear-cut to me. At the conclusion of the debate, the trustees voted to keep ROTC on campus, and suddenly I was a hero to the relatively small but certainly principled and vocal group of Princeton conservatives.

I had fallen, almost by accident, into a position of political leadership. It was my first experience of carrying the conservative agenda to the top and making my case. It would not be the last.

THE SUMMER OF 1972 WAS A VOLATILE TIME IN OUR NATION'S HISTORY as Richard Nixon's exit policy from Vietnam was being implemented. The news that captured the nation's attention, however, centered on a bungled burglary at the Watergate Hotel in Washington. Eventually, the break-in at the Democratic National Headquarters would haunt the Nixon administration, leading to the president's near-impeachment. After winning a landslide victory in 1972, Richard Nixon became the first president in U.S. history to resign from office.

Despite the widespread antipathy toward government officials and political institutions in general, my interest was piqued when I heard of an opportunity to serve as a summer intern in Washington, D.C., with Congressman Joe E. Evins, a senior Tennessee Democrat from Smithville and a patient of my dad's. Ironically, his daughter had taught me when I was in the fourth grade at Woodmont. I was intrigued by government, and the potential to make changes that could affect the community, and maybe even the world.

I spent two months living in Georgetown and working on Capitol Hill, finally meeting the congressman himself only on the very last day. Seated in his office, I asked the revered senior congressman his advice on how I might someday become involved in public service. I had liked what I'd seen and thought that maybe, just maybe, I'd like to serve my country in Washington, D.C.

His response was classic. Turning in his high-backed, dark red leather chair, he looked me over slowly, then remarked in a deliberate, grandfatherly tone, "Son, don't come here right after you graduate. Go do something else for twenty years. Be the very best at it. Then come to Washington and bring that experience with you. You'll be more successful then, whatever you do up here. Even more important, this great institution of the United States Congress and the American people will be the beneficiaries."

These words would haunt me twenty years later . . . almost to the day. It wasn't the answer I had expected, but in retrospect, I now regard it as some of the wisest advice I have received in my life. And to countless individuals who have come to see me over the years, I've offered some variant of what Congressman Evins counseled me. He unwittingly had introduced me to the simple, yet powerful concept of a citizen-legislator.

I was out of step at Princeton in more ways than simply my political beliefs. Other than Rob Mowrey, my sophomore-year roommate also from Tennessee, I was the only other member in Cottage Club—which I joined my junior year—for whom alcohol held absolutely no allure. Princeton's eating clubs were a unique feature of campus life, serving a role similar to that of fraternities at most universities. The club officers live on the second floors of the stately homes, but for most members the clubs serve principally as the center of social life—places to socialize, to have a good meal, and to either loaf or study between classes, and on weekends to party.

I ate every meal at Cottage, and often studied upstairs in the beautifully appointed, dark wood library used by the great novelist F. Scott Fitzgerald in his student days. Some of the author's early writings and personal mementoes remained on exhibit under glass as a constant reminder of the creativity that flourished at Cottage. For some of us Fitzgerald's legacy of success was something to aspire to. I loved the club and forged strong relationships that continue to this day; when I return to campus nowadays, Cottage becomes my home base. But although I enjoyed the club immensely at the time, it did not form the hub of my social life. I attended the monthly parties and enjoyed them, but I was never the one to close them down.

My conservative views and traditional outlook had a progressive streak. My senior year I was one of the people out of the 120 or so members who voted to accept women to the all-male club, a position that was not too popular at the time. It was also about this time that I wrote a lengthy letter to the trustees of my high school alma mater MBA to do the same . . . not much of a positive response there, either.

While attending Princeton, I came up with a good scheme to indulge my passion for flying and to "build time" or accumulate hours for my next aviation rating. As president of the university's flying club, I submitted a proposal to the local organ transplant centers that I use the club's airplanes to transport tissues and organs for transplantation. (This was years before I ever considered being a transplant surgeon.) All I asked in return was that the various hospitals reimburse the flying club for the actual cost of the flight. The idea fell flat, mostly for liability reasons.

One of the remarkable things about attending Princeton was the personal contact one could have with renowned professors who became mentors. A husband-and-wife team ignited my interest in health policy. Herman Somers, a senior professor of public policy at the Woodrow Wilson School, had been active in the early formulation of Medicare. He had written extensively on health-care policy and proposed one of the early foundational plans that defined what ultimately became known as managed competition. He and his wife, Anne Somers, also an established and highly regarded health policy expert, had written a book called *Health Care in Transition*, that became my bible for health-care policy. I developed a close working relationship with Anne Somers, who encouraged me to focus on the prevention side of medicine, even hiring me to run a summer health camp for eighth graders in Red Bank, New Jersey, taking me with her to New York policy conferences to meet other experts, and using me as a research assistant on her new book. But it was a young assistant economics professor from Germany by the name of Uwe Reinhardt who had the most lasting impact on my thinking and approach to health policy. Reinhardt had been at Princeton for just a couple of years when I enrolled in his basic macroeconomics class. I soon learned that he had a policy interest in health, and somehow I obtained a copy of his PhD thesis on the role of physicians' assistants in the Canadian health-care system. Professor Reinhardt was far ahead of his time, already fretting about the rising costs of health care and how, one day soon, most Americans would not be able to afford even basic health insurance coverage. With his soft German accent, sardonic sense of humor, and keen insights, Reinhardt was also a great teacher, making even the driest of subjects come alive. (I took accounting from him as well; by some magic, he even made accounting a fun and entertaining subject to learn!)

While at Princeton, I enrolled in three of Professor Reinhardt's courses—huge survey classes of 150 to 200 students, in which we studied macroeconomics, corporate finance, and accounting. I was one of those students Reinhardt whimsically thought of as his "groupies," the students in those days who came up immediately after class to ask him questions and who often hung around for an hour or so of enthusiastic, animated debate. He called me "Billy the Kid."

My politics, to the extent that I had any in those days, also appealed to Professor Reinhardt. In the 1970s, academe was a hostile environment for market-oriented economists like Reinhardt. Like the professor, I was out of sync with the times. Amid the period's Vietnam- and Watergate-born cynicism, I was openly enthusiastic about American democracy, our commitment to freedom, and the free enterprise system. Reinhardt thought I was naïve, but Princeton's vocal left-leaning culture clearly bugged him, and he found my conservative views refreshing. And he enthusiastically encouraged them by just paying attention—and sometimes by provoking me by making contrary arguments consistent with his German and Canadian heritage. I began to think that maybe I should spend my life tackling these issues of health-care quality, access, and cost.

Uwe likes to tell the story of my final exam in his Econ 102 class. Professor Reinhardt always posed the exam question this way: "You're the CEO of a company. You have promised $1.75 earnings per share. The dry run in October shows that $1.50 per share is all you'll be able to deliver. Make up the twenty-five cents and get those earnings up to $1.75, which would amount to about $10 million. You must make it up out of thin air, but in accordance with generally accepted accounting principles." Uwe paused, and with eyebrows raised, said, "The more corrupt, the better I like it!" He was only partly joking. It was the unique way the provocative young professor taught. At the time, many companies were cooking their books for shareholders and he wanted us, as students, to understand that; what better way than to make us think like the crooked CEOs themselves?

I came up with what I thought was a clever answer, yet one that was perfectly legal. It involved my imaginary company selling a useless patent it owned to a related company that appeared to be independent. This would yield a huge capital gain that would go on the books as earnings, while leasing back the patent it never intended to use for a nominal yearly fee and a note for the original purchase price, payable thirty years later.

The professor loved it! All notions of my naïveté gone, Uwe wrote on my paper in red ink, "You have the potential to be the biggest shyster I've ever had in class!" From Uwe, that was the ultimate compliment. He later described my plan as "deviously good." After class, with his eyes twinkling, Professor Reinhardt asked, "Wherever did you come up with so breathtakingly daring a solution?"

"The plan is similar to one used by the Memorex Corporation," I told the prof.

Reinhardt burst into laughter. "Devious, Billy the Kid. Delightfully devious!"

From that moment on, something just seemed to click between us, and over the years Professor Reinhardt and I kept in touch. Uwe has remained at Princeton, where he has continued to teach generations of students in his uncannily delightful and engaging way. In 2008, I returned to Princeton for a year to teach, and Uwe and I taught together a WWS graduate class on health economics, twenty-six years after he taught "Billy the Kid" how to "cook the books." The unpredictable almost serendipitous circling of life's relationships has made me a much richer soul.

I am not much one for convention, even in academics. So when I by chance heard about a little-known program in the WWS that allowed one to be exempt from all formal academic requirements of Princeton, my interest was piqued. The program, called the Woodrow Wilson School Scholars Program, was selective. In fact, only one or two students were selected each year. The idea was to provide the Wilson Scholar maximum freedom and creative license to delve deeply into a particular area of interest. The person chosen was relieved of *all* course requirements, including the most sacred of Princeton traditions, the senior thesis. In the past 280 years, no one has graduated from Princeton in the liberal arts without writing a thesis—no one, that is, except the few students in the (now extinct) Wilson Scholars program.

Interestingly, when I was running for the Senate in 1994, opposition research investigators (hired guns used by the opponent's camp to dig up dirt on a candidate) came to Princeton to try to find some scandal to use against me. When they couldn't find my senior thesis, they knew they'd found the silver bullet to bring down my campaign. Their silver bullet vanished when my campaign explained about the Wilson Scholars program. Ironically, the same issue came up again twenty years later when Sam Alito was nominated to the Supreme Court and investigators couldn't find *his* thesis. He, too, had been a Wilson Scholar.

I spent that senior year writing a series of papers on health-care policy, developing an independent study project on efficiencies of hospitals in Texas—typing up literally thousands of computer punch cards (remember this was 1974) to enter data into the massive mainframe computer at Princeton—and attending conferences and making presentations with Anne Somers. I left Princeton having completed just the basics (Dad had always said a great doctor does not have to be a great scientist) of premed and graduated from the Woodrow Wilson School with a concentrated focus on health-care policy.

Taking calculated risks and doing the unexpected—that brings me pleasure. It's the comfort zone I like to operate in. It's a philosophy I first heard articulated by Professor Hubert Alyea, who taught me Chemistry 101. Alyea was Princeton's version of the mad scientist, and a living legend at the university. He taught chemistry in the grand theatrical style, mixing huge flasks of clear chemicals to create vivid colors, blowing things up, setting blinding fires, and creating vast plumes of smoke that would envelop the audience. His final lecture, the grandest of them all, repeated each year at Princeton reunions for hundreds of alumni and their children to enjoy, always ended with a simple proclamation: "If you ever have a choice in life between one road that leads to the conventional and the expected, and another road that leads to the out-of-the-ordinary and the unconventional, choose the latter. Your life will be more rewarding, and you will never regret it."

As I have bounced back and forth between my academic passions—medicine and the sciences on the one hand, and public policy on the other—Professor Alyea's principle has colored my life. That simple, unadorned advice made going to Princeton worthwhile.

And it was about to come in handy.

*　　*　　*

I ALWAYS WANTED TO BE A DOCTOR.

It's almost impossible for an outsider to truly understand the rigors of medical school, to be followed by a year of internship, and then two to six years of additional residency training, then a year of two of specialty fellowship. Though laws have more recently greatly reduced the number of hours that can be required of an intern or a resident, the process remains physically and psychologically rigorous. You enter medical school a typical college graduate and you leave a professional upon whom people depend for their lives. Most doctors who survive the process don't like to discuss it. Instead, like veterans who have served in battle, they simply say, "No use explaining. You had to be there."

At the time I was completing applications for various med schools, Harvard was considered the premier medical school in the country. Premed students were a super-competitive lot; getting into the likes of Harvard was the goal of most, and competition was fierce. Majoring in the "soft" subjects of public policy and international relations, I felt I did not have a shot at competing with all the chemistry, physics, biology, and biochemistry majors. Going back to Nashville and attending Vanderbilt was attractive to me. And that was my goal . . . unless I could by some miracle make it to Harvard.

So I went up to Boston to see Dr. Perry Culver, one of Dad's medical study group colleagues when they served together at Maxwell Field Air Base during World War II. Dad had kept up with him over the years and he was on an alumni admissions committee for the medical school. When I finally found his office (having first searched all over Harvard's undergraduate campus in Cambridge, not realizing the medical school was four miles away across the river in Boston proper), I told Dr. Culver right up front that I did not think I had a shot at getting in but that if admitted I promised to take the education I received and apply it in as expansive a way as I could. He shared with me the fact that, yes, other applicants had much more impressive grades, had done much better on their MCATs (the standardized tests medical schools use for admission), and showed more promise as academic scientists, but no one else had on their application the statement that the Princeton premed advisor Dr. Willard Dalrymple had written on mine: "He may not be our top student this year, but he is certainly the most likely student I've seen to someday be awarded the Nobel Peace Prize."

That hyperbolic compliment was evidently enough to help me make it to the waiting list for admission. Somebody must have dropped out, because two months later I got a call, "You are admitted." I got in by the skin of my teeth.

Although four years older and more mature, I felt no less awkward as I walked onto the med school campus on Avenue Louis Pasteur in Boston than I had during my first months at Princeton. Now I had to compete head-to-head in science classes against people who had graduated at the top of their premed classes and majored in science, while I had finished somewhere in the middle in a nonscience. Even some of my Harvard professors looked at me askance. "Why would you major in public policy if you really want to be a doctor?" they'd ask. I thought them narrow and overspecialized, but I was entering their world, where they set the rules and determined the grades.

But my dual interests in public policy and medicine continued hand in hand. For instance, on weekends during my first year of medical school, when most of my med school colleagues were doing labs, catching up on their medical studies, or writing scientific papers, I was trudging back down to Princeton for board of trustee meetings. In the late 1960s, the university had modified its board policy to include young alumni trustees, including one from the graduating class each year. Just before my graduation, the junior and senior year classes and most recent graduating alumni classes had elected me to the position. Obviously, it was a heady learning experience to serve on the board of a major university at twenty-two years of age, and I loved jumping back and forth between two such diverse environments, challenging me in such different ways. I grew comfortable with operating in these two disparate worlds.

Med school demanded that students learn massive amounts of material, while perpetually reminding us that if we didn't learn it all, someone could die. It was motivating to learn, but I felt the pressure to learn it all.

I WAS IN MY SECOND YEAR OF MEDICAL SCHOOL, IN THE MIDDLE OF my first clinical rotation—that time when a med student finally gets to see patients—when I received the call from Nashville. Dad had suffered a heart attack and had undergone emergency coronary artery bypass surgery. This was a relatively routine operation even in the mid-1970s, but no surgery is ordinary when it is performed on one of your family members. I flew home from Boston immediately and went to visit Dad in the hospital. He was recovering well and encouraged me to get back to school. "I'll be fine; don't worry about me," he told me. "Just attend to your studies." I spent the night in Nashville, and then dutifully returned to Boston.

Five days later, my brother Bobby, a heart surgeon, called from Nashville and delivered the devastating news: "Billy, Dad has had a stroke." I flew back to Nashville, fatigued from the loss of sleep, and even more weary than merely physically tired. Despite my medical training, I was unprepared for what I saw and heard that first morning after Dad's stroke. Feeble-looking and drawn, my always strong father, his six-foot-three-inch frame filling the hospital bed, struggled to speak. When he finally formed some words, he spoke in a strained whisper and he could not raise his left arm. It was a sound that would haunt me and woo me back home over the years, but it was a sound I would never forget. I was distraught; I could tell that he was scared. I stayed with him in the hospital, holding his hand through the night. My own accident had caused me to face my mortality, but Dad's stroke caused me to face the potential loss of the foundation of family—from which I had drawn all strength and security.

Dad slowly recovered and over time regained function of his arm and pretty well returned to life as normal, but his voice never fully came back. He resumed work, but began slowing down his busy medical practice. A warm and charismatic speaker before the stroke, Dad's mind was still sharp; even much later in life he continued to put in ten-hour days as the cultural voice of HCA. But he was always noticeably frustrated by his impaired speech. Despite the hoarse whisper, and a slight stutter and sometimes slurred speech, he was constantly asked to speak at HCA gatherings and hospitals around the country. The whisper, however, betrayed him—and reminded me that he was not Superman, but a human being. On the other hand, the whisper worked well for him as a public speaker, as adoring audiences clung to his every word, leaning forward, straining to hear what he had to say. And he always had something good to say. It was always something simple, personal, optimistic, and patriotic. They loved it. Dad had turned his disability into a useful communication tool!

Dad soon realized that he would no longer be able to continue his work with the same intensity and devotion as in the past. To whom would he turn over his best friends, his patients, for their future care? He heard about a remarkable young physician who had developed a reputation for spending quality time with patients, who was available seven days a week. This internist, like Dad, treated each patient with respect and dignity. And he had a degree from divinity school, and before medical school had spent two years in Africa. Dad became the mentor to this young doctor, Dr. Karl VanDevender, and confidently turned his patients over to him, one by one.

Karl likes to remind people that before accepting him as a partner, Dad insisted that Karl submit to a physical exam, an exam that Dad conducted himself! Dad's real purpose in doing so was to make sure that the young physician learned how to make even the most humiliating and personally invasive procedure of a physical examination a caring, respectful, and dignified experience for the patient. ("Always warm up the stethoscope before placing it on the patient's chest." "Don't jot down notes during the exam; keep your focus 100 percent on the patient.") Dad and

Karl not only became partners, they became great friends. Karl earned the full confidence of Dad; he became like a fourth son.

I SPENT FOUR YEARS AT HARVARD. MY SOCIAL LIFE REVOLVED around my girlfriend, whom I had started dating in high school and who was now in Boston at dental school. Between going to Princeton for board meetings on weekends, my studies (where I felt I had to work twice as hard to keep up), and my relationship, I made little time to socialize with my fellow medical students. The first two years were principally academic and in the classroom, which I tolerated but didn't love. But the last two were clinical, and I was finally experiencing what I really wanted to do, care for patients. That's what I'd seen as a little boy on rounds with Dad. You never forget the first time you are introduced as a "student-doctor." The first time you examine a patient. The first time a patient dies and there is nothing you can do about it.

Even back in med school, I found myself gravitating toward a different path—a path that led to the unknown, the creative, the innovative. Although few students at that time deviated from the normal course sequence, at the beginning of my third year I asked and received permission to conduct a six-month independent research project in the laboratory of William John Powell, a cardiologist who had one of the busiest research labs at Massachusetts General Hospital (MGH), rather than do the customary coursework. I guess my experience of independent study at Princeton was still in my mind, as was Professor Alyea's advice to take the road less traveled.

During that half-year period of intensive laboratory experience in the basement of the MGH, I designed an experiment to figure out how the heart relaxes under conditions of low oxygen environment—the same conditions that occur when a person is having a heart attack. No one had ever addressed this question, which could potentially lead to therapies for the millions of people who die of heart attacks each year. Since I don't have an artistic bone in my body, I'd never felt the joy of creativity that I imagine an artist lives for. But now I did.

I could barely contain the exhilaration I felt each day at the thought that I, as a mere medical student, and an average one at that, could possibly contribute to an evolving body of knowledge that might literally change the lives of millions of others for the better. The possibilities energized me, stimulated my mind with big thoughts; they ignited a fire in me as nothing else ever had.

That research—not a standard part of the curriculum then— taught me a lot. Research can change the world. It introduced to me the excitement and passion for exploring the unknown. It allowed me to recognize that one individual willing to pursue the possibilities can make an enormous difference in the world. And it became the basis of the belief that whatever we do with health-care reform, we cannot sacrifice the innovation that makes American health care so unique and powerful.

ABOUT HALFWAY THROUGH THE FOURTH YEAR OF MEDICAL SCHOOL, you have to choose a field in medicine for your residency, the three- to six-year period of specialization after med school. I was uncertain what field of medicine I might enter. My dad had chosen internal medicine and had a special interest in the heart; he became a cardiologist. That intrigued me. But surgery held a special allure. Even Dad had said that if he'd had the money to stay in school, he would have been a surgeon. My brothers were both surgeons, and my personality seemed to fit that sort of practice. Surgeons tend to be solution-oriented; direct, cool performers under pressure, with a "let's fix things" attitude. By contrast, the general practitioner or internist is usually more of a thinker, producing a deliberate, thoughtful, and thorough diagnosis—more a thinker than a doer. These are probably unfair generalizations, but they get the point across.

I'd had the luxury of seeing both options, medicine and surgery, up close in my immediate family. During med school, I took various rotations, each for a month at a time—a month in surgery, a month in pediatrics, a month in orthopedic surgery, and others—and eventually I began to get a feel for what I really liked doing. In that fourth year, I became especially enamored with the field of heart surgery, a field that my brother Bobby had chosen. It was still a relatively young field, with the first bypass operations done in the mid-1960s. It was the dramatic field of medicine; the whole idea of starting and stopping the human heart, the seat of human life, to repair it attracted me.

So when it came time for me to make my decision, I applied for a surgical residency, leaning toward an eventual specialization (which does not occur until after five years of general surgery) in the heart. I put as my first choice the Harvard–affiliated MGH. I was admitted. I reasoned, I had come this far going to what was considered the best, so why not continue on that track if I had the opportunity? And I knew I'd get back home someday.

The Massachusetts General Hospital is facetiously referred to as "Man's Greatest Hospital." It is the origin of many marvelous discoveries in modern medicine. The list of great surgeons educated at MGH seemed endless, and our Harvard professors reminded us frequently that we walked in the hallowed halls of greatness, and it was our responsibility to carry on the rich healing traditions of our forefathers.

The walking-a-tightrope mentality that med school students learn is emphasized even more during residency, especially in surgery. Surgical residency is sometimes compared to a sort of doctors' boot camp, and rightly so: It is constant, intensive training, designed to produce supreme competence. But like boot camp, residency is also a totally consuming indoctrination period and a cutting off from the outside world. At the time, even getting married during residency was frowned upon, because there was simply no time for outside interests.

The surgical program at MGH certainly stretched my comfort zone like nothing I'd experienced previously, and in the process led to the death of many of my illusions about medical practice. The schedule at Mass General was more grueling than that in med school. We were on call in the hospital every day and every other night, often working around the clock, forty-eight-hour shifts. You develop an intense camaraderie with your fellow residents, who are all going through the same experience. MGH prided itself on a strong ward service, where the surgical residents had complete control over the patients, with the attending doctors acting only as consultants. There was some truth in the old mantra "see one, do one, teach one." The training tended to be hierarchical, with the sixth-year chief residents running the service, with the fifth-year residents supervising the fourth, the fourth the third, and so on. The years of residency were exhilarating.

Mass General's surgical residency insisted on perfection. A small error in surgery can cause someone's life to end. Therefore no mistakes are tolerated.

One of the biggest surprises for me later in life when I went to Washington was to find a much greater tolerance for error. Such mediocrity was not accepted in surgical residency; in government it was accepted as unavoidable. Moreover, in medical practice, a higher level of accountability day-in and day-out is demanded. In politics you are held accountable by elections every six, four, or two years. In surgery you are held accountable for someone's life every minute. What's more, in a political campaign, rhetoric can trump fact; in surgery, there is no rhetoric—just 100 percent accountability. When I compare the frustration of Washington's tacit acceptance of imperfection and error, I appreciate all the more the high standards of professional excellence and accountability I learned on those wards working with patients every day and night, year after year, at Mass General. I came to expect those high standards of others and, most important, of myself. They spilled over from medicine to politics and from politics to business.

In recent years, surgical residency has been sensationalized and glamorized on TV. I'm now out of the business of doing surgery every day, but I appreciate more than ever the sacrifices these medical students and residents and young doctors make every day. Few people understand the number of hours it takes to learn to diagnose an uncommon disease, to choose the specific correct surgical procedure for an individual patient, and to develop the practiced operative skills to achieve the excellent outcome that every patient deserves. It takes the every-other-night call, or its equivalent, for years in formal surgical residency to allow one to master the latest life-saving technology and advances (which change almost daily) and to manage every single complication Mother Nature will throw your way after even the most routine operative procedures.

It's just plain hard stuff. And it takes a long time—in my own case, twelve continuous years of exhausting formal training after college before I was even allowed to do my first heart transplant on my own. Twelve years. And, in part because of the time required and the dedication it demands, it requires extraordinary personal sacrifices the public never sees, but sacrifices that take their toll on relationships with others, most notably one's spouse and children.

So why do it? What are the genuine privileges of putting up with such a regimen? A central one, at least for the surgeon, is the trust you earn to care for patients whose lives have taken a turn for the worse. You enter their lives for a moment, you focus all your resources and energies on them, and you leave them better, healthier, and happier. Dad was so right when he said there is no greater profession than that of a doctor. I began to see it during these residency years. You learn what is important in life by touching intimately the lives of others in exceptional ways—and in return your own life is made richer by the shared moments.

I didn't fully realize all this until I stopped doing it every day. My political friends would later ask what the most difficult part of surgical training was. For me, it was the missed special moments with my wife Karyn and our boys. It was missing our babies' first steps, cutting short most family birthday celebrations to rush back to do emergency surgery, spending Christmas Eve not at home but in the hospital doing a transplant, and having to miss the funeral of a close, personal friend.

Dealing with death is never easy, not even for a doctor, and is perhaps especially difficult for a young doctor in training. One of my first patients to die was a little girl who had suffered severe burns and was suffering from lack of oxygen in her blood as a result. She was admitted right after the burn, and the nature of this kind of injury is that the patient gets increasingly worse over the next forty-eight hours. She came in badly injured but not disfigured. I watched her die before my eyes in spite of doing everything humanly possible to reverse the downhill course. I remember going outside the hospital by myself an hour later, sitting on the ground, just hurting and crying and feeling helpless. I even questioned seriously whether I wanted to live the remainder of my life in constant battles with death—and worse yet, in not always winning those battles.

I was dejected and discouraged, and I went back to Nashville that weekend where my entire interest in medicine was so firmly grounded. I talked with my dad and my surgeon brother Bobby. Dad and Bobby consoled me, and then Bobby gently but firmly reminded me, "Sometimes even when you do all you can, life and death are not in your hands. We are just human." I returned to Boston, determined to become an even better surgeon, understanding that our purpose was not to alter destiny, just to shape it toward a better end.

Adding to my emotional turmoil, I sensed the approaching end of a long-term relationship with my girlfriend. We had been dating since high school, remained together through college and graduate school, and it seemed a natural progression for us to get engaged. Although we both may have had misgivings about our future together, we were so wrapped up in developing our careers, we never really addressed our differences. Our relationship remained on autopilot, two Nashville kids who grew up together, loved each other, both from well-respected families; now two young adults heading steadily, inexorably, toward a wedding.

Then I met Karyn.

5

Karyn

On a crisp, spring morning in 1979, I pulled out of bed, climbed into my obligatory surgical intern's garb of white pants, white shirt, and short white coat (the outfit affectionately called "toad skins" by the MGH surgical staff—because of the "toad" work interns were required to do for the senior surgeons). Half awake, I stumbled down Boston's famous Beacon Hill to Mass General—my daily trek. It was still dark, about five in the morning, and though we were right on the cusp of summer, the air still had a slight New England chill.

At the time, I lived in a one-bedroom apartment on the second floor of an old, recently renovated brownstone at the top of Mt. Vernon Street, only a few blocks from the Massachusetts State House. I'd vary the route of my walk to the hospital each day, sometimes going straight down the dilapidated backside of Beacon Hill, at other times walking the uneven, red brick sidewalks of Mt. Vernon to pass the more charming antique shops and markets of Charles Street—but always leaving before the sun rose and returning long after it set. One thing was consistent: Each day the route ended on Fruit Street, the final stretch of about two blocks leading directly to the prominent grand entrance of my workplace, the White Building of the Massachusetts General Hospital.

Entering the modest front lobby of the hospital, I headed straight around the corner to meet my surgical team in the X-ray department to begin our early morning prerounds in preparation for what I assumed would be just another routine day. But little did I know that this day would lead to a radical turn off a long-anticipated road in my personal life. Indeed, my life was forever changed by the events that would unfold on this day.

Normally we began the day with a review of X-rays and an intern's presentation of the overnight admissions from the emergency room, before making patient rounds. Gulping a cup of coffee on the run would follow rounds, and then on to the third-floor operating rooms. By 7:00 A.M. we would be in the OR, well ahead of the attending surgeon, prepping and draping the patients, making sure all was in order for a "cut time" of seven-thirty sharp. All aspects of surgery are precise. But the routine was broken on Thursdays, when part of the team separated off to man the Surgical Clinic, treating patients for nonemergency care, evaluating for potential surgery, or conducting routine postoperative exams.

I reported for Surgical Clinic that Thursday and immediately went to Room 3 of the old Clinics Building, built in 1907 at the end of Fruit Street, just cattycorner to the White Building's front entrance. Patients checked in at the front desk and were triaged to the appropriate room, where the initial evaluation was conducted by an intern, before a more advanced resident provided treatment. The White surgical service was run entirely by residents, with a sixth-year chief resident shouldering the ultimate responsibility. I was at the bottom of the chain, no longer a medical student, yet still just an intern.

About halfway through the otherwise routine morning, I grabbed another chart on the door and entered a room to find a young woman, twenty-some years old, who had scheduled an elective visit. As I gathered information regarding her chief complaint and past medical history, and while waiting for the resident in charge, our casual conversation led to the realization that we were both misplaced southerners. She was from Texas

and I from Tennessee. Both of us were spending a transient period of time in Boston, for me to further my fledgling career, and
for her to see the world. Over those few minutes we shared the
excitement of living in such a vibrant town as Boston, although
both of us confided we were overwhelmed by the more reserved
and at times brusque nature of Bostonians compared to the more
open and friendly attitudes that we were used to growing up in
the South. I was intrigued. I didn't run into many warm, engaging out-of-towners (especially southerners) in the resident-run
surgical wards of MGH, and I was enjoying this chance encounter. In the course of our friendly yet businesslike conversation, I
learned that she had visited the clinic because, having recently
been transferred to Boston as an American Airlines flight attendant, she did not yet have a doctor in the area.

Although I'd usually see nearly thirty patients a day in the
clinic—and interacted with scores of new patients, visitors, and
staff from all walks of life every day—by the end of that fifteen-
minute conversation, I knew there was something special about
this woman.

But I had a line of patients waiting to be seen in the clinic. As
the attractive young woman was about to leave, I told her that
her test results would be back in a week and that I would call her
if there were any abnormalities. I scribbled two telephone numbers on a prescription pad—the hospital number through which
I could be paged and, if I was not on call, the only other way I
could be reached, my home number. On the way out the door I
handed her the paper and said, "If you have any more questions,
let me know. You can reach me twenty-four hours a day through
one of these two numbers." She thanked me and smiled as we
said good-bye.

I was on call the next weekend, but my brother Tommy and
his wife, Trisha, had come to Boston and were staying with me
in my small apartment (so sparsely appointed that whenever I
had guests, I slept on an extra mattress on the floor in the living room). Tommy was going to complete his seventeenth marathon, this time running the time-honored Boston Marathon on

Patriot's Day. (Last month he had a knee replacement which, as with his previous hip replacement, had nothing to do with his obsession to stay fit with running—or so the older big brother tells his forever naïve little brother!) I had traded call times so I could visit with Tommy and Trish Saturday night. I finished my rounds at the hospital and made it back to the apartment by about 10:00 P.M. Trisha was still awake, but Tommy had already gone to sleep, having loaded up on pasta in preparation for the twenty-six-mile run two days later.

I had no sooner come in the door, when Trisha said, "You had a phone call. It was a patient named Karyn, asking for Dr. Frist, but it didn't sound like it concerned a medical problem."

I was immediately intrigued. "Did she leave a number?" I asked.

"No, she didn't," Trisha replied, eyeing me with a hint of a smile. "But she seems like the nicest girl. She didn't sound like she was from here."

"What about her last name?"

"She didn't say," Trisha replied.

Now my curiosity was really stirred. Throughout the night, I kept trying to recall Karyn's last name. How in the world was I going to get in touch with her? While all this was going on, I began to remember her big, expressive eyes, the quick smile, her down-to-earth, yet subtly sophisticated southern charm, our conversation about being "misplaced southerners." Now I knew I had to get in touch with her; an urging inside told me that it was important that I call her back . . . and for some reason, I felt that this connection could not wait until the following week.

I became a man on a mission. At five the next morning, I hurried back down Beacon Hill and into the Clinics Building, where I found the stack of notes from my previous week's clinic visit. I ran my finger through the log of patients I'd seen that week. *What was her last name?* Page after page, entry after entry, I searched. Growing anxious, I began to worry that I might not find it. Then what?

Finally, it was there! Karyn McLaughlin, age twenty-five, Lub-

bock, Texas. Routine visit. And, on the next line, thank good-
ness—a telephone number.

My interest must have been strong or I would not have been
rummaging around a closed clinic to find patient records before
the sun had come up. *Should I call her back or wait for her to
call me again?* I wondered. *And why had she called in the first
place?*

I waited until that night, but when I hadn't heard from her, I
dialed Karyn's number. She answered the phone and after per-
functory pleasantries, I asked her if she was experiencing some
sort of medical problem.

Karyn replied, "Dr. Frist, I wasn't calling about a medical problem." She explained that she'd been calling for a friend who'd
been in town for the weekend, wondering about the advantages
and disadvantages of his doing a cardiology residency in Boston.
She wanted to put us in touch. Then our conversation wandered
to other subjects. She asked why I had come to Boston to do my
surgical training. After all, she'd heard all her life that Texas, not
Boston, had the best medical centers in the world! And for some
reason, we talked at length about the importance of family, a
topic we first broached that night but have shared for a lifetime.

Near the conclusion of the conversation, I took a chance and
asked, "Do you think we will see each other again?"

"I don't know," Karyn replied.

"We could get together for a cup of coffee . . . we don't need
to make a big deal about it."

Karyn later confessed that she thought, based on our brief
conversations, I was likely too cheap to spend the money for a
decent lunch or dinner, so she hedged in answering. But something else had begun to click—something beyond a first phone
call, following a happenstance meeting in a professional setting.
Nevertheless, we left the call saying we'd talk later in the week.

A couple of days went by and we reconnected: She'd pass on
to her friend my thoughts about coming to Boston for the residency, and then maybe we could get together and talk further
about it in person. I explained that due to my call schedule, it

would be best just to meet for a drink and not have dinner. I sheepishly told her that I rarely went out to dinner during my residency, because all too often, I'd fall asleep at the table, right in the middle of the meal.

Karyn laughed, and we decided to go to Warren Tavern, a historic old restaurant in Charlestown—the nicest place that I knew to have a drink, without buying dinner.

I met Karyn that next Friday evening at her apartment on Columbus Avenue, in South Boston, an enviable place to live today but at the time in its earliest stages of rehabilitation and not the safest part of Boston for a young woman to be living. When she opened the door, wearing a khaki-colored dress that highlighted her sunburned face, her beauty struck me.

We talked and laughed and time seemed to stand still. Karyn chided me once again for being cheap, first for not buying her dinner and second for having suggested that we walk to the Warren Tavern to save cab fare. Actually, I can't remember whether we walked, took a cab, hitchhiked, or rode on a magic carpet. What I do recall is that I was enthralled with Karyn's bright-eyed, contagious, easygoing personality and her rich love for life.

The minutes grew into a full-blown dinner and several hours of conversation as we got to know each other. I was mesmerized by the soft southern lilt in Karyn's voice, as I learned more about the special education teacher with deep Texas roots, who had graduated from Texas Christian University, and was now taking time to explore the world.

Over the next several months, we talked regularly and met casually whenever we could, trying to squeeze time into our busy schedules. Karyn's flight schedule and my intense program at Mass General did not always mesh well, so we simply enjoyed whatever fleeting moments we could spend together. Often Karyn would be out of town three or four nights a week, and I had my intern routine of thirty-six hours on, followed by twelve hours off. Consequently, Karyn and I didn't develop the usual type of relationship, in which a couple sees each other often, sometimes every day or evening. We rarely went out to dinner and didn't have "dates" in the traditional sense. We enjoyed each other's company, spent a lot of time talking about our values and what was important to us in life.

Much of our getting to know each other happened when I was on the emergency-room rotation; the schedule then was twenty-four hours straight on call and then twenty-four off. On the days that I was off and Karyn was in town, I'd sleep for five hours, then meet her for lunch at the T.G.I. Friday's restaurant over on Newbury Street. We'd order ice cream drinks like the banana split or strawberry shortcake to wash down nachos or potato skins.

Our evening at Warren Tavern was on April 29. During the month of May, our talks grew more intense; they were more fo-cused than those generally held between two people just getting to know each other. They were especially focused on my part. It wasn't that I was such a good communicator. No, it was because I was under a time line that I had not shared with Karyn.

Although I didn't consciously discuss it with Karyn in those early days, I was questioning and probing whether my personal life was really on the right track. I'd previously set out pursu-ing a destiny that I had recently begun to question. Amazingly, through all those early conversations with this woman I'd only just met, I confided in her everything important to me—all ex-cept one thing, probably the most important thing at that time. Something to this day I regret not being more open about sooner, with all parties concerned.

While Karyn continued to date others and our relationship was casual, still brand-new and evolving, and limited by the re-alities of two careers that so often took us in different direc-tions, the one thing that Karyn did not know was that back in Nashville, wedding plans were on a collision course with the calendar—*my* wedding plans! I hadn't mentioned to Karyn that I was *engaged*.

I beat myself up in my thoughts. Karyn and I had shared so many conversations over the previous month about substantive and personal issues. *Why couldn't I tell her about my engage-*

ment? And as the deadline drew closer, the intensity of my dilemma—and my sense of guilt and anguish—continued to grow.

Six days before the planned wedding, I finished a forty-eight-
hour shift in the emergency room. I left the hospital immediately
after rounds, went to the airport still dressed in my white toad
skins, and boarded the plane for the long, painful ride home.
I'd decided to announce to both my parents and my fiancée's
parents that "we" had decided not to get married. That things
weren't right, and I did not know exactly why. That we were
going to have to call everything off, even though we had already
received hundreds of gifts and dozens of people would start flying into town within a few days.

I went straight home and in the kitchen explained to Mother
what I had to do. Sensing my anguish, she was totally supportive,
without hesitation. I called Dad, who also never hedged in his
support, and then went to have the most difficult and painful
conversations of my life—with my fiancée's parents, and then
later that night, in the same room with all the wedding gifts,
with my fiancée.

We called off the wedding and notified our friends as best we
could. I flew back to Boston immediately, devastated and feeling
lower than I'd ever felt. My spirit was blunted and a huge cloud
hung over me. My life had gone pretty well, with the exception
of the motorcycle accident, up until then. Now it had been up-
ended for reasons I didn't understand. I'd made a decision and
acted on it. Sure, I could lose myself in my waking hours to my
harried work in surgical training. And there was some consola-
tion that I had made the right decision—but I will always regret
not waking up to the reality sooner, so as to cause less pain to my
fiancée, to me, to our families, and to our many friends.

The breakup was heart-wrenching for both of us. It was difficult, embarrassing, and painful, but it was also the right decision. Life is no fairy tale. Things don't always turn out as one
anticipates, and things are almost never as perfect as they might
seem. Loss of a relationship, like death, is always difficult to en-
dure, and some decisions leave prolonged pain and scars that not

even time can heal. I learned, though, just how imperative it is to be true to oneself, to be true in one's relationships, and the importance of never letting work or anything else take precedence over a relationship.

I also realized that slowly but surely, almost imperceptibly, Karyn and I had been falling in love. About a month after my Nashville trip, we were at a party with a lot of the people who worked together at MGH. One of my senior surgical residents was so impressed with the warm and charming Karyn that he gushed, "Oh, so you are the woman Bill is going to marry!"

"Well, we've been seeing each other," Karyn said demurely, "but nobody has mentioned anything about marriage."

"Oh, I see," the resident replied. "I must have misunderstood. I thought the wedding date had already been set."

Karyn smiled and politely answered, still not knowing I had been engaged, "No, of course not, we are just getting to know each other."

Shortly thereafter, I told Karyn the full story about my engagement. When Karyn discovered that I had been less than forthcoming, she was furious with me and made it clear how disappointed she was. More than anything, she was hurt. We had talked about so many matters, yet I had not confided something as intimate as an engagement!

I feared that I had lost her, but I was not about to give up. I called her repeatedly. I'd venture to Columbus Avenue, hoping to "bump into her" when I knew she would likely be returning from a trip. When she finally accepted my phone calls and agreed to see me, I tried to explain to her (not all that convincingly, I'm afraid) that I had not willingly tried to deceive her. I explained that though we had known each other for only five or six weeks, our conversations had led me to a greater understanding of myself. We had become great friends and had fallen in love, and our hearts had melded together. The swirl of our schedules and the intensity of my residency program no doubt contributed to the blur in which we had developed our relationship.

Slowly I worked to rebuild Karyn's trust. She continued to

date others over the summer, but eventually we began seeing each other regularly. The better I got to know Karyn, the more I realized that she was the perfect counterpart for me and that we could grow together and build a family over a lifetime. I loved her and I wanted her to love me; it didn't take me long to realize I wanted to spend my life with her. Bright, articulate, fun, loving, and kind, with a deep faith in God, she would be an inspiring spouse and a marvelous mother to our children.

Karyn wasn't so sure. Aware that my family members had all known my fiancée for years, Karyn worried that they might feel some sort of resentment toward her. I knew that my family would do nothing of the sort.

At long last, we planned a trip to Nashville so she could meet the Frist clan. I returned to Nashville a couple of days before Karyn. The night of her arrival, I drove Dad's old, black Chevrolet out to the airport to pick her up. During the drive back to my house, knowing that Karyn was already nervous, I told her that all my brothers and sisters and their spouses and children would be at our family home on Bowling Avenue to meet her and "pass judgment." I teasingly instructed as we were driving home, "Definitely don't sit down when you walk into the living room, because everyone has a specified chair where they always sit." I continued to jangle Karyn's nerves by describing my family as sedate, highbrow, sophisticated, and extremely formal—all about as far from the truth as you can get.

I maintained the façade right up to the point we arrived at the Bowling house. As I turned into the driveway, the black night was suddenly illuminated by the glaring, bright headlights of four cars parked in front of the house, all pointed directly at us. Horns started honking, and we saw a huge hand-painted banner draped across the front of the house, reading, "Welcome home, Karyn! We love you!" We later discovered that many of the grandchildren had scrawled notes of welcome to Karyn and had drawn pictures for her on the banner. Little Bobby, for example, drew an airplane, a perfect choice for us.

All my nieces and nephews, from three years to ten, came running out from behind the bushes to open the car door, nearly hugging Karyn to death before we ever made it to the front door. It was a fabulous homecoming, far from the formal reception I'd described. The ice broke and melted away immediately, as my family welcomed her. Still not sure what to make of all the celebration in light of my highly exaggerated dissertation on what to expect, Karyn was even more disconcerted by what followed.

The whole family poured into the living room, filling every available seat, and some of the grandchildren huddled on the floor, admiringly looking up at Karyn as we sat on the couch. All eyes focused on Karyn. The little girls especially loved her long eyelashes and her beautiful eyes. Everyone asked questions of Karyn, one at a time, as we went from person to person around the room.

"Tell us about your interests. What are your hobbies?"

"What about your family?"

"How much do you like watching football?"

"Where did you teach special education?"

"Why did you leave Texas to go to Boston?"

Karyn, poised as ever and smiling with each question fired her way, charmed them all. After about an hour of focused, orderly conversation, my brother Tommy inconspicuously got up and stepped into the kitchen. A moment later, he burst into the living room with a cardboard box raised high in the air, laughing and shouting that all the interviews were over.

"Stop the talking. This is the black ball box," he explained as he captured everybody's attention. "We all have had the chance to interview Karyn. We've asked her the tough questions. Now is the time for us to vote! If you think she has made the grade, put a white ball in. If not, drop in a black ball. And one black ball means she's out!"

Everyone burst out laughing. Tommy's stunt was saying exactly what everyone in the room felt: "Karyn, we love you and you are part of the family."

In the fall of 1980, Karyn's parents came to visit Boston. We drove up to New Hampshire to see the New England foliage and spent a couple of days driving the glorious countryside, staying at a small country inn. Karyn stayed in a room with her mother, and I shared a room with her dad. I had carefully planned asking Karyn's dad for permission to marry his daughter. On the last night, as Mr. McLaughlin prepared to slip into the twin bed across from mine, I placed the engagement ring I'd picked out for Karyn on the wooden bedside table between us. I'd carefully situated the opened box so the ring was plainly visible. I didn't say anything to Karyn's father at first, just letting the ring sit there. Karyn's dad could play that game as well. He saw the ring, but didn't say a word, waiting for me to formally ask for his daughter's hand in marriage. After roughly fifteen minutes, which seemed more like an eternity, I caved and asked his permission to marry Karyn.

The next morning, Karyn and her dad took a walk down a secluded country road, and along the way, he asked her straightforwardly, "Are you happy?" He and Karyn talked a bit about our potential future, but he did not tell her at the time that I had asked his consent. That Sunday night Karyn came over to my apartment after work, and we had a quick dinner. Tonight was to be the night! I was finally going to ask.

Trying the same tactic as I'd used with her dad (having not learned my lesson the first time), I carefully placed the engagement ring, in its little blue box, on a table and waited for Karyn to notice. We talked and talked, but she said nothing about the ring; nor did I. I was ready to ask her to marry me, but then, exhausted from working the two solid days, I fell sound asleep. Karyn had grown accustomed to this, but not on the night I was to propose! Karyn called a taxi and let herself out of the apartment. To this day, I'm not absolutely certain that I ever asked Karyn formally to marry me, but she took the ring that night, and it has been on her finger now for more than a quarter of a century. It was simply meant to be. And I'm still trying to communicate a little better!

We were married in Lubbock, Texas, on March 14, 1981. My entire family flew to Lubbock for the occasion, and they had undoubtedly never seen land so desolate. Mother and Dad rarely traveled out of Middle Tennessee. Dad had always said, "A day out of Middle Tennessee is a day in life lost." When Mother got off the plane in flat, dusty, treeless, brown, windswept Lubbock, she looked at Karyn's dad and asked plaintively, "Why in the world would anyone choose to live in a place with no trees?"

Worse yet, within six hours of my family's arrival in Lubbock, a powerful dust storm turned the daylight into darkness, sending tumbleweed and dust in every direction. The Lubbock folks took it in stride, just another day on the prairie. We Frists from Middle Tennessee had thought such phenomena existed only in the movies.

Because Karyn's and my schedules had kept us primarily in Boston, our parents had never met one another before the wedding week. To help bring our families together in an environment that guaranteed fun, celebration, and informality, Karyn's parents hosted the clans' first social gathering at a typical western saloon, Jug Little's Western Barbecue, complete with well-worn wooden tables, cowboy décor, and sawdust on the floor. By the end of the night, the McLaughlins had all the Frist nieces and nephews, and brothers and sisters, belting out country-western favorites with the band on a makeshift stage. The chemistry was marvelous. The same connection between Karyn and me seemed to pass among our many family members.

Despite the elements (and the barbecue), the wedding took place in the Methodist church, right on schedule. After a brief honeymoon, Karyn and I returned to Boston and set up house in the apartment on Mt. Vernon Street, where we lived for the next four years as I completed my general surgical residency.

To become a cardiothoracic surgeon, one has to complete five years of a general surgery residency and then begin a fellowship in heart and lung surgery. At the time, the fellowship for cardiothoracic surgery was only a year and a half, which was not enough time to have intensive exposure in the nonheart aspects of chest surgery. To gain that experience, an arrangement had been made to send the thoracic residents to England for more extensive exposure in noncardiac chest surgery. So Karyn and I began planning a seven-month stay in Southampton, England.

*   *   *

I'D ALWAYS DREAMED OF FLYING A PLANE ACROSS THE OCEAN, SO I figured our stint in England would provide the perfect opportunity. Not only did I want to do the flying myself, but I wanted to do it in an old 1954 twin-engine airplane that I'd bought for twelve thousand dollars the year before I had met Karyn. I'd made a number of improvements on the plane, upgrading its safety and modernity along the way, equipping it with new, more powerful engines (replacing the old 150-horsepower ones with 200s so it would stay in the air, if I lost one), a new paint job (silver to replace the faded and chipped green original paint), and more up-to-date radios (the old organ grinder radios had gotten impossible to repair). I even changed the call signs painted on the fuselage to 314KB to signify our March 14 wedding and our initials—Karyn and Bill.

Karyn, too, had always been fascinated with flying. She began taking flying lessons shortly after we started dating. While still working as a flight attendant, she went every day she was in town to the wonderful, small airfield in Norwood, Massachusetts, to take lessons from Mr. Jack Mellon. He was the ideal flight instructor—a former military man, with highly polished black shoes, an accomplished and disciplined pilot, professional, and a perfectionist. That's why Karyn always called him "Mr. Mellon."

All this goes to say that Karyn was able and willing to fly the Atlantic with me. But the best-laid plans occasionally are shuttled to the side—which is exactly what happened when we learned Karyn was pregnant with our first baby. We joyfully altered our plans and flew commercially to England, where we were to live for the better part of a year.

I had told Karyn what a great opportunity going to England would be for the two of us. We would likely have our own car to drive, and she dreamed that we might be able to live in a quaint English cottage, maybe even rose-covered. The MGH residents who'd previously been to Southampton had shared with me the rejuvenating experiences they had had with their spouses in England. They especially enjoyed having more personal time together, traveling the countryside on weekends, and spending evenings together, the sort of "regular-life" things that the days at MGH never allowed us as residents. It all sounded idyllic to me, so I reflected that to Karyn—maybe with a bit too much imagination.

When we arrived, reality set in. The car, a ten-year-old yellow Ford Escort that each MGH resident rotating through just passed on to the next, was waiting for us at the airport. The driver's-side door was bashed in, the left headlight was broken, and the passenger door was permanently locked closed, necessitating entry either through the window or through the other side. This was not a good first introduction to England. I loaded our trunks into the vehicle, as Karyn inched her way across the driver's seat to the passenger's side. I drove an hour through the countryside to Southampton and pulled up, with pregnant wife and much anticipation, to our new home.

The house was not one of the charming, rose-covered cottages we'd dreamed about, but rather a drab, cement-block apartment right on the hospital grounds, directly across from the busy Emergency Room. To top things off, just after we pulled up, I volunteered to help a neighbor push his stalled car; we got the car rolling, but while doing so it ran over the brand-new camera we'd purchased to record our experiences in England!

We made the best of the living accommodations. Karyn quickly replaced the stiff, institutional bedsheets and pillowcases stamped, with big bold letters, PROPERTY OF SOUTHAMPTON GENERAL HOSPITAL, with something a little more homey. Indeed we did have a lot more time to spend together and made a point each weekend to journey to a new region of England. We loved hosting across the countryside our close friends from Nashville, Barry and Jean Ann Banker and John and Missy Eason, and Karyn's mom and sister Trisha and her husband Ike.

Professionally, I held the position of senior registrar, similar to being chief resident in the United States, first at the old Western Thoracic Hospital, which was a single-story, hundred-year-old facility originally built as a tuberculosis sanitarium, and then later at the more modern Southampton General Hospital.

Encountering a wide variety of heart and lung cases was a magnificent experience for a budding young surgeon. I treated pathologies that doctors rarely see in the United States, including diseases such as advanced-stage asbestosis, prevalent among British workers from long-standing exposure in the nearby Southampton shipyards. More than two decades later on the floor of the U.S. Senate, as I was trying to reform the American litigation system on asbestosis, I'd think back to those long, bloody, excruciating operative cases for end-stage asbestosis—a graphic reminder both of the horrors of the disease and of the importance of tort reform, so that those in need could receive help quickly and fairly. In the 1990s a handful of greedy lawyers were abusing the tort system, putting millions of dollars in their pockets rather than in the pockets of those injured who deserved help. (We lost that battle to the trial lawyers.)

My experience in England provided great opportunities for personal growth in leadership and responsibility. The senior registrar assumed major responsibility and performed all of the surgical cases; he or she ran the surgical clinics, made all major clinical decisions, and generally acted and performed as an attending physician would in the United States. That's why the MGH surgical residents cherished their time at Southampton: They were in charge. They grew. And they came back with experiences to share with others at MGH.

This became the first of what would be many experiences in my life of going overseas to learn and observe and gather medical experiences from others, initially in the developed world but later more commonly in the underdeveloped world. Through serving others abroad, we can learn how to better serve at home.

What I found at Western Thoracic Hospital seemed foreign and strange. I could not believe my eyes the first few days in the OR; the excellent English surgeons were tackling cases just as complex as the ones we faced at the MGH, but doing so in a tiny, crowded, ancient, ill-equipped operating room devoid of the ad-

vanced technology and sophisticated monitoring that we were
so reliant on in Boston. No Swan-Ganz catheters—no measuring
wedge pressures, no atrial wires—but their results were just as
good as the ones we achieved, or better. *How could that be?* I
would wonder. Instead of the latest gadgets, the doctor and nurses
relied on careful physical exams, just like the ones Dad would do.
I soon figured out that attentive nursing and old-fashioned, thorough physical examinations of the patient would provide as much
practical clinical information as all of the elaborate (and horren-
dously expensive) equipment we relied on back in Boston. *Are
we too obsessed with technology in the United States?*

For instance, after surgery on the lungs, it is critical to get
the patient to take deep, full breaths and to cough to keep the
small air sacs of the lung from collapsing. In the States, for almost
all postoperative lung patients, we used a portable machine that
was rolled up to the patient's bed every four hours and would
"nebulize" or aerosolize a medicine called a bronchodilator, to
keep the sacs open and make the patient cough. Such contrap-
tions are expensive, and a highly trained respiratory therapist is
required to deliver the treatment.

Naturally, after my first lung case at the Western Thoracic,
a right upper lobectomy, I scratched out what to me was a routine order for a "nebulizer every four hours with bronchodilator."
Later that day, on evening rounds, I found to my astonishment the
patient sucking on a thick, sixteen-inch-long, red rubber hose inserted through a cork that plugged a polished, white earthen pot
containing eucalyptus—Mother Nature's equivalent of the cough
stimulant. How primitive! Guess what? It worked. I couldn't help
wondering, *Why use costly high tech, when low tech does the
job? Does our lack of attention to appropriate use of technology explain part of the 30 percent of the U.S. health care dollar
that is "wasted?"*

My professional experiences opened my eyes to more than
just the variations in surgical techniques. While working in England, I discovered firsthand the pluses and minuses of socialized
medicine, where government collects the funds, government de-

termines how much is spent, government owns the hospitals, and government hires and controls the doctors and nurses who provide the care—for everyone.

The advantages I experienced included low out-of-pocket expenses to the patient, with many medical services made available at no direct cost to the patient at all. For everyday health-care matters, the socialized system seemed to work seamlessly. When people got sick, they received basic care. Everyone, rich and poor alike, had his or her own assigned general practitioner. And, though they were not trained as long as the internal medicine specialists on whom so many of us rely in the States, the care by the GPs was excellent for 90 percent of the typical medical problems most people experience. It's gotten to the point it's impossible to find a family practice doctor in the United States.

Our first son, Harrison, was born at Princess Anne Hospital in Southampton. Karyn's prenatal care by the general practitioner was superb; he'd make house calls to our flat, where he'd join Karyn for tea. At the time of delivery, we just had to show up at the hospital. Paperwork seemed nonexistent; I don't even recall having to sign any paperwork as we were admitted. After twenty-four hours of labor, Karyn required a Caesarian section because of failure to progress, and again the care for the delivery was superb.

But then we began to notice a difference. One of the downsides of socialized medicine at the time was inadequate funding for nursing care. Karyn was told to stay in the hospital for a week because of her incision, but beginning the day after birth, it was Karyn who had to roam the halls to find clean sheets each day to change both her and Harrison's bed (quite uncomfortable with her abdominal incision!). It was Karyn and her mother, Kathryn McLaughlin, who had come to assist with the new baby, who together carried out all the basic nursing functions. If times are tough, the central government simply cuts the budget for health care, rationing what each hospital gets, and the hospital has no choice but to make do with the resources available. You take what you can get in times of rationing. You have no voice, and you have no choice.

I was also struck by the cultural differences in the British patients and their families' attitudes toward disease. In England, as long as everyone was getting about the same health care, even if it wasn't the best and the latest, no one seemed to complain. Americans expect more of their health-care system. My English patients were more accepting of the fact that there are limits as to what modern medicine can accomplish. For example, when I operated on a patient with lung cancer, if there was some minimal spread of the tumor discovered at the time of surgery, that would be the absolute end of therapy. I would tell the patient and their family that surgery was all that we had to offer, and share with them the statistics showing that the patient would unfortunately not live beyond a few years because of the spread of the cancer. The patient and his family understood and accepted this. They didn't ask what more could be done; they didn't ask for a referral or a second opinion.

But if I had operated on that same patient in the United States, we would have immediately recommended radiation therapy and, if indicated, chemotherapy to fight the cancer. We would routinely offer the latest scientific breakthroughs and medicines and the latest technology to fight the cancer. We doctors would not give up! And most patients would be much more demanding, expecting to get whatever latest therapy is available. Back at home, the normal questions would be: "What experimental therapy is there? Can't I get an extra year of life with some new treatment? There must be an investigational clinical trial somewhere that I could enter." The contrast was striking to me.

The rationing of health care was overt in England, whereas in the United States we had (and have) a much more covert sort of rationing based on ability to pay and on varying access to insurance. For example, in England, as senior registrar I was responsible for keeping the list of heart surgery patients whom we would treat over the following month. It would be over a hundred patients long at any one time, listed one to one hundred in order of how long they had been on the waiting list. We operated on two cases each day from the list, starting with the names at the top unless there was a clear-cut emergency. After 4:00 P.M., we were not allowed to do any more cases; the operating rooms closed, and the surgical staff went home. We started afresh on the list the next day. By the time I got down to patient number seventy or so, I noticed that some of the patients had died waiting.

In the United States, that would never have been tolerated. If we had one hundred patients who needed open-heart surgery, we'd work around the clock and get them all done within a week. Yes, some patients might have to wait a couple of weeks for purely elective heart surgery in the United States, but it wouldn't be because a government bureaucrat was rationing their care based on money available or some politician's decision to cut off the money spigot.

Another eye-opener to me was the British attitude toward the clock. Medical training in the United States was focused entirely on patient care. In those days, the hours an intern or a resident worked were always secondary to the care of the patient. If you were a resident and you had a new patient, in our U.S. surgical programs you would stay with the patient and make sure that you attended to his or her every need. There was no "punching out" at five or six o'clock. The patient was your responsibility, and you did not hand that off to others, even if it meant staying extra hours to make sure that absolutely everything for that patient was smooth.

In England, the intern-equivalents, or "house men" as they were called, working under me, with the national government their boss and the socialized system their administrator, clocked in each day, arriving not a minute before the required 7:30 A.M., and when five o'clock came around, even if we were in the middle of rounds on the patient wards, they would clock out, having fulfilled their end of their contract with the government. *But what about the patient?* I'd think in amazement. Well, the next shift could pick up the pieces.

In America today, because of the law that specifies residents work no more than eighty hours per week, residents are forced to watch the clock much more stringently. But my dad would never have understood "clocking in and out" when it came to taking care of patients. One's personal experiences in life do color one's policies and attitudes. Mine surely have.

Based on that personal experience of working directly for the British National Health Services (NHS), it seemed to me that the disadvantages far outweighed the benefits of truly socialized medicine, where the rationing of diagnostic modalities like CAT scans and MRI machines, types of treatment for cancer, availability of life-saving pharmaceutical agents, and specific number of hospital beds are all determined (and thus rationed) by some politician in government, regardless of current patient needs or medical requirements. It may just be the doctor in me, but I think the health of a person is too personal and too critical to be left to the whims of a government official, whose priorities shift from year to year, dictated by the budget cycle.

Lamenting the slowness in the system, the unavailability and inaccessibility of much of the latest useful technology, the long lines of people waiting for the heart operations that we performed every day, the inability to even offer state-of-the-art treatment for many types of cancer, and the lack of access to life-saving kidney dialysis for older people, I returned home convinced that socialized medicine could not, and should not, work in any shape or form in America.

Moreover, my experience there further developed my own philosophy on the American health-care sector—that we need to address the egregious gaps in cost and access in our health-care system, not by centralized federal government rationing but by changing the incentives within our own blended private-public system. For those unable to get insurance on their own, we need to move more toward the English concept of medicine as a "social good," but the overwhelming majority of our health care should be delivered through a private system that centers just as Dad did on *value* for the individual patient that aligns incentives for doctors, nurses, hospitals, and health plans to keep people healthy or return them to health. The "sector" must be transformed into an integrated "system" that rewards quality of the entire care delivery value chain of a medical condition and that is driven by twenty-first-century knowledge and interconnected information systems. Consumers and participants should be the drivers for quality, and basic health-care services should be available and affordable to every American. I hope, in the years to come, we'll be able to move our system much closer to this ideal that centers on value without losing any of the wonderful benefits of choice and high quality provided by our current system.

Though we never got that rose-covered cottage, Karyn and I loved our experience in Southampton; we grew closer and the joy of our life (the first of three), Harrison, arrived. I gained a more complete and much richer understanding of my own specialty of heart and lung surgery, as well as an appreciation for both the unique contribution of innovation that characterizes American medicine and of the freedoms we have in America to choose our own doctors and our own health-care plans. My time in Southampton also reminded me of the dichotomy regarding the two disparate passions with which I lived perpetually: I wanted to work hard to become a pioneering, cutting-edge surgeon who was part of figuring out innovative treatments for the really big challenges and unknowns in cancer and heart disease, who had access to the breathtaking new advances and technologies to bring hope and life to others, without losing that personal, compassionate, patient-centered, family-doctor approach to healing that my dad had modeled so well.

Better yet, I'd heard about a place and a doctor who might be able to help me bring these two seemingly conflicting passions together—a place and a doctor who embodied the passions of health, hope, and healing.

6

The Heart of the Matter

Being on the cutting edge and creating new knowledge always appealed to me. It probably didn't start in Dr. Powell's basic science lab at the MGH, but it certainly was cultivated there.

Even while doing heart and lung surgery in England, I had already taken an interest in, and started gravitating toward, the exciting new frontier of transplanting the human heart—a field with almost science-fiction-like opportunities to treat individuals bound by diseases that otherwise would be fatal. Transplantation also appealed to my passion for innovative solutions to seemingly unsolvable problems.

Ironically, in the early 1980s, Mass General, despite being one of the most advanced, highly respected hospitals in the country and being located in the very city where kidney transplantation had started some twenty-five years earlier, was not yet convinced that the risks of heart transplantation outweighed the benefits. Conventional wisdom among the physicians there was that heart transplantation wouldn't work, at least in the short term; the immunological rejection and enveloping infections made it impractical and too expensive. So, in 1980 the medical institutions and bureaucracy in Boston formally said no to the pursuit of transplanting the human heart. A moratorium on heart transplantation was announced.

This was devastating news for me. How shortsighted! How could the best of the best refuse to participate in one of the most promising new breakthroughs of the past fifty years? In effect, they were signing my traveling papers.

I immediately began searching for the most progressive, pioneering transplant program in the world. I found it at Stanford University Medical Center in Palo Alto, California, under the direction of Dr. Norman Shumway, the true father of heart transplantation.

Shumway and his associates had been working on animal heart transplants since the 1950s. In December 1959, Dr. Shumway and his close friend and medical research collaborator, Dr. Richard Lower, successfully transplanted a heart between two dogs. The dog with the transplanted heart lived for eight days, proving Shumway's theories and procedures could work.

Both doctors believed it was only a matter of time before human heart transplantation could be done, but Shumway and Lower also believed in careful, meticulous research. Through rigorous, cautious exploration and surgical precision, they proceeded, step by step, through the early 1960s.

With Shumway's blessing and recommendation, Lower left Stanford in 1965 to head his own surgical team at the Medical College of Virginia in Richmond. The two men stayed in contact and continued a friendly competition in the race to see who could be the first to do an actual human heart transplant. Meanwhile, two far more intense rivals, Dr. Adrian Kantrowitz at Maimonides Hospital in Brooklyn and Dr. Christiaan Barnard in Cape Town, South Africa, also hoped to become the world's first successful human heart transplant surgeon. The global race had begun.

All four surgeons knew and had a grudging respect for one another. Barnard and Shumway, however, were cut from radically different cloth. Barnard's ambitious, hard-charging personality had grated against Shumway's more laconic, laid-back personality when they'd worked together briefly on a surgical team in Minnesota in the mid-1950s. While Shumway preferred a team effort, graciously sharing any praise or acclaim for his accomplishments with the nurses, doctors, technicians, and scientists around him, Barnard seemed obsessed with achieving fame and glory for himself.

Over an eight-year period, Shumway and Lower had also systematically done extensive basic science research. After developing the surgical techniques of removing and replacing the heart, they turned their attention to the next challenge—the response of the body's immune system to reject foreign organs, even those implanted by well-meaning surgeons. Meanwhile, Barnard, who had done relatively little fundamental transplant research, had spent a mere three months in Richmond with Dr. Lower, carefully observing his research and techniques and planning to replicate them back in South Africa.

Shumway wisely recognized that he also needed the American public to become comfortable with the novel idea of transplanting a human heart. Two issues had to be resolved. One was the medical and ethical question of when a person was actually dead, making the removal of a heart to be used in another person's body acceptable. At that time, simple absence of a heartbeat was the accepted definition of death. The concept of *brain death* had not yet entered American law or understanding. The heart, rather than the brain, was regarded as the defining organ of life.

The other challenge was the romantic and spiritual concept of the heart as the center of a person's being. Nobody ever sent a valentine saying, "I love you with all my liver." For the average person in those days, to remove a person's heart was to take away his or her core identity.

Slowly, both of these obstacles were overcome through educational efforts and scientific research, even as Shumway systematically continued to prepare the way technically and scientifically for heart transplantation. By November 20, 1967, Shumway and his brilliant young chief resident, Ed Stinson, felt confident enough in attempting a human heart transplant that they announced their intentions in the prestigious *Journal of the American Medical Association* (JAMA). Of course, for that to happen, someone had to die without damaging the heart, and an amazing number of coincidences had to align themselves. So Shumway and Stinson waited patiently for the moment to act.

Meanwhile, on December 3, 1967, in Cape Town, Dr. Christiaan Barnard used the Shumway and Lower techniques to transplant a human heart from a young woman, brain-dead after a car accident, into the body of a fifty-five-year-old grocer, Louis Washkansky. Barnard won the race to transplant a human heart from one human being to another.

The world hailed Barnard's success, catapulting the Afrikaner to instant fame and acclaim. I vividly remember as a young fifteen-year-old seeing Washkansky's and Barnard's picture on the cover of *Life* magazine. Most within the scientific community who knew how Barnard had achieved his goal were less enthralled. They felt that because of their more than a decade of painstaking and disciplined basic science and clinical research, it should have been Shumway or Lower who had the honor of performing the first human heart transplant, not some opportunist who had stolen the glory from them.

Ever gracious, Norman Shumway publicly spoke kindly and magnanimously of Barnard, allowing only Ed Stinson to share his private anguish and disappointment. Nevertheless, he was committed to moving forward with his intention to transplant a human heart at Stanford, hoping for the right combination of a needy recipient and an appropriate donor. Shumway felt that with Barnard attracting the lion's share of the media's attention, he and Stinson could quietly go about their business, perfecting the procedures and saving lives by means of heart transplantation.

The following day, David McIntire Bashaw was born in Philadelphia to Celeste and Keith Bashaw. Celeste was the daughter of Reverend Carl McIntire, a prominent Presbyterian minister and one of America's most loved and respected radio Bible teachers. There was little rejoicing in the Christian community, however. The famous preacher's grandson, David, was an anencephalic baby—born without a functioning brain and leaking bloody cerebral spinal fluid. Yet the infant's heart continued to beat strongly.

With the permission of Celeste and Keith, their baby was flown to Brooklyn, where Dr. Adrian Kantrowitz waited in anticipation of attempting America's first heart transplant, an even more delicate procedure because Kantrowitz hoped to transplant baby David's heart into the body of a seventeen-day-old baby boy, Jamie Scudero, who was dying of congestive heart failure.

At five-thirty the following morning, Kantrowitz attempted to become the first American to transplant a human heart. But seven hours after the procedure, the heart stopped and both little David and little Jamie were dead.

Then, a mere eighteen days after performing the first human heart transplant, Christiaan Barnard watched as his patient, Louis Washkansky, turned a blue-black color and died. His immune system had rejected the young woman's heart.

Undeterred and no less confident, Shumway and Stinson performed the first successful heart transplant in America a month later, on January 6, 1968, when they transplanted the heart of Virginia White, a forty-three-year-old wife and mother of two, who had suffered a brain hemorrhage, into the body of Mike Kasperak, a fifty-four-year-old retired steelworker.

Kasperak lived for fourteen days before succumbing to multiple system failures, none of which was related to his new heart's ability to pump blood through his system, or his body's rejection of the new heart. Shumway and Stinson, though saddened and exhausted after several operations trying to repair Kasperak's debilitated body, were encouraged that the transplanted heart had continued to function through it all. A new world had opened before them.

Over the next year, heart transplants became the "designer" operation, as high-profile cardiac surgeons around the world rushed to attempt the new procedures. Shumway knew that most of these would fail, and indeed some 85 percent of the patients died relatively soon after transplantation. Only Shumway himself could boast of better results, managing to keep about 40 percent of his patients alive. Most surgeons quickly abandoned the procedure. But not Shumway. He knew the path to success: focus, systematic research, hard work, and never saying "It can't be done." He continued his systematic and deliberate approach of steady research to address each new problem that appeared along the way. When everyone was giving up because there was no way to diagnose rejection early in its course, Shumway did what any great scientist would do; he solved the new problem. He figured out a way to sample a tiny piece of heart muscle and make the diagnosis before the heart had irreversible damage. The tool to do the sampling, the cardiac bioptome, was a Stanford invention.

The next problem to rear its head was the infections that arose in the recipient, whose immune system was suppressed by medicine to prevent rejection of the organ. Solving this problem required a new medicine. It was not until the drug cyclosporine began to be used experimentally in 1980 that the odds of long-term success began to shift in Shumway's favor. Cyclosporine suppressed the immune system of the transplant recipient enough to keep the body from rejecting the new heart, yet amazingly, the drug left the rest of the immune system capable of preventing most infections. Shumway started using the new drug, and soon his patients were not only surviving for a year or more, but with the help of cyclosporine, many went on to live long and productive lives.

Cyclosporine use was still in its early stages when I traveled again to Stanford in the early 1980s. I had met Dr. Shumway a number of years earlier when I was considering going to Stanford for medical school. Shumway, whom I'd read about since I was a teenager, and whose systematic and deliberate approach to achieve great things had become legendary, surprised and impressed me with his easygoing, relaxed demeanor. I couldn't help but contrast the purposely intense and too frequently humiliating atmosphere of most cardiac surgical training programs with the equally demanding but laid-back and respectful and encouraging attitudes of Dr. Shumway and his team in California.

I kept in touch with Dr. Shumway, letting him know of my interest in heart transplantation. One day, in the middle of my thoracic chief residency at the MGH, I received the call: "Bill, in six months I'll have an opening in the heart transplant program here. I want you to come to be the senior fellow, then chief resident."

I was ecstatic. I called Karyn and told her the great news. After a few days of discussion, we decided we should leave the security of a career in Boston, apparently locked in its backward-looking ways when it came to heart and lung transplantation, to go work with the visionary Shumway. Boston killed the dream, but Shumway was making dreams become reality.

I quickly discovered that Shumway's team was an eclectic bunch of unusual personalities, each person brilliant in his or her own way. That was part of the genius of Shumway; he spotted talents instinctively and promoted them, often overlooking quiddities and frailties, or maybe even playfully delighting in them. One of the first oddities I noticed upon my arrival in Palo Alto was that every single member of the cardiac surgical team, except Shumway himself, wore cowboy boots. I had no idea what significance the boots implied, whether a rugged toughness or nonconformity to medical norms, but I soon dug out an old pair of boots that I hadn't worn since my teenage years. The irony was not lost on me that having been raised in Nashville, home of country music and the Grand Ole Opry, I had to move to California to wear cowboy boots every day.

Karyn and I leased a house from a Stanford professor who was on sabbatical. Tucked in the hills behind the university, the clay-colored stucco house seemed designed to blend unobtrusively with its surroundings. After living in a small third-floor apartment on Mt. Vernon Street in Boston, we loved that home, complete with a swimming pool and a flower garden in the back. When I wasn't working, Karyn and I walked and rode bicycles through the picturesque neighborhood.

When the professor returned, we rented a newer home in Menlo Park. The well-kept neighborhood boasted brightly colored flower beds and enclosed backyards. Karyn loved our new home, as did our young son, Harrison. Was it the warm weather, the more casual approach to life, the better living conditions, or just the healthier lifestyle? The peaceful atmosphere appealed to us, and nine months later, our second son, Jonathan, was born at Stanford Hospital.

Working with Shumway at Stanford felt like a medical paradise compared to the more traditional, hierarchical surgical experience that was the norm in cardiothoracic surgery at Mass General. Dr. Shumway demanded a team approach, motivating through encouragement rather than denigrating, belittling, or criticizing doctors or nurses. No surgical instruments were ever thrown in Shumway's operating rooms. Any time things did get tense or an operating team ran into unexpected trouble, Shumway quickly defused the situation with a joke. He imbued confidence in others—his colleagues, his residents, his nurses, the technicians.

Although he was a brilliant surgeon and technician, Dr. Shumway prided himself on being an even better teacher. Moreover, he enjoyed allowing the younger members in the OR to take the lead. Whether it was Dr. Lower, or Dr. Stinson, or much later, me, Shumway preferred to step back and with precision and confidence guide the doctors he was teaching, frequently referring to himself as "the world's greatest first assistant." By the time I arrived at Stanford, Dr. Shumway's accomplishments were already legendary, yet he seemed as proud of the accomplishments of his trainees as he was of his own. When he introduced me as "a valuable member of the team," I was thrilled. I later learned that he always introduced newcomers as "a valuable member of the team." In a world where accomplished senior surgeons are often regarded as untouchable, with huge egos, Dr. Shumway's attitude was a refreshing anomaly.

Was this approach transferable to other careers? I had no interest in politics at this time; I was too busy mastering my craft as a heart surgeon. But politicians do have big, self-righteous egos. In years to come, I'd have many opportunities to compare my Senate colleagues and others I met in Washington with Dr. Shumway. For me, he remains a model of unassuming but incredibly powerful personal leadership.

Most of the residents with Shumway spent three full years in cardiac and vascular surgery before moving up, but I'd already completed my cardiac residency in Boston, so I didn't go through the Stanford program. As I was the outsider from Boston, the other residents easily could have resented me, but instead they went out of their way to introduce me to the Stanford ways, and to make me feel welcome.

I spent a few months at the Veterans Administration Hospital, doing more routine heart surgery such as coronary-artery bypass surgery and valve replacements, learning Shumway's unique methods, and then Dr. Shumway moved me straight into transplantation. Working daily with Drs. Shumway and Stinson, I soon became chief resident in cardiovascular surgery. It was heady stuff, operating every day with surgeons who had made and were continuing to make medical history—pioneers who kept on pioneering.

A great clinical surgeon must be a great research investigator, Shumway believed. He had all of us work in the laboratory in the basement of the Falk Cardiovascular Research Center as well as clinically in the hospital. We each had our own research project that would address some unknown in the fast-evolving field of transplantation. We were expected to share the results of our investigations with others at national conferences through formal presentations and peer-reviewed papers. Shumway taught us that breakthroughs don't originate in the operating room. Rather they are the product of countless hours of experimental work in the laboratory. If a new problem arises after the last advance, design a research project and take it yourself to the lab to figure it out. And once you do, be a good enough surgeon to apply your answer clinically in the operating room to better the lives of your patients. A Shumway-trained surgeon does it all—a curious scientist who is equally comfortable in the basement laboratory and in the operating room. Shumway emphasized the value of enlarging one's comfort zone.

One of Dr. Shumway's favorite sayings was, "Cardiac surgery is not hard to do; it's just hard to *get* to do." Indeed, it took four years of college, plus four years of medical school, five years of general surgery practically living night and day at the hospital, a year or two of research, three more years of cardiothoracic surgery—all of that and more, simply to get the opportunity to be the lead surgeon for a heart transplant. But to me, it was worth every minute of the work, every step of the long, long journey. Heart transplantation was adrenaline-producing stuff.

Dr. Shumway's philosophy in the OR was, "Keep it simple." He often reminded his trainees, "The simpler it is, the less room there is for error." While Shumway expected perfection, he encouraged the doctors he mentored to be honest about missing the mark: "Never be afraid to double-dribble," he quipped when a surgeon tried to close too much space with one suture. The lighthearted approach in no way minimized the message Shumway emphasized. "Get it right—even if it means taking out a suture and doing it all over again; get it right. Don't let your pride stand in the way of perfection." Shumway also taught, "Never lose your temper; if you do, you've lost."

These are some pretty good rules for heart surgeons. I found them even better for my life in politics.

The first time I ever cut out a human heart and replaced it with the heart of another person was a night I will never forget, especially with Dr. Norman Shumway, the man who had invented the procedure, cracking jokes across the table from me throughout. It was 3:00 A.M.; the rest of the world was sound asleep. A young girl who would otherwise have been dead in six months now had a chance to live a full life. As I saw that new heart kick into gear and start beating strongly, an amazing sense of elation and relief swept over me. It wasn't pride; quite the contrary. I was humbled to have the power to protect life, to help restore it or prolong it. Through the miracle of transplantation, aided by the opportunity to be trained by the best, the discovery of modern miracle drugs, and the selfless act of the heart donor, I was blessed with the ability to prolong God's gift of life. What a privilege—a humbling privilege—to serve others.

Life at Stanford was good. I was fulfilled in my career; Karyn

and the boys were happy, and we couldn't imagine anything better. And then I received that phone call from Nashville.

"BILL, THIS IS HARVEY BENDER," THE VOICE ON THE PHONE SAID.
"Ike Robinson and I would really like to talk to you about coming
back home."

I didn't really know Dr. Bender very well. I'd spent a couple of
months after my first year of med school doing research on heart
blood flow in dogs at Vanderbilt, and knew him as the Johns
Hopkins–trained head of thoracic surgery there and a well-respected
congenital heart surgeon. I also knew that Vanderbilt hoped to develop a state-of-the-art heart transplant facility. Ike Robinson was
the vice-chancellor for medical affairs at Vanderbilt.

"Tell me more," I ventured.

Dr. Bender spoke enthusiastically about Vanderbilt's plans
for transplantation, reminding me that they already had one of
the busiest kidney transplant programs in the country under
the leadership of nephrologist Keith Johnson and surgeon Bob
Richie. He wanted to know if I had solidified my own position
after my stint at Stanford was completed.

I told him that indeed I did want someday to return home
and that I had a grand dream that included but went well beyond
what was being done at Stanford. Shumway had taught me to
dream big and then make it happen. My dream was to create a
multiorgan transplant center, housed in one location. We would
not just do hearts and kidneys, but would add liver, and pan-
creas, and bone marrow, and we would soon even do single-lung
transplants (though at the time no one had had much success in
single-lung transplants; in fact, even the Shumway program had
not yet tried to perform them).

Dr. Bender suggested that Vanderbilt might offer the ideal location for my ambitious new concept. The notion excited me.
Certainly, the idea of moving home held a strong attraction for
me, especially since Karyn and I would be returning to our
southern roots. Mother and Dad were getting older and unlike

my elder brothers and sisters, who had all gone away but by then had returned to live in Nashville not far from the family home on Bowling, I had not had the luxury of spending extended periods of time with them since leaving for college.

Beyond that, however, Vanderbilt was offering me the opportunity to develop a new type of transplant center that was integrated and truly multidisciplinary—to include all organs, with ethicists, social workers, psychiatrists, and scientists all under the same roof. The only institution that had tried anything like this at the time was Pittsburgh, and even they had individual programs separated by organ type. Almost all other existing programs were single-organ centers, and most of them were stovepiped around a single, high-profile surgeon, within a single department. But with my experiences at Stanford, which underscored working as a team, I envisioned the potential synergy of bringing together the expertise of many surgeons and nonsurgical physicians, allowing their rich and diverse ideas to feed into a single, integrated system and stimulate further advances, transplanting all major organs, and bringing in other related specialties, like infectious disease, that were more traditionally housed in separate departments. This was my big dream.

Shumway had always said focus everything on the patient, so I figured, let's do just that. Let's bring the disciplines under one roof around the patient. The casual exchange of ideas among all the disciplines that would ensue with a common location would generate new ideas to be explored and conquered.

In response to Dr. Bender's suggestion, I put together a detailed thirty-page blueprint describing how such a program could be achieved. I wrote a business plan for the new endeavor, including the personnel required, the space it would take, and how it might be financed.

The timing was perfect. Moreover, I was enticed by Vanderbilt's willingness to allow me to do a small series of transplants on patients who could not afford the high cost of transplantation. I had argued in my business plan that the medical center would have to "invest in" (that is, pay for) five heart transplants and possibly five lung transplants—about one hundred thousand dollars per patient, plus a lifetime of expensive medications. Most insurance companies still regarded this kind of transplant as "experimental." I knew we could change that by demonstrating the best results in the country. I proposed new billing and reimbursement schemes—billing over a cycle of care. The program would become self-supporting, I said, because I would see that Vanderbilt became the "center of excellence" for transplantation in the South, and thus would be reimbursed by private insurance and Medicare.

Karyn didn't flinch when I proposed that we move to Nashville. Instead, she went to work, meeting with Realtors back in Tennessee, finding a comfortable home for our family (thinking it would be the home we would finally settle in for the rest of our lives), negotiating the deal, packing up our belongings in California, and arranging every detail of the cross-country move— all while I lived in the operating room. She literally bought our new home without me ever seeing it. As always, Karyn made the wheels run, allowing me to grow professionally and contribute to my patients.

Dad had always said, "Good people beget good people." He used the line in every speech and public gathering. So, like Dr. Shumway, I insisted on handpicking my own team members, and I sought to assemble the best in their fields. When word got around that we were building a team on the Shumway model, we had no shortage of solid applicants.

I worked seven days a week, month after month, getting the program up and running. My colleague, the smart, low-key, Hopkins-trained Dr. Walter Merrill, and I were constantly dealing with patients, flying off in the middle of the night to hospitals all over the East Coast, sometimes Canada and as far west as Colorado, to personally inspect and then remove the donor hearts. In those days, we had to do all of our own donor "harvests." The field was so new that a typical heart surgeon had never even seen a heart cut out. And after a patient was successfully transplanted, it was a perpetual battle, fighting against the next round of infections and heart rejections until things settled out. Walter was the consummate partner, always gracious and volunteering to do more than his fair share, never complaining. For more than five years we were at each other's side daily and all night at least once a week as we built our rapidly growing program.

Much of the burden of the new program fell naturally to me, since it was I who had the formal training at the most respected heart transplant program in the world. It was exhilarating for our new team but tiring, and it took me away from my family too much. I spent all Christmas Eve and Christmas day in the operating room for two of the first three years of the program. You can't schedule transplants at your convenience; you do them whenever a donor heart becomes available. And to be honest, giving someone a new life on Christmas Day had special meaning. But the demands on family life were real. Our third son, Bryan, was born in Nashville, but I missed most of his early adventures growing up. Karyn never complained, but she carried a heavy load.

In addition to transplantation, there was the more routine heart and lung surgery we'd do every day . . . and the trauma call which would always bring in the unexpected.

SEPTEMBER 21, 1991, DAWNED A CRISP, CLEAR, EARLY FALL DAY IN Nashville. Karyn and I were watching Harrison play soccer, as Jonathan and Bryan were running up and down the sidelines. Shortly after noon, my beeper began to vibrate and I received a call from Vanderbilt University Medical Center; I knew that either a heart donor had become available for a transplant or a trauma case was on the way in. Either way it was clear I'd have to cut the match short.

"Dr. Frist, we have a chopper coming in from Fort Campbell. Patient has a potentially fatal gunshot wound to the chest," the voice on the other end of the line said calmly.

"What's the status?" I asked.

"A chest tube has been placed, but there is continued hemor-rhaging. Large bore IVs are in place."

I knew what that meant: Emergency surgery was almost cer-tain. "I'm on my way," I said. "I'll get to the hospital as quickly as possible."

I rushed toward Vanderbilt Hospital to be present in the trauma unit before the helicopter arrived, in the event that we had to go straight to surgery. As I raced across town, I didn't know any de-tails concerning the patient about to be delivered to the hospital. *A gunshot wound,* I thought. Shootings are commonly seen in the trauma unit, but they don't usually present with a chest tube already in place. The patient coming in could be anybody—a ci-vilian, a domestic-violence case, or it might be one of the many young soldiers stationed at Fort Campbell, located on the border of Tennessee and Kentucky, about an hour's drive northwest of Nashville and home to the 101st Airborne Division.

I arrived at the hospital, quickly changed into my scrubs, and waited for the helicopter. I didn't have to wait long. A few minutes later, the military chopper landed at the nearby Nashville Metro Fire Department helipad, and the patient was transferred by ambulance to Vanderbilt's trauma center, where he was quickly wheeled into the trauma room. A team of trauma surgeons and I went to work.

While awaiting the patient's arrival, I had learned that he was indeed a soldier who had been shot during a live-fire training ex-ercise at Fort Campbell. Apparently, another soldier had tripped and accidentally discharged his M-16 a mere forty meters from the patient. The bullet had ripped a hole in the soldier's chest just over his right breast pocket and exited his back. Bad enough for a soldier to accidentally shoot one of his own, but the person he shot was the battalion commander himself. The commander had been observing troop maneuvers when the shot pierced the air, dropping him to the ground. Although he remained conscious, he was bleeding badly.

A med-evac helicopter on site rushed the soldier to the Fort Campbell Hospital, where the military docs quickly inserted a tube in his chest to evacuate the ongoing bleeding from his lung. Recognizing the bullet had entered close to where the lung connects to the heart and that the bleeding continued after the chest tube was placed, the doctors referred the patient to our Level I trauma team at Vanderbilt for definitive treatment.

Once we got a look at him in the trauma unit, after a quick evaluation, we made a decision to go straight to the operating room. We needed to perform an emergency thoracotomy to stop the hemorrhaging from the lung. Still conscious, lying flat on his back, with various intravenous tubes hooked to his body, I leaned over the patient slightly and calmly explained the situation. "Colonel, I'm Dr. Frist, a thoracic surgeon here, and I will be taking care of you. What is your name?"

The soldier replied, "Sir, I'm Lieutenant Colonel David Petraeus, commander of the 3rd Battalion of the 187th Infantry Regiment at Fort Campbell."

"Colonel, we're going to need to take you directly to the operating room to control the bleeding and possibly remove a piece of the lung close to where it connects to the heart."

Most patients confronting the potential of going under the knife express some reticence. "Do I really need surgery?" they might ask. "Isn't there anything else that you can do?"

Not Petraeus. His eyes locked squarely onto mine as he said, "If we've got a problem that needs to be fixed, let's get on with it. Let's get it done now." His straightforward decisiveness surprised me, although I would years later learn that such a call for action and results was a defining characteristic of David Petraeus. Clearly a no-nonsense sort of guy, we went straight to the OR. On the way, he told me how proud he was of the soldiers who had treated him in the field and how he wanted to get back to the base as soon as possible. I told him we had to get him through the surgery first, but you could tell he wasn't going to stay around long after surgery.

"Where did you do your training?" he asked as we entered the OR, still bleeding at a good clip from the chest tube.

"Princeton and Harvard," I replied.

"Now I can relax; I know I am in good hands," he said. "I can entrust my life to a Princeton man."

Minutes later he was asleep and I made a large incision through his right chest. Once inside, I discovered about two centimeters of shattered rib embedded deeply in the colonel's lung, making the operation even more tricky and tedious. He had an eight-centimeter hole in his back, where the bullet had exited after blasting completely through his body. Once I was able to control the hemorrhage, I moved next to repair the wound near the heart. Finally, I reapproximated his ribs, sewed him up, and took him to the recovery room.

I estimated that Petraeus's recovery would be about a week, but within twenty-four hours, the colonel was already badgering me to get back to Fort Campbell. "I feel fine, really, Doc," he said. "I'm ready to go home."

David Petraeus was as much a scholar as he was a soldier. He had done graduate work and earned a Ph.D. in 1987 at Princeton's Woodrow Wilson School of Public and International Affairs, which explained the Princeton comment on the way to the OR. Petraeus had done his doctoral dissertation on some of the military lessons learned from the Vietnam War.

With Petraeus lobbying hard to get out of the hospital early to get back with his soldiers, I finally acquiesced and allowed him to return to Fort Campbell after only two days of recovery time. He still had a tube in his chest when he left the hospital, but he didn't seem to mind. His men mattered more to him than his own comfort.

The next time I heard anything about him was when another trauma surgeon called me a few years later, wanting to know exactly what surgical procedure I'd done on David Petraeus. Now a brigadier general, Petraeus was back in a trauma unit after having suffered a badly fractured pelvis when his skydiving canopy collapsed about a hundred feet off the ground due to a wind shear, at a parachuting drop zone near Fort Bragg, North Carolina. Tough as nails, Petraeus survived the parachute's collapse and recovered with as much aplomb as he had the gunshot wound. I remember thinking this guy really got himself into some tough situations—shot with an M-16 and falling from the sky without a parachute. No telling what would happen to him in the future.

Our serendipitous 1991 meeting would lead to our paths crossing many times in the future, as I transitioned to the Senate and Petraeus continued to climb the military command structure. We stayed in touch over the years, and I visited the general and his soldiers at Fort Campbell several times, once spending a night in the barracks with my son Jonathan to experience a bit of the soldiers' life from their perspective. At the time, we were working on appropriations in the Senate to improve the living conditions for soldiers at U.S. bases. In October 2002, General Petraeus and I ran the army ten-miler together in Washington, D.C., along with a contingent of his soldiers. Perhaps I should say we *started* running the ten-miler together, since after the first one hundred yards, the intensely competitive general whose goal was clearly to beat every one of his soldiers left me in the dust!

A few months later, David Petraeus was leading his men in Iraq. Karyn and I visited with Petraeus's wife, Holly, at Fort Campbell, while her husband was launching the assault on Baghdad. Karyn would be donating the proceeds from her book *Love You, Daddy Boy* to the nonprofit foundation Operation Eagles' Nest to support the families at Fort Campbell. And I spoke with him in Iraq by phone from my Senate office on the very day he began the assault.

In mid-2004 I took a Senate delegation to Iraq and visited with General Petraeus. While I was there, Petraeus asked me to speak to a group of fifty young Iraqi soldiers in the middle of their military exercises. Standing in the hot, dusty training compound, Petraeus gathered the soldiers around us and he told them the story of how we had met on that fateful day back in September 1991. The moral of the story was to always be prepared and to always expect the unexpected. He was a soldier's soldier; you could tell the Iraqi recruits respected him tremendously.

An intense competitor who used to challenge his men to push-up contests and almost always won, General David Petraeus is also one of the U.S. Army's brightest minds and best analytical thinkers. He combines a keen understanding of history with a willingness to try some off-the-wall, out-of-the-box approaches. One of his slogans displayed in the 101st's barracks in Iraq was: "What have you done to win Iraqi hearts and minds today?"

Interestingly, my friendship with General Petraeus is colored with many intersections and many parallels. From emergency surgery, to our common interests at the Wilson School at Princeton, to our time in Iraq together, to our mutual commitment to winning the war on terror—the fibers of our lives have been woven into a marvelous tapestry with a similar commitment to serve.

When the true and accurate history of America's wars in Iraq and Afghanistan is written, General David Petraeus will join the ranks of Dwight Eisenhower and Douglas MacArthur.

OUR EFFORTS AT VANDERBILT ACCELERATED PROGRESS IN THE transplant field through our unique multiorgan, multidisciplinary approach, sharing information across subspecialties, allowing more efficient and better use of resources, incorporating an infectious disease expert who did nothing but transplantations, and bringing a hospital ethicist onto the team—an innovative, forward-looking step at the time. As a result, the entire field of transplantation benefited. And we developed a model of integrated health-care delivery, called today *value chain care delivery*, which I believe addresses most of the major problems of cost, access, and quality we experience today.

Walter and I coordinated all of our initial transplant runs. We went wherever a viable donor could be found, if—and it was a big *if*—we could get there, excise the heart, and bring it back to Nashville and transplant it into another human being, all within the strict limit of four hours. Through years of experimentation, Shumway had discovered that the human heart could survive outside the body for up to four hours if kept sufficiently chilled. It would restart if transplanted within that extremely narrow window of time. The key, of course, was that there could be no wasted time and absolutely no mistakes—a challenging standard to meet, but one that transplantation made essential.

The tension of a transplant run—racing against the clock to retrieve a still-beating heart from the body of a person who has already died, and then returning to the hospital to insert that heart into the body of another person being kept alive by a machine—is matched only by the sense of fulfillment you feel in saving a life through means that were impossible only a decade before. Nevertheless, the math of heart transplants tended to be depressing. Somebody had to die so another person could live. That was the constant dilemma we faced. We always had more patients needing transplants than we had available organs to transplant. So each week I would helplessly watch some of my patients waiting for transplants die.

Hoping to educate the public on the need for donors, I began traveling around Tennessee talking about the moral/ethical issues of transplantation, dealing head-on with questions such as, "Who should decide who gets to live and who dies?" I encountered substantial resistance to the concept of transplantation from certain elements of the public. Insurance companies remained reluctant to fund the procedure, declaring it experimental long after the procedures were proven effective. Medicare moved even more slowly, taking eight years before finally agreeing to pay for the procedure.

Some people opposed transplantation on religious or philosophical grounds; others simply felt it was too morbid to take an organ from a dead person and place it in a living body. Many potential donors wondered whether a physician—despite the Hippocratic Oath—might work less strenuously to save their lives if the doctor knew the patient had signed a donor card. Still others were concerned about the possibility of doctors compromising care to *provide* a donor, or worse yet, the possibility of organized crime or other unscrupulous parties bidding high for body parts. I did my best to assuage everyone's concerns, while throwing myself into making more people aware of the need for organ donors.

Nowadays, the profiles of recipients and donors are matched on a national computer base, but in the 1980s, I carried an index card in my white physician's coat front pocket every day. On the card would be written the names of approximately twenty patients, all who would be dead in a few months if I didn't find them a heart. I knew personally every one of the patients listed on that card, along with their spouses and families. It depressed me but at the same time it inspired me to act. Somehow, I had to find a way to make the unrealized potential supply out there meet the growing demand for this new, poorly understood, life-saving procedure.

I'd been hired to be a surgeon, not a spokesperson. But I had to get the word out. My goal became to reach as many people as possible, especially community leaders who in turn could educate others, through whatever means possible. So at nights and on weekends, I left the hospital to travel far and wide speaking about the dire need for organ donations. I spoke to Rotary Clubs and other civic groups; I visited with hospital staffs all over Tennessee. I wrote articles for newspapers, magazines, and newsletters. My efforts were having an impact, but not nearly enough. Too many of my waiting patients were still dying.

Up until this point in my life, I'd always felt that if you just worked hard enough you could always accomplish your goal. But now, just working hard was not enough. I needed a louder, more far-reaching megaphone. I began to wonder what role my interest in public policy might play in making the miracle of transplantation more widely available. Were my parallel interests of science and policy back at Princeton beginning to intersect?

Kidney transplantation, unlike heart, had been performed fairly routinely around the country for about twenty years. The director of kidney transplantation at Vanderbilt, Keith Johnson, had presciently realized the huge potential of pubic policy in transplantation years before. He spearheaded the initiative in the late 1970s that led to Tennessee's being the first state in the country to put an organ donor form on the back of the driver's license. But by the mid-1980s the form had been taken off, allegedly for financial reasons.

Now, with Keith's support, I initiated a statewide grassroots campaign to return the donor form to every new driver's license. With no political or grassroots organizing experience, I jumped into this new arena of public policy headfirst. With the help of Tracy Frazier, my energetic administrative assistant at the transplant center, I organized committees in the seven major cities across the state and set up community generated letter-writing campaigns. We planned and implemented a lobbying effort in Nashville, another first for me. I'll never forget the thrill when I went to see the distinguished and long-serving lieutenant governor John Wilder. After what I remember as my nervous and poorly organized presentation, he stood up and shook my hand firmly and said in his rural southern drawl, "Boy, I don't really understand the transplanting body parts, but I love y'ur passion, and if it'll he'p others like you say, I'm your man in the Senate."

Our grassroots effort paid off. Three months later, legislation was passed, and the organ donor card was back on the Tennessee driver's licenses—for good. Wow! Even a doctor can get involved and influence public policy to change the course of peoples' lives. We now could reach millions of people in a new way and so thereby save hundreds of lives.

Could the healing of an individual be expanded to the healing of a community through public policy and public service? Suddenly, public policy began to seem like a powerful way of expanding what I was already trying to do as a physician.

7

The Unlikely Candidate

I can't really explain it, John; I just feel it is something that I want to do. It's something *somebody* should do," I said as I lifted my cup and took a sip of hot, freshly brewed coffee at Shoney's over on Murphy Road in Nashville.

"Yes," said John Van Mol, "but why does it have to be *you*?"

I had come to know John when his public relations firm Dye, Van Mol & Lawrence volunteered to help me with spreading the word across the state on organ donation. On a pro bono basis, he had personally put together a bicycle tour for my heart transplant patients, lead by inspirational patient Jimmy Moore, who traveled over five hundred miles, from Mountain City near the Virginia border to Memphis. What better way to tell the world that transplants work than the visual of a bevy of patients cycling across the state? Then, when I wrote the book *Transplant*, John helped with the Tennessee book tour. John and I got together periodically for breakfast meetings throughout the late 1980s, and I found myself talking about my future possibly leading in a different direction—toward politics.

John, whose business in life required him to get down to the core of a matter before deciding how to sell it, would listen to me, sip his coffee, and then ask, "Now, really, why do you want to do this?" Over and over again he would press me on that point.

"You have it all right now. A great reputation, the satisfaction of knowing you are saving lives every day. You give up a lot of things to enter politics, and in exchange for what?" he wanted to know. "Will you really have more of an impact in politics than you can have in medicine?"

I knew I finally got through to John one morning, when I said, "John, this heart transplant business is a good thing. It's fun, it's important, and I think I've made a contribution. But when you get right down to it, I've now trained many others to do the surgery—now maybe I should try to expand service to a larger community."

Bing! I could see the light come on in John's eyes. Thinking, no doubt, that I was talking about job burnout rather than putting my skills to work in politics, John at last began to talk to me about public service. In fact, he got excited about the possibilities. "What about governor?" he asked. "Just from the little I know about the job, and the governors I've worked with, it looks to me to be among the best jobs. You get to be the CEO of the state, you're at the top, setting the agenda, as opposed to Congress, where you are one of 435 people, or the Senate, one out of a hundred."

John was on a roll, so I didn't even try to interrupt him. "You know what we need to do?" John gushed. "We need to come up with a list of people you should talk to to see if it is really right for you. You can see Governor Ned McWherter, and you should probably talk to former governor Winfield Dunn, and former governor Lamar Alexander. And you know Al Gore, don't you?"

"Yes," I said. "I've talked to him a few times since I moved back to Tennessee and I've worked with his staff on transplant issues, but not about this. Dad even told me that one day he would be president."

John was exuberant now. "I can go to my friend Don Stansberry, who is best friends with Howard Baker, and then we can see Howard himself. We'll come up with a list of all the people you know and all the people I know . . ."

I liked the idea of talking to Howard Baker, a former U.S.

Senate majority leader, White House chief of staff to President Ronald Reagan, and 1980 presidential candidate, but one who never forgot his deep roots in rural Tennessee. Not only because he was the most respected statesman in Tennessee, but also because throughout his career, Howard Baker had emphasized the notion of the *citizen legislator*—the ordinary citizen who steps up to serve the community, state, and nation. That was a civic ideal that appealed to me.

And that's how we wound up in East Tennessee on March 6, 1990, visiting with Howard Baker. I finished an all-night case, repair of a torn thoracic aorta, at about 8:00 A.M. and rushed out to the airport to fly over to Knoxville for the meeting. I grabbed a couple of my *Transplant* books on the way out the door as gifts for my hosts.

Senator Baker had lunch with John and me at a restaurant in his hometown of Huntsville, about an hour from Knoxville. Also joining us was Donald Stansberry, an experienced Tennessee political insider and a partner in Senator Baker's law firm.

"Well, what are you?" Howard Baker asked me between mouthfuls of delicious country cooking. I must have looked puzzled, because he clarified his question. "Are you a Republican or a Democrat—or does it matter?"

Up till then, I simply hadn't thought about the implications of party affiliation that much. I swallowed hard, and replied, "I'm a doctor."

The three men around the table laughed. "I mean," I went on to explain, "you know my father, Senator. Our family is traditionally quite conservative, which means I guess I'd say Republican, but I haven't been all that active in politics since I was in college. I didn't vote until I was thirty-two . . . I was working all the time to be a great surgeon . . . but when I voted, I voted Republican."

Howard Baker smiled his best Andy-Griffith-Matlock-country-lawyer smile, the one he used to veil his wise insight into matters. I could tell he was a little taken aback by my statement of not voting while I was in surgical training. He tilted the conversation toward his own voting record. Most of the time, Howard Baker had hewed to the conservative line, supporting the Vietnam War, championing nuclear power, favoring increased defense spending, and arguing for a balanced budget. But he always followed his conscience, which led him to support Lyndon Johnson's landmark Great Society programs on civil rights and open housing. Similarly, much to the chagrin of folks from the coal-bearing hills of East Tennessee, including his own family members who made their living by mining, he helped write the tough 1970s environmental legislation on clean air, clean water, and strip-mining. A man of legendary integrity, he was, according to Tennessee senator Jim Sasser, "too well adjusted" to become president, and I found his pragmatic approach to politics very congenial.

I took a stab at explaining my attraction to public policy and politics, talking about my years at the Woodrow Wilson School, my family's strong commitment to serving others, how I had always lived with a thought in the back of my mind that I wanted to spend some part of my life doing some kind of public service. Baker was affable enough. "You know," he said, "I think public service is the most important second undertaking that a public-spirited citizen can engage in, and I wish more bright men and women would do it. But the political process and what you have to go through and the effect it can have on your life—one word sums it up: demeaning. You must be secure in your own skin and know who you are. And if you do something like this, be prepared to quit. At any point. The true citizen legislator should look on public office as if it's an out-of-town visit, not a move. And not only that, you've got to be prepared to lose."

"Well," I said as the waitress refilled my glass of iced tea, "in my case, it's pretty clear what I would do if I lost. I'd go back to transplanting lungs and hearts." Then I moved on to what truly bothered me about what Senator Baker had said—the demeaning part. I was worried about Karyn and the boys. I had already put them through more than they deserved with my time away from home during my surgical training and now my time at Vanderbilt. "What about your family?" I asked. "How does a campaign affect one's family, one's wife and children?"

"Campaigning can be infectious," he said. "You and Karyn might find yourself together day and night, on this effort. The major danger comes later, after the election. You can get captured by the city, by Washington, and by the system. Even though you go home every weekend—and most members do—in effect, you are going home as a tourist. You don't really live there. And that can be terribly hard on a family.

"But if you decide to run for office," he told me, "you've got to make a clean break. You can't be a candidate and do your surgery at the same time. A clean break will reflect a real commitment on your part, and will let people know you're serious. And you will be able to figure out how much you really like being a candidate. Two years before the primary, certainly not later than Christmas, two years in advance, you've got to make that commitment. Take a year and travel the state. You have no political background, so you're going to have to cover every town, every spot, by car, by airplane—you love to fly, use a plane. But talk to people, get ideas. You don't have to have an agenda. Listen to them, let them tell you what they want in a senator. Everyone will just assume you agree with them. They'll argue with you, and maybe even dislike you if you disagree with them, but if you look them in the eye, and listen to them, they'll give you a chance. Doing this, you'll figure out for yourself how much you really like the people of Tennessee, and how much they like you. And you will discover whether a life of politics is for you."

Senator Baker cleared his throat and spoke sonorously, "Now, about this party thing. You need to talk to people, listen to them, but you have to make up your own mind. You've been rather apolitical up till now—that's the nature of being a doctor. But there is a grand opportunity in the Republican Party right now. I assume that's your inclination, or you wouldn't be talking with me. But talk with Lamar Alexander. Go by and see Winfield Dunn, and others. And I'd ask Lewis Lavine, Lamar's former chief of staff when he was governor, to help you understand the politics of Tennessee. Talk to Congressman Quillen in East Tennessee. Whatever you do, you're going to need East Tennesseans' votes."

(East Tennessee has historically been the state's Republican stronghold. As a Republican, you can't traditionally win Tennessee without winning by a large margin in East Tennessee.)

"I strongly urge you to consider serving in the Senate," he said. "Go to Washington rather than stay in the state. Washington is where the action is. You can influence the whole country. You can deal with world issues. And for all I said about getting enamored by the city, it's a great place to live. Beautiful, good schools, inspiring culture, a great place to raise a family."

We continued talking about the nuts and bolts of politics— finding a staff, opinion polling, and the like. All too soon, it was time for John and me to head back to the Knoxville airport.

Just before we left, Senator Baker touched my arm. "Let me ask you, son," he said in a fatherly tone. "What do your dad and Tommy think about all this?"

No doubt the senator noticed my countenance drop. "I haven't talked to Tommy about this," I said. "Nor to Dad, either, really. I've dropped a few hints, that's all."

"At the end of the day," he said with the bottom-line advice, "don't overanalyze all this. Your gut will tell you if it's the right thing to do."

And his final words: "You know," he said, shaking his head as he looked from man to man in turn. "I think this is doable."

The seed had been planted.

I wasn't overly worried about a political race. It couldn't be more grueling than seven years of surgical residency. I was a risk taker by nature; I relished a tough challenge, gravitating toward goals that seemed out of reach. A much greater concern was Karyn and my sons. I didn't know how Karyn would react when she fully realized the seriousness of my thoughts about entering the political arena, but my guess was that after all the family sacrifices that accompany a life with a heart surgeon, her response would not be positive. Karyn cherished our family and our privacy. Harrison, Jonathan, and Bryan were the most precious things in her life, and she would never jeopardize their happiness or their opportunity to grow up with normal childhood experiences. She knew politics would throw up challenges that we would simply not have to face if I stayed a surgeon. Both family and privacy would in some way be sacrificed on the altar of politics if I were to run. You don't run and serve as an individual; you run and serve as a family.

And then there was Dad. I recalled how he had reacted to Tommy's bold decision to focus on the business side of health care, in Dad's mind "deserting the noble practice of medicine" for business. And that was entrepreneurship, something Dad instinctively admired. Dad had never been one to look up to the values of typical politicians. He'd have trouble understanding why anyone would abandon medicine for politics—least of all his son.

But my real worry was that I could well be handing them— Karyn and the boys, my brothers and sisters, and especially Mother and Dad—public humiliation and defeat. If I ran for the governor's seat or for the Senate and I lost, they all would have to suffer through the loss with me. And why put them through that? And if I won, their lives would be subjected to more public media attention; the media tends to disparage successful people.

All these concerns gave me pause. But the thought of the good I might be able to do in public life kept me interested. As a heart surgeon I had the good name, the income, and the ability to heal individuals—but I didn't have the reach of public policy to improve the lives of others. And I had a passion to do so.

Over 1991 and 1992, while growing the transplant center and operating daily at Vanderbilt and the Veterans' Hospitals, I slowly and deliberately engaged myself in political life. I talked to people and wrote letters—to Howard Baker and Winfield Dunn, to Al Gore and Lamar Alexander, to former U.S. ambassador Joe Rogers and Nashville-based Republican fundraiser Ted Welch, to former Senator Bill Brock and Republican National Committee Chairman Richard Bond. I attended a Bush-Quayle fundraiser in Nashville and had my brother-in-law, Lee Barfield, write to his friend Al Hubbard, Dan Quayle's chief of staff, for advice. I talked with political professionals, election strategists, and campaign managers like Bill Roesing, Jim Cannon, and Emily Reynolds. At Princeton board meetings, I bent the ear of Missouri senator Jack Danforth, an Episcopal minister, hoping to get a better feel for his world. (If an Episcopal minister could jump into politics, I thought, surely a heart surgeon could.)

I let some of these people know I was generally interested in public service and asked them to keep me in mind if they heard of a good appointive position, which would avoid all the potential negatives of a campaign. To others, I talked candidly about positioning myself for a possible electoral bid in 1994. Doggedly, systematically, carefully, I approached those identified as the authorities in the field. I literally went down my long list, checking each name off as I talked to them. Gradually I learned the right questions to ask, and then I listened with the same intensity with which I listened to a patient who had come to see me with chest pain and three-vessel coronary artery disease.

I had worked closely with the staff of fellow Tennessean Al Gore on some of the public issues dealing with transplantation in the 1980s, so I was interested in his take on my political considerations. Gore was still Tennessee's senator at that point, although he was trying to secure his party's nomination for the presidency. I had never met Gore, yet had deep-seated respect for his family tradition in service to Tennessee. Also it was he who helped author the landmark legislation that established the United Network for Organ Sharing, the successful public-private partnership that oversees the equitable distribution of organs across the country.

Gore graciously spent an hour with me in his Washington Senate office, one whole wall lined from floor to ceiling with books, answering my questions about entering a life of public service. Years later, when I had young people request to see me in my Senate office, I frequently thought back to that meeting, remembering all the time Gore spent with me, just a constituent who had a vague interest in serving others.

Gore pointed out that there was a real opportunity in those days for thoughtful, intelligent, substantive people within the Democratic Party. It was advantageous, he felt, to be a Democrat in Tennessee, as demonstrated by the long, rich history of Democrats who had dominated Tennessee politics for generations.

On the other hand, Lewis Lavine, Lamar's former chief of staff, who had grown up a Democrat but had become a Republican, told me he just felt more comfortable around Republicans. Although he thought that in Tennessee a mediocre Democratic candidate could still beat an excellent Republican, he emphasized that ultimately you had to feel comfortable with your party, especially among those who would advise and support you. That gut feeling, Lavine said, was what really was most important.

And just to confuse matters, there were the folks who suggested that political ideology and party affiliation were not nearly as closely related in Tennessee as they were at the national level. The conservative "blue dog" Democrats in the South, they'd argue, were no different in ideology from run-of-the-mill Republicans.

Of all the new people I met during that period, Jim Cannon was to have perhaps the greatest influence on my ultimate decision. A tall, lean, distinguished-looking man, with a full head of sweeping hair and patrician manners, Cannon had a deep, philosophical reverence for public service and a pragmatic understanding of politics. A former editor of *Newsweek*, he'd served as Nelson Rockefeller's chief of staff for fifteen years when Rockefeller was governor of New York; he held the same position with Howard Baker when he was majority leader in the U.S. Senate. Afterward, Jim worked with President Gerald Ford, and was actually writing a book about Ford and his family that day in June when Howard Baker called him to suggest a meeting with me.

Sitting in Howard Baker's law office on Constitution Avenue and listening to him and Jim Cannon discuss and expound upon the significance of politics, campaigns, and the workings of the American government, I got a good sense of just how noble public service could be when someone took the job seriously and did it right.

In the months to come, Cannon and I spoke frequently by telephone, and whenever I was in Washington, I'd go by his wonderful Georgetown home or get together with him for lunch or coffee. When we both were on vacation in Nantucket in August, we met for breakfast at the local favorite, Downy Flake, just as all the neighborhood fishermen were returning from their daybreak ventures. He took me under his wing and educated me with his experiences.

During one of our summer telephone conversations, we discussed party affiliation. Jim came up with the kind of pithy observation I learned to associate with him—and to value. Keep it simple, as Shumway had always said as we were sewing in a new heart. "The difference between Republicans and Democrats," he said, "is that the Democrats think that government can solve problems, and the Republicans think that individuals can solve problems. That's it, that's the real difference."

That idea was not new to me, of course. Perhaps I was just ready to hear it at that point.

In a sense, I realized, I had been a Republican all my life. My personal milieu—my family, my friends, my acquaintances—was generally Republican. More important, I believed in individual responsibility and accountability and a limited role for government; I was pro-business and valued hard work, freedom to choose, competition, and entrepreneurship as the wellsprings of happiness and prosperity. I valued the dignity of the individual.

Simply put, I was a Republican. And, yes—it mattered.

By midsummer, I began participating in Republican Party activities: attending Statesmen and Lincoln Day dinners, sitting on committees, raising funds for the party, and contributing to Republican campaigns. I was still extremely self-conscious about these activities, however, and I remember being somewhat embarrassed by the fact that I was such a Johnny-come-lately to the grassroots efforts that were building a stronger GOP foundation across Tennessee. No one made me feel unwelcome, but I did not fool myself. Many in the Republican Party establishment were happy to see me merely because I came from a prominent family and might be a conduit for filling campaign coffers. Few, I'm sure, considered me a possible (much less plausible) candidate for public office.

I was still trying to decide whether to campaign for an elected position or seek a political appointment within the government. From pundits, players, and party members far and wide, I received some encouragement and many suggestions. Some told me to make health care my issue, and to ride it to national prominence, while others warned me to be wary of health care as an issue, because consensus on the subject didn't exist and probably wouldn't exist for years. Republicans have never led on health care issues, many would advise. Others urged me to spend time on local issues, while others warned me not to get bogged down in local matters but rather to keep my eye on statewide and national concerns.

After the Democrats nominated Al Gore to share the ticket with Arkansas governor Bill Clinton in the 1992 presidential race, there was a lot of speculation about the 1994 election in Tennessee. Who had a chance to win Gore's old seat in 1994? Who might vie for the governor's office, since the incumbent Democrat Ned McWherter, would be term-limited out of the running? And would anyone dare to take on Democrat senator Jim Sasser, the powerful Senate Budget chairman and three-term incumbent already touted as a front runner to become Senate majority leader?

To say I was fascinated by all this would be an understatement. I remember especially the personalities. There was the ebullient Haley Barbour, with his good humor and his wild, colorful, Yazoo, Mississippi, language, charismatically leading the Republican Party. And the two low-key, down-home Tennessee boys, Howard Baker and Ned McWherter—both by then regarded as the statesmen of their respective parties—on opposite sides of the aisle politically, yet so much alike in their common sense ways. There were the serious and sophisticated politicos like Al Gore, although Gore's style, especially his use of language filled with polished, prep-school periods, would be labeled "stiff" by a news media addicted to punched-up, often ungrammatical sound bites. There was the hard-nosed professionalism of Bill Roesing, and the intense political and fundraising savvy of Washington-based but Nashville-raised Emily Reynolds.

To a lot of folks nowadays, the world of politics seems alien to their day-to-day reality. So I was surprised to hear so many of those already in the business tell me that you did not so much need a highly articulated and particular reason, a pet issue, or an explicit agenda to enter politics as you needed a deep passion to serve and an unshakable faith in representative government. Looking back, those two distinct points of view had special relevance in my case.

I had, of course, my own opinions on certain issues, like anybody else, and those opinions were often tied to my quotidian experiences. My years in medicine have given me a unique prism through which to view the realities of everyday living for all Americans, rich and poor. One could hardly work in a hospital and fail to see each day the effects drunk driving, or illegal drugs, or violent crime had on the fabric of American life. Behavior drives the health of an individual and behavior drives the health of society. Patients opened up and told you their life stories and the challenges they faced. They would vividly and emotionally describe the out-of-control welfare system that paid people not to work, stripping them of their individual dignity. Often, too, my particular brand of medical practice helped me to see better than many others the explicit link between broad public policies and specific, individual lives.

For instance, a man had come to me the year before who was in need of a heart transplant, but he did not have the insurance to pay for it. A transplant in those early days of the new procedure cost about a hundred thousand dollars. He and his family might possibly come up with that amount if they pooled all their resources, but that's all they had. If he spent the money, or could come up with about half of it for the hospital portion, the hospital would allow us to give him a new heart, and he would live, but his family would be impoverished. I can recall clearly sitting with him and painfully discussing the costs of the operation, what the hospital could cover, what he would have to contribute, and the long term impact spending that kind of money would have on his wife and two children. Such conversations are powerful and heart-wrenching. They hurt.

The man was forty-three years old, just about my age at the time. He had a family about the size of mine, and his kids were roughly the same ages as Harrison and Jonathan. And, after a lot of thought, he said, " I won't do it." That day he made a conscious decision not to go after the transplant. He chose to die rather than leave his family penniless.

It's not right, I thought. And this scenario was playing out every day in some shape or fashion in every community all over the country. Not just for transplants, but even for basic forms of care like prenatal counseling or treatment for hypertension. I remember thinking specifically that if we only had some system of health insurance coverage for every American, he would have lived a full and productive life watching his kids grow up and get married and have their own families. We are the richest and most generous country in the world, we have the know-how to save lives, yet we still can't offer every man, woman, and child the security of a basic level of care. You can't change that by operating on one person at a time. Can you through policy?

Thus, I had a direct personal interest in the national debate that had been mounting in recent years over health care. In the off-year Senate election two years before, a little-known professor in Pennsylvania, Harris Wofford, had soundly defeated the high-profile U.S. attorney general, Richard Thornburgh, for the seat vacated by Senator John Heinz, who had died in a plane crash, solely by championing health-care reform. A little-known political strategist named James Carville (whom sixteen years later I would join in a Coca-Cola commercial during the Super Bowl promoting bipartisanship) had sensed the unease among the American people on the issue and made it the central defining issue of the Wofford campaign. By the summer of 1992, health-care reform was rising to the top of the national agenda as well.

Anne Somers at Princeton had always told me if there was ever a field that you felt passionately about, that you wanted to really learn about, write a book about it. Writing will force a discipline, she told me, that makes you a lot smarter on the topic, and your passion will then have a way to spill over to others. It's the best way, she said, to translate your passions into action. So I decided to write a book about health-care reform, one that would describe the problems of the health-care system from the inside out in a clear, easily understandable fashion, and that would outline the various approaches to reform being bandied about and weigh their strengths and weaknesses. A number of those already involved in the health-care debate told me that such a book would be helpful, since it might give some realistic shape to the amorphous reform effort being talked about in Washington.

I put Topper Doehring, an inquisitive and industrious Vanderbilt medical student working for me that summer, on the project and partnered with my friend Charlie Phillips, who'd assisted me with *Transplant*, to help Topper and me with the research, interviewing, fact-checking, and outlining of the issues. Together we dove into the public policy of health care. In fact, exploring health-care reform took up most of my time that summer outside my day job as a heart surgeon. What talking I did to politicians and political advisors about my own political plans was often done in conjunction with these research trips, jammed into lunches or dinners or afternoon appointments between interviews for the book.

We interviewed doctors, patients, hospital administrators, government officials, and policy mavens, and we gathered fact sheets, bulletins, insurance brochures, medical plans, agency documents, newspaper articles, magazine pieces, proposed legislation, research studies, opinion polls, policy pamphlets, histories of medicine, think-tank tracts—anybody we could get to and

anything we could put our hands on. I was falling back on the
foundation I had laid with my independent study of health policy
during my senior year at Princeton.

We got to know the health-care lobby rather well. We visited
the headquarters of an organization formed by primary physicians who favored a single-payer universal health-care system
like the one in Canada. Tucked away in a run-down building up-
town with locks on the shared bathrooms in the hallway, the
outfit's small offices were empty except for a secretary and their
spokesman, a young policy wonk with disheveled hair, a rumpled
sports jacket, a photocopied agenda, and a David-versus-Goliath
sense of determination.

We made the rounds of the K Street crowd interviewing the
major private insurance and health-care industry lobbyists. They
wore designer dresses and custom-made suits and confidently
welcomed us to their plush offices, where they plied us with
coffee and four-color brochures that outlined their easy-to-read
positions with clever graphics and studies. We even visited the
major doctors' organization, the American Medical Association,
although we had to travel to Chicago to do it and make our way
past the guards and the security checks to reach the upper floors,
where we were passed from one legislative specialist to another,
in a series of carefully scheduled meetings.

We also managed to observe those directly involved in policy
making, which interested me beyond our investigation of health-
care reform. In fact, these visits provided me with my first real
glimpses of Congress at work, as it were, day to day. There were
myriad position papers, draft legislation, and proposed bills on
health-care reform floating about Capitol Hill that summer, but
the best, I thought, had come out of the office of Tennessee's
own Representative Jim Cooper, a conservative, pro-business
Democratic congressman. I knew Jim casually at the time (since
then we have become colleagues and close friends and are both
teaching today at Vanderbilt) because his chief of staff was an
old high school buddy of mine. Over lunch he kindly hosted us
at an outdoor café in D.C. I enjoyed talking to him and to his staff

about health-care reform, but what fascinated me as much as the policy he had come up with was *how* he had come up with it: how he—a junior congressman—had recognized the health issue long before other legislators were paying much attention, then deployed his staff to intensely cover the issue; how he then had shaped their work and his own thinking about the subject into a specific piece of proposed legislation; and, finally, having produced the draft bill, how he went about gathering support for his proposal both on the Hill and around the country. This may all sound pretty boring to some, but I thought, *Here is exactly what I do every day, yet in an entirely different world. This fellow really knows how to take a problem, study it, and then fix it.*

In a similar way, I found myself being drawn to the work of Tom Scully, another young man about my age in President George H. W. Bush's budget office, who had been charged with handling current health-care costs. Not surprisingly, he had a good handle on the current system, its inconsistencies and its wastefulness. I interviewed Tom at length about such matters. In doing so, I became interested in the mechanisms of the Office of Management and Budget, in how the process worked, how Tom and others balanced the views of the Bush administration with the demands of the various groups, the parties, and the public, in short, in the way civil servants, appointed to office, wielded administrative power. It was Tom who, twelve years later, then in President George W. Bush's administration, worked with me and congressional leaders to pass the legislation that made prescription drugs more affordable for seniors, the Medicare Modernization Act of 2003.

What we learned that summer could indeed have filled a book. As it turned out, the book we planned never got written, because events themselves overtook us. The health-care system touched almost every aspect of American life and, for that reason alone, reform efforts were destined to get caught up in a swamp of conflicting interests. The more we looked into the issue, the more it seemed to me that many of the reformers wanted to behave like overly aggressive "surgeons," all too ready to operate before the specialists could even agree on the exact nature of the disease. Let's make the diagnosis, get that right . . . and only then do the operation. More than that, I thought, maybe I should personally get a little more involved as an active participant, not just a passive observer.

The book was not to be, but during the 1992 presidential campaign, I used the information we had gathered over the summer to draft a series of articles for *The Tennessean*, Nashville's most widely read newspaper. In the articles, I described the current state of American medicine, reviewed the history of health-care reform, and spelled out the different positions of the two candidates and how those positions related to more detailed proposals already before the public. I was still a full-time, very busy academic and clinical surgeon, but I was now equipped with information and understanding of a national problem that was growing worse and that, in fact, was inconsistent with the greatness of America. And I had seen it all from the inside, where few other politicians had.

When Bill Clinton won the presidential election that fall, he announced plans to launch a major health-care initiative immediately. James Carville, now an adviser to the president, had noticed the power of the issue in the Pennsylvania Senate race. The day after the election, on November 9, I received a telephone call from Tennessee's governor, Ned McWherter, a Democrat. He had read my articles, and he remembered a conversation we'd had about my general interest in public affairs. He was putting together a bipartisan task force to study the sustainability of the Medicaid program serving the poor in Tennessee. The major goal of the task force would be to answer the question of whether major state reform was necessary. He wanted to know if I would be interested in chairing this committee.

Governor McWherter's offer meant that the world of politics and the world of medicine—the two worlds in which I was most interested—had suddenly come together for me in a way I could not have anticipated almost two decades before, when I was shuttling back and forth at Princeton between the chemistry building and the Woodrow Wilson School. I accepted the governor's invitation.

My experience chairing the Medicaid commission accelerated my interest in public service and my belief in its potential. I saw how policy could promote health, hope, and healing. The problems were staggering: the number of patients without government coverage or private insurance who slipped through the cracks and suffered from it, the rising chunk of a family's resources that had to be devoted to health care that meant less money for food, education, and housing, and the stark differences in health outcomes by race and socioeconomic status, all this complicated by where in the state one lived.

The governor's commission was set up to address these issues and more, and in particular to answer the question: Can the Tennessee Medicaid program address the health-care needs of Tennessee in a way that is both adequate and sustainable? Our job was not to make a specific recommendation for the future, but rather to predict, based on the best information we could find, what would happen if the then-current structure of Medicaid were to continue without being reformed.

We spent a year studying the problem, held hearings once a month, and interviewed policy experts from across the country. I'd do my surgery four and a half days a week, then spend a half day chairing hearings down at Legislative Plaza. I'd literally strip off my scrubs and jump into a suit, run to the Capitol, and pick up the chairman's gavel. Our conclusion: Medicaid, as then configured in the state, could not financially be sustained. Its rapid growth would so radically consume the state budget that basic responsibilities like police protection and education would have to be cut in half. Though it was not a part of our commission's mandate to make specific recommendations, it was clear from our conclusion that our state government had overpromised on what it could deliver and that substantial reform would be required to improve availability of basic health care and lower growth in health spending to within reason and affordability.

What happened over the next six months was what really

blew me away. Although our committee was dissolved and not involved in the planning, the governor and his staff designed a bold, revolutionary program built on the model of "managed competition," the same concept in health-care policy that was also being touted by the policy team of First Lady Hillary Clinton at the national level. For Tennessee, the governor's goal was to markedly increase the number of people insured in the state by placing those traditionally covered by Medicaid (mostly people with very low incomes), others who were "uninsurable" because of pre-existing illnesses, and still others who were uninsured be- cause they couldn't find an affordable policy into managed-care plans across the state.

As a result, practically everyone in the state would have health insurance, making Tennessee the first state in the country with universal coverage. The care for each person would be managed by about ten managed-care companies across the state and thus, the state officials reasoned, covered more efficiently and less ex- pensively. The doctors and hospitals would get paid a little less for every patient, but they would no longer have to take care of the uninsured for free, so at least initially they were happy. The plan was called TennCare. Tennessee would implement exactly the same kind of program Hillary Clinton was designing at the same time in Washington, D.C. Tennessee would lead the way for the president's health-care vision.

These optimistic forecasts proved illusory. The Clinton pro- gram failed before it got off the ground, and unfortunately, over a ten-year period, TennCare, the state version of the federal model by the Clintons, ultimately failed as well—not in greatly expand- ing the availability of care, which it did, from about eight hundred thousand to 1.2 million Tennesseans—but in managing efficient delivery. When the program began, there were essentially no existing managed-care companies in the state. In the years that followed, the newly created managed-care plans went bankrupt, in large part because of mismanagement and lack of experience. Care was not "managed"; instead, doctor reimbursement was drastically cut. Meanwhile, TennCare's costs exploded. Lawsuits to expand coverage (and thus costs) were successful, so even when prudent management was attempted, it was preempted. In 2007, the program was abandoned. The lessons learned from this bold yet unsuccessful attempt to improve care at the state level are applicable today as we discuss how to expand coverage to the uninsured at the national level: You can't responsibly expand coverage without addressing the growth in costs.

All this is the policy. But it was the process that had the greatest impact on me. I observed one individual (the governor) take on a major problem (health care) in the state. Because of his vision and the power of his office, he was able to single-handedly pick up $2.8 billion—one-fourth of the Tennessee state budget—and radically reshape the way it was spent to realize his vision. That is the power of policy and politics. I realized that despite the poor public perception of politicians, individual political figures had vast potential to do big things, significant things, to directly and forcefully improve the lives of millions. I saw how a single politician with the right motives could help heal some of the major problems of our society. I saw, for the first time, the potential of politicians as healers.

THE MEDICAID COMMISSION EXPERIENCE LEFT ME MORE READY than ever to take the plunge into full-time public service. But there were still some interesting medical experiences for me to encounter along the way.

In December 1993, Uwe Reinhardt, my college professor from twenty years earlier and now one of America's leading economic advisors, had come down to Nashville to attend a small Princeton alumni gathering at our home and to speak to a group of health company executives about American health care.

Uwe seemed embarrassed that I was waiting at the airport to give him a ride. "You surgeons are supposed to be a busy bunch," Uwe quipped. "Besides, I would have been happy to take a taxi." No doubt, Uwe probably viewed me showing up in my old jeep as, well, real down-home. But, otherwise, I would not have been able to give him the grand tour of my hometown Nashville and spend the morning catching up with him.

After the briefing, where Uwe did his usual iconoclastic and witty job of puncturing our assumptions about the financing of health care in America (with the same style that had made his accounting class fun), I dropped him off at the Loews Vanderbilt Plaza on West End and went back to the hospital on the other side of the Vanderbilt campus to check on my patients before the alumni dinner with about sixteen people that evening.

The dinner was perfect. Karyn was a wonderful and charming host as always, making everyone feel comfortable. Uwe hit it off with my family as I knew he would, but with the Princeton crowd there, and sitting at opposite ends of our dining-room table, I did not have much chance to talk to him, especially about the decision I had so recently made that was going to radically change my future.

Then the black paging beeper on my belt began to vibrate. Karyn looked knowingly at me. She knew exactly what that meant. I excused myself and went to the kitchen to call the hospital operator.

"Dr. Frist, we've got a heart for you," said the caller from the regional organ-procurement agency. "It looks like a perfect match for Meadows," she said as I traced down my list. Robert Meadows was the sickest person listed on my index card of potential transplant patients, and had waited the longest. Blood type matched.

By the time I'd come back through the dining-room door, Karyn had already explained that in all likelihood the call meant that I would have to leave immediately and that she would not see me for twenty-four hours. Transplants are unpredictable, she told our guests, and they might occur once a week, or three nights in a row. And they always occur at night. I walked over to Uwe and whispered, "I'm so sorry. I have to leave when you are the featured guest in my home. I've gotta go take out a heart that just became available in Chattanooga."

"I understand," Uwe said, nodding. "You go on and I will carry the Princeton flag."

I kissed Karyn good-bye and out the back door I went, rushing to the hospital to quickly see Robert and give him the good news before going to the airport. My brother Tommy and Trisha agreed to give Uwe a ride back to his hotel. But once at the hospital, I decided I really wanted to talk to Uwe before he left town the following morning. There was no guarantee I would even be out of surgery by then, so I called Tommy on his car phone.

"Tommy," I said, "why don't you bring the professor on out to the airport? I'll take him along on the transplant run."

I could tell by the hollow tunnel sound of Tommy's voice that he had the car phone on the speaker, and I knew Uwe could hear me.

"No, no," came Uwe's disembodied voice. "Billy, I can't stand to see blood. I'm sure I'll faint or throw up."

"C'mon," I said. "I'll teach you some real health-care economics tonight. You'll get a real-life perspective that no other ivory-towered academic in the world has."

Uwe finally acquiesced. "Great!" I declared. "See you at the airport in a few minutes."

These transplant runs are precise and finely tuned, but appear a lot more casual than one might think. We didn't look like a highly trained transplant team that night as we walked out on the tarmac to board the plane. I was wearing khakis and a parka, the nurses were in casual dress, and so was the procurement specialist. I saw Uwe eyeing the Igloo ice chest I carried.

"That's not my dessert I left on the table, Uwe. That's where the heart goes," I told him.

He smiled, as though he didn't believe me. I shrugged and motioned the group toward the King Air. We climbed aboard the six-passenger prop plane, and I grabbed the right rear seat, which I superstitiously claimed on every donor run. "Better buckle up tight," the pilot said. "The skies aren't too friendly tonight. Looks like we might hit some turbulence."

Turbulence doesn't bother me. But thunderstorms mean delay on the return home and that is something we could not afford. Once the heart is cut out and in the cooler, every second counts.

The pilot's warning soon proved correct. Nasty storm clouds covered most of the sector east of Nashville and before long we had to skirt to the south of a full-fledged thunderstorm. The small plane frequently shuddered as we bounced along through the rough weather. Uwe looked as though he were riding a roller coaster, holding on white-knuckled tight.

It was difficult to talk over the din, so I punched on a reading light above me, and pulled out of my briefcase reading materials to fill the time. Wondering how I could possibly read with the constant lurching up and down, Uwe asked, "Are you looking up where the heart is?" he quipped, as though trying to deflect some of his nervousness with humor. "No need, I can tell you that much. It's right here," he said, pointing to his own chest.

I looked up at him and said as casually as I could over the noise of the props, "No, it's a survey. Sort of a rundown of the top current political issues important to Tennesseans. I need to know what they are thinking. You see," I said slowly, watching Uwe's face for a reaction, "tonight is my last transplant. I'm going to run for the U.S. Senate."

Uwe responded with a quick smile, but when he saw I was dead serious, he asked with a disbelieving expression, "What'd you say? Leave surgery for politics? You've got to be kidding."

OF COURSE, I WASN'T KIDDING. THE SURVEY I WAS READING HAD been conducted by professional pollster Whit Ayres. I had hired him, along with a seasoned and aggressive campaign manager, Tom Perdue, both out of Atlanta, to help design and execute my first campaign for public office. Whit, who specialized in southern races, had comprehensively surveyed the attitudes and views of Tennesseans. Jim Sasser, the current senator from Tennessee, a three-term incumbent Democrat in line for Senate majority leader, was well known, enjoyed broad support from Tennessee voters, and was—according to conventional political wisdom and all the pundits—certain to be re-elected. I was an unknown Republican in a traditionally Democratic state who had never run for office. But Ayres had concluded that when our positions, records, and political beliefs were described without benefit of "name recognition," the polls indicated that I, or someone like me, had a real chance of winning the election. The pilot in me said trust what the instruments tell you. The scientist in me said trust the data.

Some of this I explained to Uwe as we tossed and turned in the December skies over East Tennessee. Uwe knew and respected Jim Sasser, the sitting senator I would challenge. Moreover, Uwe, like most people, assumed that Sasser was unbeatable, that I—a political unknown, a campaign naïf—was a little crazy to take him on. Uwe told me so. As did almost everyone in the weeks to come.

I told Uwe he was probably right. The political consultants and campaign experts I had talked to in the last few months had warned me that before I could face Sasser in the general election, I would have to distinguish myself somehow from a crowded field of Republican candidates if I hoped to win the party's primary. They cautioned that I couldn't count on much support from the Tennessee Republican Party, since there were others with more experience than I had, and the party leaders (understandably enough) would want to put up a candidate they thought had the best chance against Sasser, probably someone from East Tennessee where the bulk of Republican votes lie. Besides, even if I managed to win the primary, Senator Sasser—in line for the most-powerful leadership jobs in the country—would put up a terrific fight.

"Maybe I *am* crazy," I told Uwe, "but it's taken me nearly twenty years to get where I am in medicine, and I'm willing to give myself another twenty to do what I want to do in politics."

These were just the kinds of things I had hoped to talk to Uwe about. Of all those I knew well, Uwe was the one who most clearly loved public policy for its own sake. But he was a friend as well, and I could tell that he was worried—and not just about whether I had bitten off more than I could chew. (In fact, he would have understood that was part of the fun.) He was also worried that political life might not live up to my expectations. As he later said, he was sure I was capable, but he wondered whether I would be fulfilled in the cat-and-dog fights of the political arena.

"It's really your fault," I said to Uwe. "At Princeton, you were always harping on one's marginal work product, the need to improve it. At this point in life, I think mine would actually be better in the political world; I can affect a lot more people. As you say, I've reached the top of my profession, and in the course of my career, I've probably changed a few thousand lives, and these people have gone on to live good, productive lives. And their families are happy. But more people than that were shot and killed in America last month by gang members in our major cities."

Perhaps I was naïve, but I was still a true believer. I sincerely thought that a good legislator, a good governor, a good president, or a good senator could make a difference in the lives of millions of Americans. I thought good people should run for office, smart people, honest people, people with common sense and with vision, the kind of citizen legislators our founding fathers had always imagined would serve in the Congress. And now I wanted to be among that number.

"OKAY, ONLY FOUR THOUSAND MORE ENVELOPES TO STUFF," TRACY Frazier said to the group of us sitting around her kitchen table, inserting copies of my first political letter into envelopes. Tracy had been the administrator who helped me set up the transplant center. Now we were on a new mission. No mailing machines for us, no headquarters office, in fact. We were starting the campaign from scratch, working at Tracy's home because we didn't even own a campaign desk yet.

The odds against me winning a seat in the U.S. Senate were staggering. I had no prior experience in government; I was virtually unknown outside Nashville, even though I had spoken to countless groups across the state about organ donation. Moreover, it was one thing to talk about the need for organ donors, but I was not in the habit of talking about myself or what I thought about the controversial current issues of the day. My mind was more engaged with using Positron Emission Tomography with the glucose analog Fluorodeoxyglucose to detect cardiac rejection than with the policy intricacies of welfare reform. Nor was I a favorite of the Republican Party, since I was not a traditional party product. Large financial backers for my campaign were nonexistent when I started out; they preferred to invest where they could win.

As friends and family members gathered around my parents' kitchen table on Bowling with increasing frequency on Saturday mornings to have breakfast and to discuss the possibility of my candidacy, it slowly dawned on my parents that I was serious about entering public service. Thinking perhaps that Senator Howard Baker had unduly influenced my decision, Dad called the senator and said, "Howard, please don't try to talk my son into running for the United States Senate. He's spent nearly twenty years becoming a great heart transplant surgeon, and is doing a great service here."

Senator Baker respected Dad immensely, but he didn't back off a bit. "Dr. Frist, I'm not about to tell your son not to run," he said. "I won't encourage him too much, but I'm not going to discourage him, either." I think that was enough to signal to Dad that my candidacy was not a mere pipedream.

In any case, few political observers gave me a chance—not the head of the party, not the forefathers of the party in Tennessee, no one. Instead, nearly everyone said, "Don't be foolish. You have a good job; you're making a difference in people's lives, doing something worthwhile, people respect you. Let well enough alone." The most highly regarded fundraiser in the state said don't run. No one said, "Do it; go for it. We believe that you can win."

No one, that is, but my family members (though some of them were understandably skeptical at first) and closest friends. Gathered at the Bowling home, my brother Tommy, my sister Mary

and her husband Lee Barfield, and boyhood friends such as Barry
Banker and others talked about the possibilities. Amazingly,
starting at the very bottom, we put together a first-rate political
campaign team—albeit quite unconventional.

For instance, we initially did not use any Washington consultants, pollsters, campaign managers, or media people. We
built our team from local Tennesseans, for the most part, most of
whom had never before worked on a political campaign. I now
know that such an organization is unheard of in the world of
major political campaigns, but at the time, we were just a bunch
of friends out to do the impossible. We didn't know enough to
know what we didn't know. We set out with a simple campaign
slogan: "Frist First!"

Eventually, I realized that just as Howard Baker had advised,
I needed a few experts from outside Tennessee to help run our
campaign. But where does a novice politician find such help?
I talked to a number of potential campaign managers, but was
unimpressed. Then, along with Karyn, Lee, Barry, and Tracy,
we attended a large National Republican Senatorial Committee
(NRSC) conference in Washington, where a number of people
had gathered who planned to run for office, as well as individuals whom the Campaign Committee were hoping to convince to
run. Oliver North's group was there, as was Senator Phil Gramm,
then head of the NRSC, who had his sights on an eventual run for
the presidency. For me, it was an inspiring conference. One of
the speakers was a seasoned campaign manager, Tom Perdue.

If I had been trying to find someone whose personality was
almost totally opposite from mine, Tom Perdue would have been
the perfect choice. Blunt, rough around the edges, tough as nails,
with a perpetually wide-eyed, intense look about him, Tom had
run Paul Coverdell's successful 1992 Senate campaign in Georgia,
upsetting Democrat Wyche Fowler. For all his gruffness, Tom
had a southern good-old-boy appeal, although he often sounded
more like a Marine Corps drill sergeant than a politician. Even
Tom's humor was brutally honest and brusque. But in listening
to him, it was obvious that he knew the nuts and bolts of how to

put together a campaign. And his focus was totally on winning. I loved his focus.

I invited Tom to Nashville to meet with me and our small nucleus of supporters and assess my chances. Our first organizational meeting actually took place in our garage. Tom came in loaded with ideas; he had read and heavily underlined my book *Transplant* and had absorbed its message. Tom brought with him Whit Ayres, the Atlanta-based pollster with whom he had previously worked, and Whit had prepared some preliminary information on the feelings of people across the state on issues such as abortion, the death penalty, and other hot-button issues. Tom and Whit quizzed me about my positions or opinions on those issues, and all my answers were quite conservative, but not satisfactory to Tom.

Tom rubbed his chin and spoke directly. "Well, you're not going to win."

"Why? What do you mean?"

"If you are the least bit wishy-washy on these issues, the conservative base will kill you. Do you want to win, or not?" Tom urged me to spend some time to clarify my positions in my own heart and mind.

Despite Tom's bluntness, I recognized that he possessed an adroit understanding of what issues truly mattered to the public and how I could best express my heart and mind on those issues. Eventually, we brought Tom and Whit on board, and together they mapped out what they saw as a potentially winning campaign strategy. Basically that strategy was to be everywhere in Tennessee, talking to voters. Knowing my work ethic in transplantation and the not-uncommon thirty-six-hour days, they said you must outwork them all. "You need to be willing to stand out in front of Wal-Mart, hand out flyers, and ask people for their votes one by one, day after day," Tom told me.

So that's what I did. In seven years of hierarchical surgical training that began at 5:30 A.M. every morning and continued through most nights, I had learned it pays to follow orders.

Another person I began talking with early on about joining

our team was Emily Reynolds. A Nashville native, Emily had risen
to a prominent fundraising position within GOP circles, playing critical roles in several Senate and presidential campaigns.
She had recently helped engineer the fundraising for Senator Kay
Bailey Hutchison's winning campaign in Texas. Emily was (and
still is) one of the most capable women in American politics.
(Emily served as secretary of the Senate during my tenure as
majority leader.) Wooing Emily back to Nashville, and asking her
to lead the difficult task of raising funds for an unknown candidate, a doctor no less, was asking her to take an enormous risk.
But she did it. For some reason, Emily believed in me and caught
the vision of what we might be able to do. And, luckily for me,
Nashville was her home.

On March 1, 1994, at Kitty Moon's video production studio in
Nashville, with my family at my side, as well as a number of my
former patients, I announced my candidacy for the United States
Senate. (It's a small world—Kitty was the daughter of Dr. Moon,
the pharmacist who answered Mother's calls for Dad's patients
when I was a little boy.) Somewhere, Senator Sasser's campaign
consultants must have been chuckling at the thought of a politically naïve forty-two-year-old doctor with no experience running
against an eighteen-year veteran senator and future leader of the
Senate. The day before my announcement, the local newspaper
ran a derogatory article talking about the audacity of my running
for senator. As a result, I spent most of the following day in Knoxville answering questions. At a press gaggle in the Knoxville airport as I left to return home, the chief question posed was, "You
are a wealthy doctor. How in the world do you know anything
about helping people who live in the real world?"

I looked over to my side and there were four people there,
all of whom had received transplanted hearts by my hands. As
I acknowledged their presence, they stood up, and I reminded
my audience, "Individuals can make a difference in this world.
Through excellence and a commitment to hard work and serving others, individuals can make a profound difference." That
became a theme of our entire campaign, that it is not the political

professionals who have changed society, but rather individuals with a heart to serve, acting with whatever their God-given talents might be, who have truly transformed the world. And every one of us has a role to play.

Most of my campaign was spent crisscrossing the state of Tennessee. I mostly avoided Washington. But I did go to Washington on a single trip for an early campaign event, a fundraiser. I walked into the NRSC Building, where the event was to be held a couple of blocks from the Capitol, and noticed a large group of people gathered in the inner meeting area. I thought, *Wow, all this crowd just to meet me. I must be doing a lot better than I thought.* But I was quickly ushered into a side room off the atrium by a junior staffer who politely told me, "Dr. Frist, your event is in here." The tiny room was empty. A small TV was playing my campaign bio on a continuous loop over in the corner. The boisterous, packed house fundraiser in the adjacent room was for an incumbent senator. No one came into my event (except for Senator John Warner, who kindly stuck his head in as he was leaving his colleague's event to give me a word of encouragement—something I will never forget). That settled it. I said, "Washington . . . never again. We are running a Tennessee campaign."

I returned to Tennessee even more obsessed with proving that the impossible could be achieved. I traveled the state from 6:00 A.M. until midnight, day after day, just listening to people's thoughts, ideas, and opinions. We had ninety-five counties to cover, and I set out to spend time with the people in every one of them. I heard a lot of "You can't do it" in my meetings every day. Many refused to take the time to see me. Again and again, I heard, "You won't win; don't even bother." Interestingly, the more I heard such pessimistic voices, the more convinced I became that I could do it by working harder. Surgical residency had been good practice for all this.

I faced five opponents in the Republican primary, the most popular being a successful self-made businessman from Chattanooga, Bob Corker, who now serves in the Senate. I ran on a conservative platform, which was relatively easy for me, because I truly believed in the need for better fiscal responsibility in government and in keeping taxes low. Welfare reform, term limits, and allowing prayers in school were other causes in which I strongly believed. Most of all, I emphasized my belief in an individual's responsibility and dignity, rather than government providing everything for people, at the taxpayer's expense, of course.

And, naturally, I spoke often about health-care reform. The bloom was already off the 1993 Clinton universal health-care plan, which was plagued by a overly bureaucratic morass—the proposed bill was more than one thousand pages long—and, even more important to the American public, the restriction of patients' choices. I had lived socialized medicine in England, so it was easy for me to discuss the shortcomings of so-called Hillary-Care. None of the other candidates in Tennessee (or elsewhere) could speak from the direct experience of having actually worked for and operated within a socialized health-care system.

My nephew Chet Frist, who volunteered to be my travel aide for the year, traveled the length and breadth of Tennessee with me, meeting and talking with real people. As Howard Baker had predicted in one of our early conversations, I soon came to love the people of my home state. I hoped they loved me, but even if they didn't, it was worth the effort to get into the small towns as well as the larger communities and really share experiences with the people in ways that I never had done before. What a privilege it was to go to every nook and cranny in Tennessee and be able to have substantive, and many times very personal, conversations with others from all walks of life. Everywhere we went, I told people, "My American dream has come true. I set out to be a transplant surgeon, at a time when heart transplant surgery was in its infancy, and lung transplants had never been done. But the real American dream in my family started with my dad. He has been the inspiration behind me and almost everything I do, including medicine, my commitment to Karyn and the boys, and to this new goal of running for the Senate. Without Mother and

Dad's inspiration, I would not have the goal of helping change this country."

The press made a big deal about the fact that I had not voted in recent Tennessee elections (they were correct to do so!), and my opponents attempted to make political capital of the fact that I had not served in the armed services, foisting on the public the illusion that I had been hiding away in the safety of Ivy League academia while other young men my age were dying in Vietnam. My opponents rarely mentioned my years of studying medicine, except to imply that because I was a doctor, I must be an elitist who couldn't relate to everyday people.

In turn, my campaign team worked to turn that image around, to explain that because I was a doctor, I had spent my life trying to help hurting people, that I knew well the issues relating to abortion and health care and the need for investments and markets to lead the way in scientific discoveries that helped everyday people. Beyond that, as a doctor, I was accustomed to listening to people; most politicians are too busy to listen—really listen—to their constituents, but listening was something I practiced daily. I emphasized that we needed a change in Washington, that I was not interested in becoming a career politician, but that I wanted to serve as a citizen legislator. I pledged to go to Washington if elected, serve two terms at the most, and then return home to Tennessee to live under the same laws that I helped pass.

That message resonated. Slowly, but surely, the tide began to turn, as more and more people in Tennessee began to see the potential of a citizen legislator going to Washington and actually representing *them*, rather than himself or herself.

I could barely talk above a whisper when Karyn and I joined our key team members at the Loews Vanderbilt Plaza the night of the primary election. I had talked with so many people, spoken to so many groups, my vocal cords finally said, "No more." I was nervous, but confident as the election results started showing up on the three television screens in the room, each TV tuned in to a different local station. I wore my lucky tie, given to me by an eight-year-old boy, a trademark Save the Children tie with a stars-

and-stripes pattern that I had worn at campaign stops all across
the state.

One of the local television stations interviewed Karyn as the
returns began to mount in our favor. Karyn had done yeoman's
work for months balancing personal and campaign life and taking care of our three young boys, as we traversed Tennessee
throughout the hot summer of 1994. Yet when the interviewer
asked her if she was ready to launch into a major Senate race,
and another stretch of campaigning with me, Karyn was surprisingly upbeat. "Oh, yes," she said. "I actually see him more now
than I ever have before. He never asked me for advice when he
was doing surgery, but he does in this, so it has been fun to work
together."

The interviewer pressed, "What are your plans if he wins tonight?"

Karyn responded, "We'll get up in the morning and go around
the state to meet as many people as we can, to get conservative Democrats and Independents on our side. We're not going
to slow down."

By midevening on August 4, 1994, the election returns showed
that of the six candidates in the Republican primary, I had received 48 percent of the vote—enough for an eighteen-point victory margin. As I mounted the platform to thank a roomful of
supporters, the astounding truth hit me: I was now the Republican nominee for U.S. senator from Tennessee! We were now in
the major leagues of politics. It was like graduating from medical
school and finally becoming a doctor—and realizing that the grueling surgical residency was still to come.

The next morning, just as Karyn had said we would, we
started out on our Victory Bus Tour, crossing Tennessee to meet
the people, listen to their concerns and needs, and ask for their
votes.

Winning the primary election in Tennessee was difficult
enough, but as we geared up to throw ourselves into the fracas
against Senator Sasser, we knew the campaign had to take on renewed energy. Among our slogans in the general election against

Sasser, we used "Eighteen years is long enough" and "Dump Sasser!" (Tom Perdue hired a dump truck to travel the state to get the point across) and one of my favorites, "Listen, Diagnose, and Fix."

I continued to emphasize that in contrast to the incumbent senator I was challenging, who after eighteen years had become entrenched in the Washington political machine, I planned to go to Washington for no more than twelve years before stepping aside for another citizen legislator to take my place. I had no intention of becoming addicted to the constant cycle of trying to get re-elected to maintain my position on Capitol Hill. Quite the contrary, I wanted to go to Washington and operate much as I had as a physician: to listen, to diagnose the problem, and to fix it. I hammered on the point that many Washington politicians became so enamored of holding on to political power, or their careers, that it clouded their judgment and decision making. No longer were they serving the country primarily so much as serving themselves. It was a simple message, but a message that resonated with the people of Tennessee.

Political language guru Frank Luntz as well as Karl Rove, strategist for Texas governor George W. Bush, both popped in for a couple of days to express interest. Phil Gramm gave us the National Republican Senatorial Campaign's financial support. The national party sent us some encouragement and reinforcements in the form of a group of bright young campaign workers, fresh out of college. Their energy added to that of our group of novices and was refreshing. Prolonged campaigning is for the young, the young at heart, or the well seasoned; in any case, it is not a high-paying job. But our team worked tirelessly.

Oddly, the newcomers rarely referred to me as Dr. Frist. Instead, they insisted on calling me "the candidate." When they questioned our local regulars, the people who had been with me from the beginning, about what I believed about this or that issue, they always phrased the question: "What does the candidate think about this?" Or, "When did the candidate do that?" After a while, we all realized that to the people who started out with me, I was a friend; to the political professionals, I was a product to be packaged and sold to the public—I was "The Candidate." It struck me as funny, but most of the people close to me almost resented the impersonal attitudes demonstrated by the young kids who were helping us. Had it not been for their sincere desire to see me elected, the homegrown, loyal team might not have put up with the outsiders.

In their defense, the newcomers were merely doing their jobs; they were looking at the polls, studying the numbers, looking for trends, searching for ways to exploit our positives or our opponent's negatives. They were not being rude or intentionally disrespectful; this was how most elected candidates succeeded. Moreover, time was short. The Tennessee Republican primary took place on August 4, and the general election day was November 7, just a few short months away. We had a lot of work to do in covering the state. Once again, we set out by motor coach, traveling the state in a forty-foot, Greyhound-type bus, stopping at every town we came to.

A steady flux of Republican senators passed through and joined us on the campaign bus. Only recently did my good friend and colleague, Senator Kit Bond, tell me what he said to the folks in Washington when asked to report back to them on the status of my campaign after a visit in 1994. He said: "Well, for a Senate candidate . . . he makes a pretty darn good heart surgeon." I guess my campaign style wasn't exactly polished by Washington standards. But Tennesseans were beginning to respond.

At our last staff meeting on the morning before the election, Tom Perdue thanked the members of our team, saying it was one of the finest groups of which he'd been a part. Tom talked about my desire to serve being a unique aspect of our candidacy. The night before the election, Karyn and I went to a service at Two Rivers Baptist Church, in Nashville. A friend who attends the church suggested the service, as it would be an opportunity to reflect on the past year and pray. Now, Tom alluded to the possibility of divine providence guiding our steps. "It's almost like the Good Lord wants this man to succeed," Tom said, nodding toward me. "We have had so many needs, and we have been up against the wall so many times, and we have wondered how it was going to work, when out of the clear, one of you has emerged. Those of you who have worked on campaigns before know that is not the norm."

On election night, once again we gathered at the Loews Vanderbilt Plaza to await the returns. Karyn and the boys, Mother and Dad, Tommy and Trisha, sister Mary and her husband Lee, sister Dottie, brother Bobby and his wife, Carol, Karyn's mother, Kathryn, and other relatives and a throng of our closest supporters gathered in an upstairs suite, while supporters from across the state waited downstairs in the hotel ballroom. The mood in the suite was one of reserved confidence; we knew we had done all that we could do, and now it was up to the voters.

Shortly after the polls closed, Vice President Al Gore called to congratulate me on winning the Senate seat. He had been following the vote and knew that the numbers told the story. I thanked him for his call and quipped, "That thousand dollars I gave your campaign in 1988 has sure caused me a lot of trouble over the last several months!"

Within minutes of my hanging up with the vice president, Senator Sasser called our suite at the hotel. The room quickly grew quiet as everyone in the suite watched with bated breath as I talked to the eighteen-year Senate veteran. Senator Sasser graciously congratulated me, and I thanked him and wished him the best. He had served Tennessee and our country admirably, and I told him so, thanking him for his service and asking for his help in the future so I could do likewise. "I know this was a hard-fought campaign on both of our parts; give [your wife] Mary my best, as well." As I hung up the telephone, I looked at Tom Perdue and gave him a thumbs-up sign. Then I hugged and kissed Karyn as the people in the crowded room burst into cheers. "What time is it?" Karyn asked, surprised that definitive election results were in so soon after the polls had closed.

"Eleven after eight," someone else said.

I was overwhelmed with restrained emotion as the reality set in: I was the new United States senator from the state of Tennessee. "Golly . . . ," I finally managed to say. Everyone in the suite started hugging one another and gushing congratulations. It was an incredible experience for our entire team. We had started with no political acumen and no political experience, and yet here we were, victorious. Anything in life is possible.

Tom and I went into the inner room of the suite to talk briefly about the acceptance speech that I would be giving in a few minutes. Neither of us was given to emotional expressions; in both of our lines of work, we had learned to control our emotions, but that night, we hugged like two brothers who had won the big game, because in a sense, we had. "You took the lead and you never lost it," Tom told me, as I thanked him. And I could not have done it without his faith in me and leadership of our motley crew of a campaign. I likely would not have won without Tom Perdue.

We remained upstairs in our suite until Senator Sasser went on television to formally concede the election, then we went downstairs to greet the enthusiastic supporters who were absolutely jubilant in the ballroom.

With my family on the platform behind me, as well as longtime friends and supporters, including graciously and enthusiastically supportive Bob Corker and his wife Elizabeth, I stood before the cheering crowd. My brother Tommy stood just over my shoulder; Mary and Lee were on my other side. Karyn and the boys were right next to me, and right down front in a wheelchair sat my mother and my frail but excited eighty-three-year-old father.

"It's a political earthquake in Tennessee in 1994!" I began my thanks and acceptance speech. Then I turned to Karyn. "I love you," I said as I hugged and kissed her and the crowd erupted in cheers. "I cherish your values, and I appreciate your unwavering support over the last year." I looked at our three young boys. "And these guys, Harrison, and Jonathan, and Bryan, you guys are my inspiration." The crowd burst into applause again.

I spoke briefly to the crowd. "From day one, this campaign was a venture of faith, and everything we have done since that

day has been based on the belief that one individual, one person in America today, can truly make a difference. And now tonight, what the political experts predicted could never happen,
has happened! One person can make a difference . . . and I will
carry good, commonsense, old-fashioned Tennessee values to
the United States Senate."

As the room filled with cheers again, I took off the stars-and-
stripes Save the Children tie, the same well-recognized tie I had
worn on so many occasions over the preceding months. "I'm
going to do something special," I said. "This tie . . . is symbolic
of the American dream, of the American spirit. Today, I want to
give this tie to someone who means more to me than anybody in
the world, someone who embodies all that is good about America, who is actually the personification of the American dream. It
is somebody I love, somebody I respect, and somebody who has
served his fellow men and fellow women over the last fifty-five
years in the practice of medicine."

The audience suddenly realized who I was talking about
and burst into spontaneous applause. "I want to give this tie to
someone who, without his teachings, and without his lessons,
I would not be before you today—I want to give this to my father, Dr. Thomas Frist." I walked off the platform, leaned down,
and wrapped the tie around Dad's neck. Weak as he was, Dad
hugged me emotionally, our faces touching, as I steadied him in
my arms.

When the votes were fully tallied, the political pundits were
shocked to discover that we had upset our opponent by two hundred thousand votes, the largest margin of votes of any statewide
election in Tennessee history. The victory, of course, made national news. I was the only challenger to beat a full-term incumbent senator in the 1994 election. What did that feel like? It was
a combination of elation and exhaustion at the same time.

Looking back, it is easy now to see that the timing was right
for my election, as well as those of other conservative candidates.
The 1994 election became a referendum on big government; the
Republican victories were won in part because of the threats

posed by the specter of the Clinton health-care plan. Newt Gingrich did a stellar job of putting together the so-called Contract with America, a clear-cut, understandable plan for what the Republicans would do if elected. Although the contract was a great prop for those based in Washington, inside-the-Beltway talking heads greatly overstated its significance in the hinterland. I know the contract itself played essentially no role in our Tennessee race and, I expect, in most Senate races around the country. Most Americans had no clue what the contract was; indeed, it became famous *after* the election. We won in 1994 because Americans rejected the big-government solutions and the reflexive liberalism that dominated the first two years of President Clinton's term.

In 1994, Republicans rode to a sweeping victory, regaining control of the House of Representatives as well as the Senate. Gears had shifted from earning the opportunity to actually serving. Thrilled that I would be going to Washington to serve the people of Tennessee, I also knew that there was little time to rest on our laurels. We had much work to do, and we needed to set up a Senate office in Washington, something nobody on our campaign staff had ever done before. The response of friends and family members as we watched the news reported on television was, "We won! *We won!* Now what are we supposed to do?"

8

New Kid on the Hill

Between the election and Thanksgiving, I convinced Mark Tipps, the bright, young Nashville attorney who had played an instrumental role in my campaign, to move to Washington and serve as my chief of staff—a staff that, at that point, consisted of Mark and me. Mark and I essentially lived together during those first few weeks. Karyn, Mark, Tom Perdue, and I traveled to our nation's capital in late November. My first day in Washington as the senator-elect, I was to check in at the Russell Senate Office Building for an orientation meeting with Georgia senator Paul Coverdell.

That morning Tom, Mark, and I stepped out of the Hyatt Hotel on New Jersey Avenue and were nearly overwhelmed by the majesty of the U.S. Capitol looming nearby. We began walking up Constitution Avenue toward Capitol Hill. "Okay, where are we going?" I asked.

Tom pulled out our agenda for the day and read the office address for Paul Coverdell. The three of us looked at each other sheepishly. It was obvious that none of us had any idea how to get to the Russell Building. "I'll bet it's one of those big white marble buildings," Mark ventured.

A young woman was passing by, carrying an armful of papers, and looking as though she might be headed to work somewhere on Capitol Hill. "Excuse me," I said. "Could you please tell us how to find the Russell Senate Office Building?"

I could feel my face turning red from embarrassment when the young woman pointed directly behind me. We were standing right in front of Russell, less than a hundred yards away. We were as green as you could get.

From Russell, we set out to search for our first transition office, really not much more than a cubbyhole in the basement of the adjacent Dirksen Building, with a telephone, a desk, and a few folding chairs. While I attended various orientation meetings, Mark immediately began the interviewing process, attempting to pull together a staff before I took office officially on January 5, 1995. We had little to work with. We didn't even have a secretary, so I dictated the letters and sent them back to Nashville via FedEx to be typed and mailed by campaign volunteers.

Throughout December, Mark and I traveled back and forth to Washington for two or three days at a time, interviewing a plethora of applicants for the relatively few staff positions we had available. Since my predecessor had been a Democrat, no existing infrastructure was intact from which we could draw skilled, experienced staff members. Thanks to the "Republican Revolution," there were so many new Republican senators and congressmen in town, there was a scramble to hire experienced staff. Consequently, the number of available people on our side of the aisle who knew the way things needed to be done was relatively slim.

In reviewing resumes, Mark noticed that "everybody in Washington was somebody really important," or at least one would think from reading the job descriptions. Only by personally interviewing applicants could we discern that the job seeker who had "personally attended to numerous high-ranking government officials" was actually a waiter in the Senate dining room. Mark carried the load there. It was a long, tedious process of wading through the pile of job applications, hoping to find qualified personnel who would be able to help us hit the ground running.

Fortunately, Mark was able to recruit some excellent staff

members, including Ramona Lessen, a sixteen-year veteran of Capitol Hill. Ramona was a godsend, since she knew how things worked in Washington and whom to see to get things done. She became my right hand for the next twelve years.

Several veterans of Capitol Hill told Mark, "You better get yourselves an office manager who knows what's going on around here," so we also considered hiring Donna Beck, who had recently been the office manager for retiring Senate majority leader George Mitchell. She was highly qualified, but when word got out that we were interested in hiring her, we received a phone call from one of the Washington conservative "think tanks," warning us, "You know, of course, that she is a former Democrat staffer."

"Yes, we know," Mark replied, "but she knows what needs to be done." It was our first brush with how things work in Washington; it doesn't matter who is the most talented person, or who can do the most to help the country. What matters most in Washington is a person's political affiliation. But that didn't matter to us. We hired Donna because she was the best, and she did an excellent job. Donna's work was exemplary, and she really helped us get up and running quickly.

In the same way, we hired Ginger Parra to help run our Tennessee state office. Ginger was also a Democrat, and she and I had worked together when she was the executive director of the Tennessee Medicaid Commission. She was a talented woman who helped us immensely in the early days of my new career. Overall, we tried to hire a blend of people, some like Kathy Fine, our first legislative director, a Vanderbilt Law School graduate who had worked for Senator Coverdell, and others who had little to no Washington experience at all, but who could bring fresh ideas from the private sector to our staff. Yes, we were elected as "a breath of fresh air," but we knew that experience in Washington was critical for survival.

I was sworn in on January 5. My entire family, including my octogenarian parents, traveled from Tennessee to attend the public ceremonies, and then–vice president Al Gore accompanied Karyn and me to the old Supreme Court chamber within the

Capitol, where I laid my hand on Karyn's dad's Bible as the vice president conducted the private swearing-in ceremony.

Dad was excited for me, but he felt less than excited about my putting medicine on the back burner. When he saw my name on the front entry door of my Senate office, he walked down the hall, waited for me to come out of a meeting, and walked me back to the nameplate where he deliberately pointed. "Bill, something important is missing, isn't it?" asked Dad. I looked at the nameplate and knew immediately what Dad was referring to—there was no "MD" after my name.

I immediately had Ramona request a new sign, and kept the "MD" on both my door and my official desk on the Senate floor throughout my terms of office as a constant and visible reminder of who I am, where I came from, and who I will always be. To me those letters behind my name reflect my personal and professional values and ethics; beyond that, they place the emphasis where it ought to be in government, on helping *individuals*, not simply the majority or the loudest voices.

Walking into the chamber of the U.S. Senate as the new guy was like stepping into a whole new world. I was breathless. Anyone with even a rudimentary appreciation of history and the remarkable leaders who have served our country in that stately room could easily be overwhelmed. The blue-carpeted floor, the one hundred personal, carved wooden Senate chamber desks, forty-eight of which date back to 1819, the two (one Republican, the other Democrat) side-by-side cloakrooms at the back, and the second-floor galleries for visitors, lined with the white marble busts of the American vice presidents (who are the presidents of the Senate), and the inscriptions above the presiding officer's desk, *E Pluribus Unum* (One out of many), and above the doors— *Annuit Coeptis* (God has favored our undertakings), *Novus Ordo Seclorum* (A new order of the ages), and our national motto, "In God We Trust" over the south-central entrance—all speak of the rich history and traditions of the U.S. Senate.

As the new kid on the hill, I was literally number one hundred on the Senate seniority list—after all the incumbents, as well as

the newly elected officials who had held government office previously. Yes, I started at the absolute bottom. It reminded me of
that first day of medical school, as a misplaced southerner humbled even further by the hallowed halls of Harvard, but at least
there, I was not *junior* to the other 125 in my class. In the Senate,
even though my freshman class of eleven incoming Republicans
was larger than usual, I was the lowest man on the totem pole.
(There remains some friendly debate about who was lower in
the pecking order, my colleague Spence Abraham, senator from
Michigan, or me. We flipped a coin to determine who was number one hundred, and I won! Regardless, both of us were looking
up from the bottom.)

Being last in seniority mattered. It meant that our tiny, tight
transitional offices (the second ones) were tucked in the attic of
the Hart Building, with no outside windows, while we awaited
the completion of our permanent offices in Dirksen. We even
had to cut six inches off our hallway flagpole because the ceil-
ings were so low. We didn't have a conference room, so all of
our staff meetings were held out in the narrow attic hall. Some
conferences and interviews between female staffers were even
conducted in the women's restroom! When we moved into our
permanent location in the expansive Everett Dirksen Building
a few months later, we felt as though our modest offices were
palatial.

One of the first committees on which I was assigned to serve
was the Senate Banking Committee. I had served on the board
of Third National Bank in Nashville, so I was comfortable with
my knowledge about the issues with which we were dealing. My
first day in office, I attended financial hearings at which Arthur
Levitt, chairman of the Securities and Exchange Commission,
and Federal Reserve chairman Alan Greenspan were questioned
by our committee. Before long, I was also on the Small Business
Committee, the Labor and Human Resources Committee, and
the Budget Committee.

I was serious about my role as a citizen legislator, as the old
bulls of the Senate probably realized when I offered my first piece

of legislation to the Senate—a proposal for term limits. I extolled the desirability of term limits, quoting Harry Truman, who said that limiting the amount of time an official could spend in office would "cure both senility and seniority, both terrible legislative diseases." It was like sticking a hot firebrand in the eyes of the old bulls.

It got worse. During my first term in office, I supported a constitutional amendment requiring a balanced budget, as well as extending a line-item veto to the president. Convinced that the 1994 Republican revolution at the polls had been a mandate for a fresher, more vibrant vision for the future, I also strongly supported Senator Trent Lott's ascent as majority whip.

I was eager to represent my state well, so during the first few months in office, I tried to read, answer, and sign as much of the mail from my Tennessee constituents as possible. Before long, I was signing stacks of mail every day. We had no standard letters, no letters to state my positions on various issues, no staff members who could help shape my responses to the issues—I didn't even know what the real issues were yet! We were all learning on the job. Fortunately, under the dedicated leadership of Mark and with the help of Ramona and the experienced staff members who had worked for Senator Coverdell and Senator George Mitchell, we started to get our bearings.

Several senior senators also helped me find my way in the dark. Majority Leader Bob Dole was a strong influence, and a good role model when it came to maintaining civility in the Senate, never hesitant about stepping across the aisle of the Senate floor to engage a Democrat on an issue demanding bipartisan support. Senator Pete Domenici came alongside me early on, not just as a mentor, but as a good friend. And Trent Lott, the heir apparent to Bob Dole's position when Dole decided to run for president in 1996, helped me better understand the way things worked in Washington.

Nevertheless, my early days in the Senate were challenging. Similar to med school, an enormous amount of information needed to be assimilated quickly and accurately, so I asked questions constantly and I listened—a lot.

One of the first controversial issues with which I had to deal was President Clinton's nomination of Dr. Henry W. Foster Jr., to fill the office formerly held by Joycelyn Elders as surgeon general.

Many senators don't like the position of surgeon general in the first place. In 1995, many Republicans especially didn't like President Clinton's previous use of the office, particularly Joycelyn Elders's active lobbying for the distribution of contraceptives in public schools, as well as her suggestions that perhaps drug legalization should be encouraged. So when President Clinton nominated Dr. Foster, the conservative guns came out firing. False accusations swirled about the man, and much of the acrimony was politically driven. It was character assassination and I detested it.

The abortion issue surged to the forefront of every discussion about the nomination, because Dr. Foster was an obstetrician who had performed thousands of healthy deliveries, but had also performed abortions associated with medical necessity earlier in his career. He was not an "abortionist," as his critics wrongly claimed. Although strongly pro-life—I opposed abortion—I felt that Dr. Foster's detractors, mostly my fellow Republicans, purposely and maliciously twisted the facts surrounding the doctor's medical practice to destroy his reputation.

Making matters even more delicate for me, Dr. Foster was the chairman of obstetrics and gynecology at Meharry Medical School in Nashville, my hometown, and I knew him personally. He and I had served together on a medical ethics board in Nashville and he had impressed me as a knowledgeable doctor and a good, moral man, with the highest professional ethics. I was aware of his record of being involved with abortions, but I was also aware of his vocal support for sexual abstinence programs, and that he had founded and directed the successful "I Have a Future" program in Nashville, ironically one of President George H. W. Bush's "Thousand Points of Light." The program designed by Dr. Foster was an effort to reduce adolescent pregnancies through education, especially in economically depressed areas where teens were considered more at risk for HIV/AIDS and other sexually transmissible diseases.

I gathered and read assiduously Dr. Foster's writings, scrutinizing them through the prism of his alleged advocacy for abortion. Though he did not deny that he had performed abortions, or was listed as the doctor of record (a term in academic teaching centers for the senior surgeon in charge of the case, whether or not he or she actually did the procedure) for thirty-nine abortions, he had publicly stated that he abhorred abortion and advocated abstinence as a means of stemming the tide of teen pregnancies. I then met privately with Dr. Foster, and we discussed how he viewed the surgeon general's position and what he hoped to accomplish if confirmed. Dr. Foster told me that his priorities would be full-scale attacks on teen pregnancy issues, youth smoking, screening for breast and prostate cancer, and AIDS research. Whether or not Dr. Foster was simply telling me what I wanted to hear, I became convinced that I would support him, in spite of the strong conservative opposition. The issue to me became bigger than Dr. Foster's nomination or my position on it. Before getting involved in politics, I had been appalled by the disrespect, scorn, and derision Democrats had hurled at Supreme Court nominees Robert Bork and Clarence Thomas, castigating good, intelligent men as though they were repugnant criminals. The Democrats' crass comments and actions filled me with revulsion. It didn't seem right to me to condone that same sort of politically biased shredding of a doctor (or anyone else) simply because he had been nominated by President Clinton rather than President Bush.

Beyond that, the simple truth was that the surgeon general did not set the nation's policy regarding abortion. When the Senate had confirmed as surgeon general Dr. C. Everett Koop, an outspoken opponent of abortion, his service did not outlaw abortion in our country. Neither would we change the laws regarding abortion by nominating Dr. Foster. To me, the bottom-line issue was: Is the person qualified to do the job and serve with integrity?

Conservative groups came out in strong opposition to Dr. Foster, while organizations such as Planned Parenthood and the National Abortion Rights and Reproduction Action League supported him. When word got out that I was supportive of Dr. Foster, some pro-life groups felt as though I was betraying them. Several prominent Republicans called Mark and told him straightforwardly that if I wanted to end my political career quickly, I should decide in favor of Foster. Suddenly, I was torn between supporting my senior Republican colleagues and standing for what I believed to be right. *Welcome to Washington.*

During my first meeting with Bob Dole in his majority leader's office, I was asked to vote against Foster's nomination. I told Senator Dole that I could not do so in good conscience and I explained my position. To his credit, Dole told me to vote my heart, and he would respect that. In Bob Dole, I saw a true statesman in action.

As a member of the Labor and Human Resources Committee, I took part in the hearings in which Dr. Foster was first officially questioned about his qualifications and his positions. The committee had the power to squelch the nomination right there or send it on to the full Senate for a vote. During the hearings, I posed many questions to Dr. Foster, allowing him to make or break his own case. I did, however, come to his direct aid when a hysterectomy Foster had performed was described by my Republican colleagues as an abortion. I felt the questions asked Dr. Foster about that case were misleading, so I cross-examined him almost like a trial lawyer, allowing him to clarify the facts. No doubt my support of Dr. Foster "rehabilitated" him in the eyes of several of my Senate colleagues and helped propel his nomination out of the committee with a nine-to-seven vote in favor, one yea vote being mine.

Afterward, Ted Kennedy sang my praises, saying what a magnificent job Senator Frist had done in the hearings. Naturally, that didn't sit well with my more conservative constituents back home.

When the nomination reached the Senate floor, it was met with resounding opposition by most members of my party. President Clinton eventually withdrew Dr. Foster's nomination following a filibuster led by Senator Phil Gramm of Texas, so a full vote of the Senate was never taken. Ironically, although I was on the losing side of the Foster nomination, my positions began to define my place in the Senate. Perhaps I had demonstrated that I had truly come as a citizen legislator, an independent thinker, willing to buck my own party if necessary to do what I felt was right. Consequently, members of both parties began to seek me out privately with queries about various medical and health-care issues. They didn't always agree with my prescriptions, but at least they were willing to consider my diagnoses of the problems.

Later in 1995, Senator Dole appointed me as chairman of the Medicare Working Group, a task force charged with developing policies that would strengthen Medicare. It was a natural fit for me, drawing upon my experience chairing the state Medicaid task force back in Tennessee. I soon discovered that both the Medicare and Medicaid programs were growing at more than 10 percent every year, double the rate of the budget as a whole, and fueling the growth of the national deficit. For the first time, Medicare spending was exceeding the funds coming into the Medicare Trust Fund. As a government, we simply were overpromising to the next generation what we could deliver. Although nobody wanted to talk about it for fear of repercussions in the upcoming 1996 elections, if we didn't impose some limits on the ever-increasing spending, and do it soon, the entire hospital trust fund would be depleted and bankrupt within seven years.

Naturally, the Democrats, who loved to spend, seized on our proposed limits to future increases in spending and labeled them (using the press) as "cuts" in spending on Medicare, in an attempt to give the impression that those heartless Republicans were taking care away from the elderly who desperately needed it. I realized that we were going to get little accomplished on the issue until after the 1996 elections. My colleagues on the task force suggested that as a doctor, I could help calm the situation by appearing in a series of television ads refuting the Democratic charges that Republicans wanted to cut Medicare coverage. I was glad to do the ads, but I was beginning to understand what some people referred to as Washington's voodoo economics. Only in Washington political circles could reducing the amount of *increased* spending be interpreted as a spending cut.

An important step I took during my initial days in Washington was to join the weekly Senate prayer breakfast in the Capitol. It was attended by twelve to twenty senators each Tuesday morning as well as by the distinguished and beloved chaplain of the Senate, Dr. Lloyd Ogilvie. The prayer breakfasts were a fifty-year tradition in the Senate and they offered a time of personal exchange, prayer, and fellowship among senators of both parties. I soon came to find it my favorite hour of the week, in part because of the intimacy of the discussion and in part because it was one of the few times you could find Republicans and Democrats in the same room, talking civilly with one another.

I learned quickly not to take the Capitol Hill wrangling personally. Much of the public bombast by certain members is nothing more than that—bombast designed to get a sound bite on the evening news or to appeal to the voters back home. Nevertheless, it still hurt when we worked so hard trying to convince people across the aisle to vote for some measure that we truly believed would benefit the entire country only to see it go down to defeat due to a lot of hot air. Usually, I took either victory or defeat in stride; if we lost a vote, I refused to give up or get depressed, regardless of how much effort we'd put into trying to pass the legislation.

At first, it was frustrating to realize how slow and tedious accomplishing anything in the Senate was going to be. Part of that, of course, is intentional, and was designed to be so by our Founding Fathers. The Senate is meant to be a place of debate, a place for the nation to slow down, stop, think, and make sure the government is not acting impetuously. But as a heart surgeon, I was accustomed to fixing things—not merely talking about them. I had said in my campaign that people in Washington tend to have a two-year outlook, worried more about the next round of elections, rather than a twenty-year plan; too many politicians seemed to be more intent on maintaining power than concerned about what was best for the country. The reality of that short-term thinking hit me hard during my first months in office.

Nevertheless, I looked at the situation as a magnificent opportunity. Because I'd told my constituency in advance that I would serve two terms and then come home, Mark and I felt that we didn't have to do business as usual; we could change things.

ON SEPTEMBER 14, 1995, I WAS SUPPOSED TO FLY BACK TO NASH-ville for a midweek fundraising event and return to Washington the following day. I was running late, and I still had to go over to the Senate floor to vote. Perhaps it was providential.

Just about that time, Graeme Sieber, the director of a home for troubled boys in Cleveland, Tennessee, was visiting my colleague Fred Thompson and the Tennessee House members, lobbying them to reconsider budget cuts that would affect charities like his. Sieber had just gotten off the elevator outside the Dirksen office of Rhode Island senator John Chafee when he keeled over with a heart attack, falling partially in the elevator doorway and partially in the hallway. A woman staffer from Senator Chafee's office raced around the corner to my office and called in to Ramona, "Is your boss here? I think a man in the hall has had a heart attack!"

Ramona burst into my office to inform me, and I grabbed an emergency medical kit I kept in my closet, rushed down the hall, and pushed through a small crowd in front of the elevator. I found a man ashen gray on the floor, his head in a pool of blood. Had he been shot? No, I found a gash in his scalp, resulting, I concluded, from his fall to the hard marble floor.

Chafee's office manager had been a Girl Scout leader, and she had already begun administering CPR before I arrived. I dropped to my knees, felt the patient's neck for a pulse, and immediately cleared his airway and began mouth-to-mouth resuscitation. "Can someone else give her a hand in compressing the chest?" I said, looking up between breaths, knowing the woman would soon grow tired. "Has someone called 911?" I knew it'd be impossible to get him back without a defibrillator. I was worried because it had been several minutes since the man on the floor had passed out. I checked his carotid pulse again and felt nothing—a bad sign. I made a fist and delivered a strong thump to the chest—nothing. I had grabbed an airway tube from my emergency kit. I inserted the clear plastic tube down his windpipe to force air into his lungs, attached the big black air "ambu" bag, and instructed a bystander to squeeze it once every five seconds. I knew if we didn't get him turned around quickly he would die.

The on-call doctor from the Capitol Physician's Office arrived with a heart defibrillator. I stripped open the man's shirt, slapped on the sticky electrode pads, and read the wildly irregular electrical activity on the screen as ventricular fibrillation (which is incompatible with life). We shocked the patient once . . . his body jerked into the air. No pulse. Twice, nothing . . . I glanced up at the clock, thinking maybe it had taken too long to begin CPR. I thought for sure that he was gone. Then I turned up the power on the defibrillator and shocked him once again. Suddenly, his heart kicked back into a regular, normal sinus rhythm. The squiggles on the screen normalized into a repetitive, steady pattern. He was alive.

"Stop CPR," I said.

We watched and he took a breath on his own. His color slowly began to return. As I looked up, the District of Columbia emergency response team was arriving on the scene. I filled them in on what had happened and turned the situation over to them.

I stood up from the marble floor, my white shirt disheveled and soaked with sweat from all the activity. I hurried back to the office where Ramona greeted me with a "What in the world happened to you?" expression on her face. I looked a mess, blood still on my hands, but I still had to go over to the Senate floor to vote.

I cast my vote in favor of an amendment to a bill and then raced off to the airport.

On the way, I called Ramona. She told me that Senator Chafee had gone to the Senate floor, proclaiming something like "Bill Frist has saved a person's life, bringing him back from the dead, right outside my office door!"

"No, he can't say that!" I replied emphatically. I was horrified, first because of the senator from Rhode Island's compliment, but second, because I wasn't so sure the man was going to survive or not have brain damage. I called the hospital emergency room and relayed to them the details of the procedures we had used to resuscitate the patient. The hospital reported that Mr. Sieber was in the emergency room, stable, and that all signs were that he was going to make it.

I arrived in Nashville just in time to clean up, change clothes, and make my speech. The following morning at five o'clock, I was back at the airport headed to Washington to make a 9:30 A.M. vote in the Senate. When I walked into the Senate chamber that morning, I received the surprise of my life. The members of the Senate broke out in spontaneous applause. I sheepishly acknowledged the senators' congratulations. In truth, I had just done in public what hundreds of doctors all over the country do anonymously every single day in America. Here, among this collection of lawyers and politicians, it was an extraordinary feat.

A day or so later, I visited Mr. Sieber and his wife in the hospital. They both thanked me profusely. We talked briefly about the surgery scheduled for the following day, when an automatic internal defibrillator device would be surgically inserted under the skin to prevent the life-threatening event from occurring again. If his heart went into fibrillation, the remarkable device would automatically give his heart a shock of electricity to normalize the rhythm.

As I was leaving the room, Mr. Sieber called out, "And by the way, Dr. Frist, don't forget why I came to Washington . . . to see that you support my boys back home. We need that money." Despite his close call with death, Sieber was most concerned about those he'd come to Washington to serve. Indeed, constituents have passion. I smiled as I waved good-bye. Graeme was my kind of man.

As an interesting byproduct of my newfound notoriety in the halls of Congress, Ramona began an entirely new file she labeled simply as "Referrals." Everyone from my fellow senators to the Capitol Police to the catering people knew somebody with some sort of medical problem. "Do you know somebody who might be able to help?" they'd discreetly pull me aside to ask. I tried my best to connect people to the best doctors around. But I began to realize how hard that is to do, even for a doctor. Which doctors in the Washington region are really the best? How do I know for sure? No objective, accurate measures of quality of doctors existed then (and little exists today). Yes, even senators have a hard time navigating our irrational and fragmented health-care system.

Probably all this attention to my "medical side" reminded me of my roots. Having become acclimated to my new surroundings, I found myself longing to be able to help people as a doctor. I got my medical license to practice in Washington, D.C., and decided to do volunteer medical work in my off-hours in a traveling medical van in Southeast Washington—a notoriously dangerous section of town almost totally lacking in health resources. I was aware that a man in Southeast would on average live seventeen years less than a man five miles away in suburban Maryland— seventeen years less. Maybe I could make a difference there.

A fellow Tennessean living in D.C. had befriended the Southeast community and saw the need. She scrounged up enough money to buy a secondhand van to provide free health screening on the streets; the problem was that she didn't have a doctor. I heard about her plight through some friends back in Nashville and volunteered to join her on a regular basis. We'd park on the street, in what would seem to be the worst part of town. I knew for a fact that the adjacent block was the site of the most drug arrests in the city. People would line up outside the van, from which we saw and treated patients. The people we served were among the city's poorest. This was life in the trenches with real hurting people. No money, little food, no home, no family—and no help with their diabetes or treatment for their high blood pressure. Being uninsured matters; you die sooner. *Even those with Medicare could not get life-saving prescription drugs; maybe someday I can help change that. Maybe someday we can provide afford-able coverage for the medical needs of these patients.*

I doubt the press was even aware that I was working with the free clinic, and frankly, that suited me just fine. The Washington media is much more interested in covering the partisan shouting matches on TV than in the plight of poor people.

I often found myself in the right place at the right time. For example, after speaking on health-care issues and participating at the Republican National Convention in San Diego in August 1996, Karyn and the boys and I attended a barbecue in Montecito, California, where an eighty-four-year-old woman slumped to the floor, grabbing her neck with both hands as she fell. A shout went out for help. A quick sweep of her mouth with my finger followed by the standard Heimlich maneuver of upper abdomen compression and she was able to breathe again. Once she calmed down, she continued to enjoy the evening.

On another occasion, I was returning home from Indonesia when my connecting flight got delayed in Los Angeles. When we finally got airborne and I had just settled back in my seat to do some reading, the announcement came over the plane's public address system: "Is there a doctor on board?" I identified myself as a physician to the flight attendant, and she informed me that a man on board had passed out and seemed to be having trouble breathing. I quickly checked his vital signs, and while checking his heart, I felt a prescription pill bottle in the man's pocket. Amazingly, I recognized the physician's name on the prescription from my Stanford days. I had the pilot contact Ramona in our Washington office, and Ramona connected me to the doctor at Stanford, who explained why the medication had caused the adverse reaction and how to overcome it. We were able to revive the man, and he survived just fine.

I was reminded once again that although I was now a United States senator, I was still a physician at heart.

I KNEW THAT BOB DOLE WAS GOING TO BE DISAPPOINTED IN ME. It was 1996, and Dole was fulfilling his longtime dream of running for president. Now he'd asked me to introduce him in my hometown of Nashville at a major Tennessee fundraising event at our close friend Alynne Massey's magnificent home on Belle Meade Boulevard—in the same zip code that for years was the highest per-capita Republican fundraising area in the nation. Although Senator Dole had been to Nashville many times, this was to be his formal introduction as a presidential candidate to the Middle Tennessee community. It was only appropriate the home-state senator welcome and introduce his good friend and Senate colleague, especially at such a prestigious event.

Months ago I had told Bob that I'd love to host him in Nashville. But now I had a serious conflict. I knew that I had to tell Senator Dole no . . . again.

For the past few months, whenever I could get home before the boys had gone to bed, our youngest son Bryan and I had been carving a Pinewood Derby car for the big Cub Scout race. Although I had little to add to nine-year-old Bryan's work, every night for two weeks he and I had worked with the slowly changing block of wood and the chisel, weights, and sandpaper so we could together plan and accomplish the next step. Finally, we were ready for the trials for our troop.

Unfortunately, because of the Senate's haphazard and random schedule, when the night came, a vote was called for on the Senate floor. Having been in the Senate just a couple of years, it was important for me not to miss a Senate vote. I had to call and tell Bryan I couldn't make the trials. Karyn would have to take him instead. Bryan didn't say much, but I could tell he was disappointed.

Bryan finished in the top third, I learned from Karyn as I sat in one of the Senate cloakroom phone booths. As I walked around the Senate chamber, still waiting for the Senate vote, I thought, *I should have just skipped this vote to be with him.* At home later that night, I told Bryan, "I'll make the finals for sure," remembering how my dad had always showed up for my Little League baseball games no matter how busy he was at the hospital.

Now, as I checked the calendar for the date that Senator Dole was requesting, my schedule was clear except for one appointment—Bryan's final Pinewood Derby race.

I looked up at Mark, my chief of staff, who was standing in the doorway, waiting for my answer. "I can't do it," I said, as much to myself as to Mark.

"What do you mean, you can't do it?" Mark asked.

"The Dole kickoff event is now the same day as Bryan's Pinewood Derby race," I said. "I promised Bryan that I would be there. I am simply not going to break that promise."

Mark stared back at me with an incredulous look for just a second. Then he nodded and returned to his office without even attempting to talk me out of my decision. He understood. I set about the task of writing an apology to Senator Dole. Dole, the political pro, also understood—and even had the letter I'd written read at the event in Tennessee. Meanwhile, I went to Bryan's Pinewood Derby race over at St. Patrick's School. We finished in the middle of the pack, but our wheels didn't fall off and Bryan had a blast, celebrating with his friends, their dads, and a number of moms, the many weeks of father-son work in friendly competition.

It comes back to priorities. I had seen too many politicians, preachers, doctors, and businessmen spend their lives trying to win the accolades of the world, while losing in their relationships with their own family members. I didn't always do it perfectly (far from it!), and if I had it to do all over I would have done much better than I did, but finding the right priorities was constantly on my mind.

*   *   *

ANY TIME I RETURNED TO NASHVILLE, I TRIED TO SPEND SOME
extra time with my parents, then in their late eighties. Both remained sharp mentally, but neither was in good health. By then,
Dad had suffered a heart attack, two heart operations, a stroke
following his second heart procedure that had left him with the
frustrating stutter, a broken neck from an automobile accident
that required a metal "halo" brace screwed into his skull for six
months, colon cancer that required a surgical resection, and progressive loss of hearing, but he remained active and he was always his usual upbeat self. With each health insult, he would
bounce back and waste no time in getting back to counseling
others and giving inspirational talks to people in medicine and in
health care the country over. In every talk, he would open with a
joke about all his past maladies to put his audience at ease.

On every visit, my siblings and I gently urged Dad and Dodie—as
the family had taken to calling Mother after the first grandchild
arrived—to put down on paper some of the things that we could
pass on to the great-grandchildren who would never have the
opportunity to be in their presence. By now, there were fourteen grandchildren and five great-grandchildren who hung on
every word Mother and Dad said. Every Christmas, Thanksgiving, and Easter, all of the next several generations, most of whom
lived in Nashville, would gather in the living room on Bowling
where we'd all grown up and listen to the family stories, most
related to the enduring lessons of life, that Mom and Dad would
share. Harry Hollis, an author and a close friend of the family,
had observed the personal and powerful impact that Dad had
had over the years on so many thousands of people, both in his
large medical practice in the community, and globally through
his work with HCA. To capture and preserve Dad's simple philosophies for future generations, he began a tape-recorded oral
history project with Dad.

As we approached the Christmas season in 1997, I pushed Dad
to put some of his philosophy on paper. Karyn's and my grandchildren would never know him. He hesitated, saying humbly that
he really didn't have any profound philosophy worth sharing. But

on December 15, Dad finally took time to write some of the things about which he felt strongly. In a letter headed, "For my family and for future generations, with great love," he wrote:

Dear great-grandchildren,

My children have asked me to write down what I believe. They want their children and their children's children to know about some of the things that are important in life. That is why I have written you this letter. I am writing it to you, even though I cannot know you. I hope, as you read it, you will know me, and know your parents and grandparents, a little better. . . .

I believe in a few simple things. I learned about them a long time ago from my mother and my father, my sisters and my brother, my teachers and my friends. I learned a lot in life, but I have never changed these beliefs all the way through. This is what I believe.

I believe that religion is so very important. I was raised in the Presbyterian Church in Meridian, Mississippi, and I never missed a Sunday from when I was three to when I was eighteen. I believe there is a God and in Jesus Christ. The only prayer I ever pray is thanking God for all the blessings I have. I never pray when I'm in a tight spot because I think God, in his wisdom, knows what you need. I believe in the morality of religion—the Golden Rule. I say something nice to people when they deserve it. When they don't deserve it, I say something nice about other people, so they know how to act and they always smile.

I believe that culture is so important. My mother was so kind, so giving, so unselfish. My wife, Dorothy, is the same. When you marry, marry someone who believes in the same things you do.

Be happy in your family life. Your family is the most important thing you can ever have. Love your wife or your husband. Tell your children how great they are. Encourage them in everything they do. I never punished my children, never ever raised my voice with them. If they know you expect them to do right, they will do right. If you praise them for the good things they do, the bad things will disappear.

Be happy in your career. I was a doctor. I loved being a doctor because it meant helping people, being with patients every minute. All my sons were doctors. It's a great thing to be a doctor. Whatever work you do, do it well. Remember any job worth doing is worth doing well. Always do a quality job. . . .

I believe good people beget good people. If you marry the right person, then you will have good children. But everywhere else in life, too, good people beget good people. In your work, when you hire good people, they, in turn, will hire good people and right on down the line. That's how we built Hospital Corporation of America. From the board members right on down to the man in the boiler room and the woman who makes the beds, we wanted good people with integrity and high moral standards. We made such a difference in the world with HCA, and we did it because good people beget good people. . . .

Finally, I believe it is so terribly important in life to stay humble. Use your talents wisely and use other people's talents to help other people. Don't think about the reward; that will probably come along if you don't go looking for it. (I always said at HCA that if we just concentrated on doing the best job we could of giving quality care, then the bottom line would take care of itself. And it did.) Always be confident. But never be cocky. Always stay humble.

So, my great-grandchildren, I hope you will live happy and long lives like I have. I hope this letter will help you. Maybe you will give it to your children, and they will give it to their children right on down the line. The world is always changing, and that's a good thing. It's how you carry yourself in the world that doesn't change—morality, integrity, warmth, and kindness are the same things in 1910 when I was born or in 2010 or later when you will be reading this. And that's a good thing, too.

Love,
Granddaddy

These are simple truths. They reflect core values that served well this man and those who had contact with him. They became the riverbed for the lives of his five children. To this day, we gather around the table at holiday times to reread these simple truths.

That Christmas was a low point in terms of health for both Mother and Dad. For the past three years, they had lived downstairs in a bedroom set up in the large, back game room, where growing up we five children had played Ping-Pong and had so many memorable times with neighborhood friends. Mother had been confined to a wheelchair for bad arthritis in her hips. Dad had been hospitalized for progressive congestive heart failure in November and was now recovering at home. Though physically both were ill, they were as alert and optimistic as ever.

Just after Christmas, Karyn and I took the boys out to Snowmass, Colorado, to stay in Tommy and Trisha's condominium. Mary and Lee and their family were there as well. Just before New Year's Day, we received a call that Mother had been in a serious accident and had broken both of her legs when her wheelchair broke loose while being transported in a van. We immediately flew home to be with her as she recovered.

When it rains it pours. On the day of travel back home, Harrison developed severe headaches and neck rigidity, the telltale signs of spinal meningitis. On landing in Nashville, we went straight to Children's Hospital, where the diagnosis was confirmed and Harrison was hospitalized for treatment with high-dose antibiotics.

The following day, Mom was rehospitalized for treatment of her leg fractures and a low-grade lower-lobe pneumonia. Karyn and I spent that week in constant rotation from Harrison at Vanderbilt, to Mom at Centennial Medical Center, and to Dad at home.

Less than three weeks after Dad wrote the letter, on January 4, 1998, I was downstairs with him at the Bowling home when he told his devoted attendant, Brenda, that he was tired and wanted to go to bed. I said good night to him and continued working

Frist family on Mother's Day, 1952. (Left to right: Bobby, Mary, Dorothy Cate Frist, me, Tommy, Dottie.)

Me at age eight.

Riding with my father on Tony in the front yard of our home on Bowling Avenue, 1954.

Karyn McLaughlin, then a special-education teacher, and I walk along a wooded beach in Bimini one year before we were married.

(Photo credit: Ed O'Lear)

Karyn and I were married on March 14, 1981, in Lubbock, Texas.

(Photo credit: Bill S. Weaks)

The founders of Hospital Corporation of America in 1983. (Left to right: my dad, Dr. Thomas F. Frist, Sr.; businessman Jack Massey; brother Dr. Thomas Frist, Jr.)

Dr. Norman Shumway, the pioneering father of heart transplantation and my mentor at Stanford, taught me lessons I carried through my years in the Senate.

Vanderbilt Hospital's heart and lung transplant recipients' reunion, 1991.

In transplantation, every second counts. No team member, from ambulance driver to surgeon, can make a mistake.
(Photo credit: John Howser, Vanderbilt Medical Center)

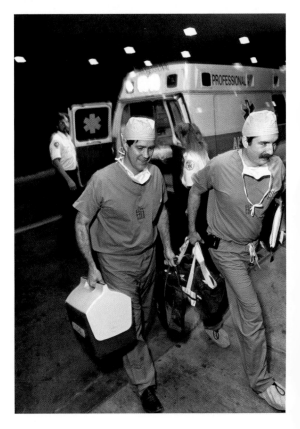

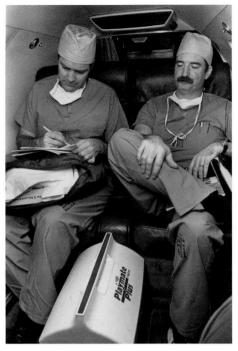

Organ procurement specialist Doug Martin and I fly through the night on a "donor run," 1992. Heart to be transplanted is in the cooler. (Photo credit: John Howser, Vanderbilt Medical Center)

On September 21, 1991, I performed an emergency thoracotomy on a patient shot through the chest with an M-16. The patient was Lieutenant Colonel David Petraeus, commander of the Third Battalion of the 187th Infantry Regiment at Fort Campbell. (Photo taken in Iraq, January 2005.)

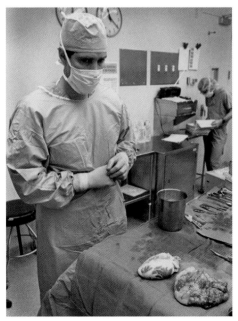

Preparing to replace the diseased fifty-three-year-old heart (right) with a healthy eighteen-year-old heart (left). (Photo credit: John Howser, Vanderbilt Medical Center)

My brother Tommy and me on a campaign bus trip across Tennessee in October 1994.

Presenting my campaign "Save the Children" tie to my dad on election night, November 8, 1994, with my sons Harrison and Bryan looking on. (Photo credit: Nashville Public Library, Special Collections)

Swearing-in ceremony conducted by president of the Senate and former Tennessee senator Al Gore, witnessed by former majority leader (and Tennessee senator) Howard Baker, 1995. Karyn is holding her father's Bible.

Frist family planting the bicentennial tree of Tennessee, the tulip poplar, on the Southeast lawn, of the U.S. Capitol in 1996. (Left to right: Bryan, Harrison, Karyn, me, Jonathan.)

Volunteering medical services in low-income Southeast Washington, D.C., after voting on the floor of the Senate. The free-care clinic was operated out of an old medical van.

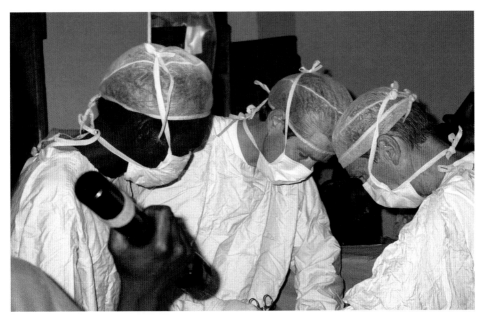

Dr. Dick Furman and me operating by flashlight in war-torn Lui, Sudan, in an abandoned schoolhouse with no electricity or running water, 1998.

In Northern Uganda delivering food with Franklin Graham's Samaritan's Purse in July 2007. Thirty-five thousand Ugandans received supplies on this day. (Photo credit: Samaritan's Purse, Photographer: Steve Starr)

President Clinton in the Capitol Rotunda delivering the eulogy for John Michael Gibson and Jacob Joseph Chestnut, Capitol police officers killed in the line of duty. Ramona informed me, "Senator, something terrible just happened over at the Capitol."

With President Bill Clinton, Senator Tom Daschle, and former majority leader Howard Baker aboard *Air Force One*, en route to Tennessee to attend the funeral of Albert Gore, Sr., December 8, 1998. (Photo credit: White House photo.)

Bono (of U2) and me traveling throughout rural Uganda in January 2001, investigating the impact of recent U.S. debt forgiveness. We continue to collaborate on HIV/AIDS policy and global poverty issues.

2001: The Frist home on Bowling Avenue with the extended family, following the Thanksgiving dedication of a prominent flagpole and flag to honor Dorothy and Thomas F. Frist, Sr.

Discussing strategy for the 2002 Senate elections with Finance Director Linus Catignani and Tennessee Finance Chairman and close personal friend Steve Smith.

President Bush signing the Medicare Modernization Act into law in December 2003.

Senate and House leadership met regularly with President George Bush in the Oval Office. (On sofas left to right: me, Tom Daschle, Tom DeLay, Nancy Pelosi, Denny Hastert. In foreground left to right: President Bush and Vice President Cheney.)

(Photo credit: White House photo)

Speaker of the House Denny Hastert, President Bush, and me in the Oval Office at our regular morning leadership meeting. (Photo credit: White House photo)

John Roberts in 2004, just days before the vote on his confirmation as Supreme Court justice. Former Tennessee senator Fred Thompson (background) was his escort. Two Supreme Court justices were confirmed during my tenure as majority leader.

The Frist Family celebrating at the 2004 Republican Convention just prior to my address on health-care issues. (Left to right: Jonathan, Harrison, Karyn, me, and Bryan.)

The Indian Ocean tsunami struck Sri Lanka on December 26, 2004, killing thirty-one thousand Sri Lankans. In response, I hand-delivered financial emergency aid from nonprofit, Nashville-based Hope Through Healing Hands and PUR clean water packets from Procter & Gamble.

Hurricane Katrina, the largest natural disaster in United States history, struck landfall on August 29, 2005, and 1,836 people lost their lives. I chartered a plane to volunteer my medical services for evacuees at Louis Armstrong New Orleans Airport and Morial Convention Center, both sites of humanitarian and rescue operations.

Karyn and me on the balcony just outside the majority leader office (the Howard H. Baker, Jr., rooms) on the west side of the U.S. Capitol.

Tennessee senator Lamar Alexander (on sofa) and I join President and Mrs. Bush aboard *Air Force One* in June 2006 on a trip to Memphis, Tennessee, to meet with Junichiro Koizumi, prime minister of Japan. (Photo credit: White House photo)

President Bush and me in a quiet moment in the Capitol, ten minutes before the president gave his 2006 State of the Union Address. (Photo credit: White House photo)

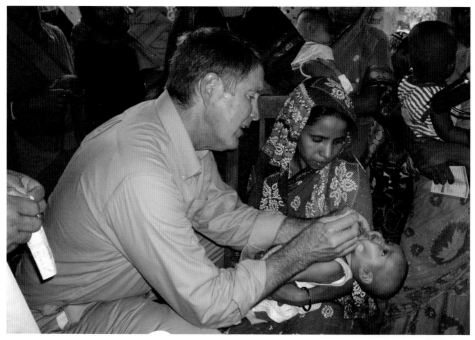

Administering vitamin A to an infant in rural northern Bangladesh during a 2007 medical mission trip with Save the Children. Sixteen thousand children die every day of preventable causes. (Source: UNICEF)

The dedication of the Dorothy Cate & Thomas F. Frist, Sr., Family Life Center at Cumberland Heights, the alcohol rehabilitation center founded by my dad in 1964 at the suggestion of a patient. (Left to right: Bobby Frist, Mary Barfield, Dottie Eller, me, Tommy Frist, Jr.)

on an upcoming speech, sitting in his big reclining chair in the adjacent living room. About an hour later, Brenda urgently called for me from the back bedroom, shouting that Dad had stopped breathing. "Should I start CPR?" she asked.

"No," I said, joining her at his bedside, "Dad wouldn't want that."

Dad had died peacefully in his sleep. And at that moment, a huge chunk of my life was instantly gone. The foundation of security that I could always rely on no matter what happened to me, no matter how many risks were taken, was ripped away from me.

I immediately called Karyn and the other family members, all of whom gathered at the house. In tearful, somber tones, we discussed how to tell Mom. None of us had envisioned them ever not being together, and Mother literally had focused her entire life on her husband, Tommy, supporting him in his profession and caring for him daily over more than sixty years of married life. We all decided to go as a family to the hospital to tell her.

Bobby volunteered to be the spokesman, so as we gathered around her bed late that night, waking her up from a deep sleep, he told her gently, in a compassionate and controlled way that only he could have pulled off, that Dad had died. She was quiet and you could sense the spiritual loss she felt. She said she understood us, but in some ways you could tell she just didn't believe us. We talked a bit and then let her go back to sleep.

The visitation was held two nights later at our lifelong family church, Westminster Presbyterian. It was packed. It was raining hard, so to accommodate the visitors, we had five separate receiving lines, one to a child, rather than a single long one. Karyn slipped out a few minutes early to go be with Mother at the hospital.

No one could possibly have guessed what would happen over the following twenty-four hours. While still at visitation, I got an urgent call from Karyn saying that Mother was not doing well, and that I should come right over. I said some hasty good-byes at the visitation and headed toward the hospital, just a few miles away. But while I was still in the car on the way, my cell phone rang again.

"Dodie just died in her sleep," said Karyn sorrowfully.

We will never know the exact cause of Mother's death. What we do know is that she was never the same after she learned of Dad's departure. Her heart simply slowed and stopped.

As our family reflected together on Mom's and Dad's lives later that night, we all recognized that as much as we grieved losing her, there was something extremely appropriate about Mother's passing so close to the same time as Dad. It was fitting that two people who loved each other so much should pass into eternity together.

Dad's funeral was to be held on the day following the visitation, now a brief fifteen hours after the death of Mom. Mary suggested, "Why don't we have a joint funeral and have them buried together, at the same time?"

"Impossible," the funeral director emphatically declared. But Mary insisted, explaining that they had lived inseparably, thus they should leave this world still inseparable.

When people arrived at the church for Dad's memorial service the next day, they were astonished to find something unexpected. At the front of the church there were two simple wooden caskets, not one, side by side, almost touching. They soon discovered they were at a service honoring not one but *both* of our parents. It was raining heavily the day of the memorial service, but the church was crowded with people. Eulogies were offered by former Tennessee governor and close family friend Winfield Dunn, our longstanding church pastor K. C. Ptomey, and Karl VanDevender, Dad's doctor, medical partner, and, more important, in his later years his closest friend.

In his eulogy, it was Karl who best captured in eloquent words what everyone was thinking: "While the loss of one person we so greatly loved should be met with a chorus of words, I feel as if the loss of two has brought about a reverential silence. The death of Mrs. Frist last night makes this moment something else entirely. Even though we may have said at times she could never live without him, the fact of it has left us stunned and over-whelmed. One death is the story of an end of a long and illustri-ous life. Two deaths is a love story." And a love story it was.

Today, years later, I still think of Mother and Dad every day, lis-tening for their voices in how to handle a certain situation, com-menting on something they said or did, attempting to honor their legacy by living my life in accordance with their examples.

Leaving this legacy for our children is the central reason Karyn and I decided to renovate the home I was born and grew up in on Bowling Avenue in a quiet residential section of Nash-ville after I left the Senate: to pass on to the next generation the values that played out there for almost fifty years among two unselfish, humble, and loving parents and five children. In our library today as a reminder of my father's enduring values you will see inscribed on the wall, "Good people beget good people," "The curve is always going up," and, in the corner—"Two deaths is a love story."

The image of my dad growing up in a "boardinghouse" envi-ronment extends to our home yet today. Just as our family home was a haven for my friends and me as we were growing up, so is our home a place where our sons' friends are always welcome. Now that we have moved back to Nashville to live in the family home, our family feels a sense of continuity with our heritage, a connectedness to our roots, as though we have come full circle. As Dad said so simply, "Your family is the most important thing you can ever have."

9

Capitol Crossfire

I could tell by the ashen look on Ramona's face that this was no ordinary interruption. Ramona was glued to the television set propped on the filing cabinet in the corner, as I stepped through the doorway of her office in the Dirksen Senate Office Building on Capitol Hill in Washington.

"What is it, Ramona? What's going on?" I asked.

"Senator, something terrible just happened over at the Capitol," she managed to say, as she raised her hand to her heart.

It was a sunny, blue-sky Friday afternoon, July 24, 1998, near the end of the business day, and I had just returned from the Senate floor, where I had been presiding. I had gaveled the Senate closed until Monday, and then Senator Rod Grams from Minnesota and I had headed back toward the Dirksen Building.

Rod and I were walking through the tunnel that connected the Capitol to Dirksen when my cell phone rang. I glanced at the phone and immediately recognized the number of the Capitol Physicians' Office. We had an informal agreement that if the Capitol physician received word of a medical emergency on the Hill, they would give me a call in case I was already in the area and could possibly administer emergency aid before the official response teams arrived.

This was one such call. Details were sketchy, but someone had said something about hearing gunshots in the Capitol.

I hurried to my office, where I watched the chilling newscast with Ramona for a few moments. Then I was on my way. Gus Puryear, my new legislative director from Nashville, who had come up to work with me, had pulled the car out of the garage and was waiting for me on the back side of the Dirksen Building. He was on his cell phone as I hopped into the car. "Ramona just called and said there has definitely been a shooting at the Capitol."

"Okay, get me as close to the Capitol as you can," I replied. Gus whipped the vehicle out of the parking slot and headed behind the Russell Building on the way to Constitution Avenue.

"Do you know how many shooters there might be?" Gus asked.

"No, I have no idea," I replied, peering out the window, trying to see what was going on. The streets were clogged due to summer tourists and the Friday afternoon rush hour, as we approached the north entrance to the Capitol. A Capitol police officer stopped us at the intersection.

"Senator Frist," I identified myself to the officer. "I'm trying to get to the Capitol."

"Well, you won't be able to get in this way," the officer explained. "Emergency vehicles are on their way."

I threw open the car door right in the middle of the intersection and jumped out. "Wait here for me, Gus," I said, nodding toward the southwest corner of the Russell Building. I left my suit coat in the car and ran toward the Capitol, my tie flapping in the late-afternoon sunshine. As I sprinted past the guard station on the side of the Capitol grounds, I called out to the guard without slowing my pace. "What happened?"

The guard recognized me and waved me through. "We have men down inside!" he shouted. I kept going, racing across the east perimeter of the Capitol lawn. The ambulances and emergency responders had not yet arrived, but I could hear the sounds

of screaming sirens in the background. Other than the Capitol
Police, I was one of the first on the scene.

In those pre-9/11 days, the U.S. Capitol was one of the most
accessible federal buildings in America. Unlike the White House,
which was surrounded by wrought-iron fencing and accessible
only through tightly controlled security entrances, the "People's
House" was largely open to the public. We loved it that way.
Capitol Police were stationed at the doorways, along with a mag-
netometer—a metal detector—but once visitors cleared those
checks, they were free to roam as they pleased, to sightsee, run
into their representatives in the hallways, or watch Congress
from the gallery. While some entrances to the Capitol were designated for lawmakers and staff only, on most days, anyone could
enter the door now in front of me.

But not today. A Capitol Police officer raised his hand to stop
me, then recognized me and pointed toward the "Documents
Door," a busy lower-level entrance, just to the left of the majestic
main steps leading up to the Rotunda. One of the Capitol Police
hurried me inside and whispered hoarsely, "Men are down on
the floor. We think three people have been shot, but there may
be others."

Although I didn't know it at the time, a few minutes earlier,
Russell Eugene Weston, a man with a history of mental illness,
had walked through the same door. When Weston attempted to
go around the metal detector just inside, Capitol Police officer
Jacob J. Chestnut stopped him and instructed him to go through
the detector. Instead, Weston pulled out a Smith & Wesson .38
handgun and shot Chestnut in the head.

Further inside the hallway, bustling with visitors young and
old, another officer heard the shot, grabbed his own pistol, and
opened fire in Weston's direction. The gunshots echoed through
the cavernous marble halls, and seasoned Capitol regulars as well
as tourists screamed in panic. One or more of the shots may have
hit Weston; another struck twenty-four-year-old Angela Dickerson, who was visiting the Capitol that day with relatives. The bul-

let fragment creased her face, just missing her right eye; another bullet pierced her shoulder, exiting the other side.

Ronald Beamish, a seventy-year-old British tourist, was the first to reach the fallen Officer Chestnut. Mr. Beamish's family members took cover in a restroom while he tried to assist the fallen officer. Beamish never saw the gunman.

Another woman tried to flee the crossfire by running into a small side corridor a few feet from the metal detector. She passed by an alcove with an elevator and a stairwell leading to the crypt, the basement area below the Capitol Rotunda, and pushed through a door marked PRIVATE. DO NOT ENTER. Weston followed close behind her.

The door was the back entrance to the suite of offices occupied by House Majority Whip Tom DeLay and his staff. Just inside was Special Agent John Gibson, a member of DeLay's plainclothes security detail. When Gibson heard the gunfire out in the hallway, he jumped to his feet and shouted for everyone in the room to take cover. "Get down! Get down!" he yelled. Several staffers ducked under desks; others ran into an inner office area that housed the offices of DeLay and several staff members.

The rear door to the office suite opened, and the frightened female tourist tumbled into the room. Right behind her barged Weston.

With lightning reflexes, Agent Gibson pushed the woman out of the way. Weston was firing already as Gibson pointed his nine-millimeter pistol at the intruder. Weston's bullet blasted into Gibson's chest, dropping him to the floor, but not before the officer had squeezed off several rounds, hitting Weston in the chest, thigh, shoulder, and abdomen. The rampaging Weston fell in a heap, up against the back wall as his blood quickly soaked the carpet where he fell.

I knew none of this, of course, as I bounded through the Documents Door. The scene inside was horrific. Seeing the first man lying on the floor in a pool of blood, I recognized immediately that his condition was critical. The head wound was massive. I turned him on his back and did a ten-second exam; I began re-suscitation efforts immediately.

Amidst the sounds of multiple sirens and the roaring noise of a helicopter overhead, an emergency team arrived, and we lifted the fallen officer onto a stretcher. A member of the Capitol Physicians team inserted a breathing tube to keep his airway open. "You've got to get air into the lungs," I called to the medic above the din of the sirens and an approaching "lifeflight" helicopter. "I can barely feel his pulse. About thirty and thready. Let's compress his chest and get an IV in to get his pressure up." We hurriedly carried the stretcher out the door and then rolled it across the hot pavement to the waiting ambulance. I held the man's wrist the whole way, monitoring his still weak pulse, knowing that his only chance would be to keep his heart and lungs going until we could get him to the emergency room for a full assessment of his likely fatal head injury. I climbed into the back of the ambulance, continuing my resuscitative efforts. He was unresponsive, but his heart rate had stabilized, his blood pressure was slowly coming up, and we had control of his airway. Another doctor showed up, introduced himself as an emergency physician who had just started working with the District, and offered to travel with the injured patient to the hospital. Someone rushed up to the ambulance and through the back door of the ambulance called to me, "Dr. Frist, can you come back inside the Capitol immediately? We have other victims still inside who need help!" I jumped out the back of the ambulance and paused for a brief moment. *How surreal*, I thought, as I looked up at the massive dome of the Capitol, silhouetted by a bright blue sky, with the American flag waving so proudly. *How could this human tragedy be unfolding here, now?*

Satisfied that the first patient was stabilized and in excellent hands, I sent them off to the hospital and ran back inside. As I was re-entering the hallway, I saw another emergency team carrying a second gravely wounded man from the Capitol to a helicopter with rotor whirling thirty yards from the building in the east parking lot, waiting to transport the man to a hospital.

I'd walked peacefully through that parking area a thousand times on the way to voting.

An officer led me to the DeLay office suite, where I discovered yet another man lying sprawled near the back entry door. The man on the floor had been shot several times by the looks of it. The walls and floor all around him were spattered with blood, and he had severe injuries to his extremities and chest. I immediately dropped to my knees to begin resuscitation in an attempt to save the man's life. I focused on his airways, making sure the man could breathe, stabilizing him until the paramedics arrived. We lifted him to the stretcher; by then my white shirt was covered with blood. Unlike the other two patients, he was still spontaneously moving and would wince when we moved him. Having taken care of scores of people with injuries like this in trauma rooms, I knew that if we could stop the bleeding, control his airway, and keep him out of shock, we could keep him alive. We got him into the back of the ambulance, and with sirens wailing we headed to the district's General Hospital.

Since I had been so involved in the emergency response from a medical standpoint, it was still unclear to me what had actually happened. The only thing I knew was that there were three people seriously injured, all with gunshot wounds. As we made the bumpy ride in the back of the ambulance, I asked the paramedic riding in the back with me if he had heard what happened. He looked up and said he didn't know the details, but from what he understood, nodding down toward the man whose femoral artery I was at that moment compressing to stop the bleeding, this individual was the shooter, the man who had perpetrated the deadly acts inside the Capitol.

Back in our offices in Dirksen, rumors ran rampant. By now nearly everyone knew there had been a shooting—the sound of sirens below and helicopters above attested to the seriousness of the situation—but no one knew how many shooters might be on the loose. There was a real scare that armed gunmen might be running through the tunnels of the Capitol complex. Ramona and other staff locked the office doors to the outside hallways.

When we arrived at D.C. General Hospital, I systematically reviewed with the doctors in charge the history, physical findings, and current status of the patient. The emergency room doctors and nurses took over. My job as doctor was complete. I waited until they no longer needed any information from me, spoke briefly with the police, and then called Ramona to have Gus come pick me up at the hospital. Gus was new to Washington and another staffer, Meredith Medley, rode with him to give directions.

As I got into the car, the press waiting outside the hospital rushed forward and asked for details of the events over the past hour. I politely said "No comment" and that the police and hospital would be issuing statements. On the way to the airport, Meredith noticed blood on my white shirt and was full of questions, wanting to know all the specifics of what had happened. Many of those details were too graphic to share, and even attempting to describe clinically what had transpired was difficult, especially since I had no idea what was behind the shooting.

At Reagan Airport, we met Karyn and the boys, who had been following the live news as it unfolded; they had spotted me in the background in the news coverage carrying one of the patients out to the ambulance and got a glimpse of me moments before at the hospital as we were departing. They were, of course, accustomed to my responding daily to trauma in my "real life" at Vanderbilt Hospital before the Senate, but even they were a little taken aback by my being in the middle of all this at the nation's Capitol. We hopped into the small plane and took off for the tranquility of a brief family getaway to Nantucket.

I leaned back and reflected on the nightmarish scenes I had just witnessed. Already our office was being bombarded with interview requests from major media. I had told Gus and Meredith to refuse all interviews for the next several days out of respect for the families.

Sadly, Officer Jacob Chestnut never regained consciousness and was pronounced dead at George Washington University Hospital. Officer John Gibson died during emergency surgery at

Washington Hospital Center later that afternoon. They had sacrificed their lives in the line of duty of service to others, dying to protect my congressional colleagues and their staff, as well as innocent bystanders. Flowers and wreaths began showing up at the Capitol almost immediately, sent by a shocked public as well as congressmen, staff members, Capitol employees, and fellow law enforcement families. Both Jacob Chestnut and John Gibson were popular men in the Capitol; both left behind wives and children. The officers received the high tribute of lying in honor in the Capitol Rotunda as hundreds of mourners passed by to pay their respects. I sat alone in the back of the Rotunda during the service to honor these men and their families, reflecting on these men's sacrifice for our country. Afterward I introduced myself to their children and told them how much I respected their dads. I told them their dads had hearts to serve, and that our country is a better place because of their service. That brief conversation inspired me to contribute for the next five years to a fund established to support their education and well-being.

Early in the week after returning to Washington, as the most controlled and efficient way to respond to all the media requests, I held a short press briefing on the east lawn of the Capitol in an area designated as "the press swamp." I believed it important to clarify what had happened in a way that would be sensitive to the families involved. Afterward, as I was walking underneath the huge maple tree back to Dirksen, a young Capitol police officer approached me, carrying a baby girl, his daughter. He thanked me for trying to help his friends, the fallen officers inside the Capitol, and we talked briefly about his daughter. "She is so lovely. How old is your daughter?" I asked.

"Six months," he said proudly.

I nodded. "I once did a heart transplant on a little girl who was only six months old," I said. "You are a very lucky man to have a beautiful baby girl in good health. Thank you for your service and sacrifice of being away from her so much to keep all of us safe and secure." The officer nodded appreciatively. Somehow, in the midst of all the Capitol chaos, everything reminded me of medicine and healing.

In an unusual twist, Russell Weston recovered but was deemed incompetent to stand trial due to mental illness. No plausible motive explained Weston's deranged attack, other than his mental instability. He was not part of a terrorist group, or even on the Secret Service's "watch list."

The vivid memories of the event and questions about whether Weston was a product of a health system that underinvested in treating mental illness and failed to ensure access for the disadvantaged surfaced regularly over the ensuing years as I worked with my colleagues Pete Domenici, to ensure better access for those with mental illness; Ted Kennedy, as we addressed health-care disparities that lead to unpardonable gaps in health-care delivery; and House Speaker Denny Hastert, as we worked to get affordable and necessary prescription drugs to millions of seniors in need. Such efforts don't solve all problems for the Russell Westons of the world, but they do make all of our lives more promising.

Weston was remanded to the psychiatric center at Butner Federal Correctional Facility for treatment. He was a diagnosed paranoid schizophrenic who apparently had stopped taking his medicine before the murders, and his case took another bizarre turn when a judge ruled that he could be forced to take his medicine, especially if it allowed him to be mentally competent enough to stand trial. In 2004, the court determined that Weston was still not competent to be tried, despite treatment. The judge suspended but did not dismiss the criminal charges against him. Russell Weston has yet to stand trial for shooting to death two noble and courageous law officers.

Some people saw my actions that fateful day as ironic—the man who gunned down two Capitol police officers was himself saved by a U.S. Senator. A few, to my surprise, were even critical of my actions. Of course, I merely did what any doctor would have done. Let judges be judges; but let doctors be doctors. Our focus is to treat and heal, regardless of the circumstances. And that's as it should be.

ALTHOUGH I STARTED MY POLITICAL CAREER AS A NOVICE, I FOUND myself quickly climbing the political ladder and becoming better known to the American people through a series of events that were, for the most part, not of my making. For example, in 1997 and 1998, I worked with several fellow legislators and outstanding health-care experts to more fully understand the federal Medicare health program for seniors: its strengths, its shortcomings, and options for its reform. Many of the people I worked with through this process were influential players in federal health-care policy, and while the Clinton administration veered away from the more consumer-directed and patient-centered types of ideas we explored, these people and their progressive ideas would resurface a few years later in future health-care battles.

On January 27, 2000, Senate Majority Leader Trent Lott asked me to present the Republican response to President Clinton's 2000 State of the Union Address, along with Senator Susan Collins of Maine. Susan spoke about education and the economy; my job was to talk about health care, and in particular, to rebut the Clinton plan that at the time was strongly proposing much more government control of health care through thousands of new mandates and weighty new bureaucracies. The State of the Union responses by the party not in power are notable mostly for the criticisms the speakers receive from commentators afterward. Relatively few people want to watch a response by two Congress people taped hours before in a sterile office setting after an hour-long, choreographed speech by the president of the United States presented in the majestic House Chamber live before an adoring, enthusiastic audience of seven hundred cheering political figures. But I had fun putting my thoughts together, working with Susan, and going through the process.

In Washington, success in the Senate meant not just success in policy. You also needed to be successful in politics.

In the spring of 2000, I became cochairman of the Republican National Convention platform committee, a group of about 110 Republican activists from around the country charged with developing the official platform for the 2000 presidential campaign, describing our positions on the major issues of the day. Paul Coverdell, the junior senator from Georgia, had become Trent's right-hand man in day-to-day Senate floor operations. He had also become the formal liaison between the Senate Republicans and the presidential campaign of Texas governor George W. Bush. Early on, the Bush people, all from Texas, weren't comfortable with many of the Washington regulars. Surprising to most, in those days very few people in the Senate (or in all of Washington for that matter) had had much contact with Governor Bush. He had not been involved in affairs at a national level. Paul, not officially in elected Senate leadership, had become acquainted with the young George Bush years earlier when Paul had worked for President George H. W. Bush at an event at the Bush compound in Kennebunkport. When the campaign said they needed a point person in the Senate, Governor Bush said to go with Coverdell. In that capacity Paul each week in his office would pull together senators to meet with representatives of the campaign, making sure each senator had the opportunity to access them. Paul was the ultimate team player and was trusted by all. Paul tapped me to be his assistant in his capacity as Senate liaison for the Bush campaign.

My selection to be platform cochair created a stir. The typical pattern over the years had been for the Senate Republican Policy Committee Chairman to fill this slot. But serving in that capacity at the time was Idaho senator Larry Craig, a well-liked senator viewed by many as rigidly conservative and seemingly dominated by the National Rifle Association, imagery the Bush folks were anxious to avoid in those early days. That I was selected effectively broke protocol.

But then in mid-July, we were still on the Senate floor late one night when Paul mentioned to some of his staff that he had a splitting headache. Nobody thought much of it, since it had been a long, tension-filled day on the floor. Paul's doctor resided in Atlanta and he would see him the next day. The following day Paul flew home, where shortly after arrival he suffered a massive cerebral hemorrhage, a type of bleeding brain aneurysm that threw him into a coma.

He had been in the cath lab for diagnostic studies for several hours and was about to go into a second procedure when the family called me in Nashville for advice. Hours later I flew down to Georgia. I went straight to the hospital and was met by the hospital administrator, who walked me through a side door to avoid the press parked outside the front. After meeting with the family the neurologist took me down the hall to review the angiographic studies and the CT scans. The X-rays told the story: Paul had suffered irreversible brain injury from an abnormality that there was no way to prevent. Modern medicine had nothing more to offer.

Lloyd Ogilvie, the Senate Chaplain and a close friend to Paul, arrived later that morning to be with the family. Lloyd played a powerful role in the spiritual and personal lives of so many in the Senate family. Later that night I returned to Washington knowing, as did Paul's family, what the inevitable outcome would be. Paul clung to life for another two days, dying Tuesday evening, July 18, 2000. Word of his death came to many of my colleagues early the next morning as they were arriving for the weekly Senate prayer breakfast in the Capitol, which Paul had so loyally attended in his years in the Senate. The hour was spent memorializing the truly great man and friend to all, the individual who worked tirelessly behind the scenes to make sure that the legislative trains ran on time; the chair he had occupied in that small room on the ground floor of the Capitol for the past eight years of weekly fellowship gatherings would remain empty.

When I received the news of his death on Tuesday night, I was on my way to the Washington Metropolitan Club for an organizational meeting of the Republican platform subcommittee chairs. As I stood in front of the fireplace in the dark paneled room on the second floor, I announced that Paul Coverdell had died the hour before. The audience, who knew of his commitment to the principles of the party and the platform being put together, was in shock. I remember explaining that his death reminded me of a transplant, the loss felt in one family and the hope felt by another, and that Coverdell's vision and commitment to freedom and truth would be incorporated in the platform document, like a beating heart.

The fundamental challenge in working as a platform chairman was to give the delegates confidence that they owned the platform content and were controlling it, yet ensure that the candidate's voice was given great weight. The most important element of the platform was to make sure no bad stories flowed out of the process, since the committee proceedings peaked just days before the kickoff of the convention. That was a first, second, and third objective. Bush advisor Karl Rove and campaign policy director Josh Bolten basically told platform executive director Mitch Bainwol, an experienced and highly respected political operative, that his job working with the platform cochairs was to make sure everything stayed under control, out of the media limelight, and in the background. In some ways, putting together the party's platform can be an exercise in containment. For example, in San Diego, at the 1996 Republican National Convention, the prolife plank had become a sore spot with many people and created division among our own members that the media tried to use, with some success, to further divide us. We were intent on preventing a repeat performance.

Under Mitch's astute leadership, one of the most critical things we did in managing the platform process was to call every one of the delegates just after their appointments simply to listen to their ideas, to hear them out, and to pick their brains. Mitch assigned a third of the delegates to each of the cochairs. I took careful notes of each conversation. Through strategic exercises like this, day after day, Mitch and I really got to know and respect each other. We shared a focus on demanding an incredibly granular sense of the schedule, the strategy, the process, and the personalities.

Josh helped formulate the ideology expressed in the document, and Larry Lindsey and Condi Rice had great influence, as well. Karl crafted the political strategy. When there was a debate that we could not settle, we took it to Josh, who in his even-handed, steady, smart way brought closure. What could have been a divisive process began to flow seamlessly. The usual high-priority conservative issues drove the platform: prolife measures, tax cuts, and national security. Thanks to much work with committed platform delegates representing all points of view on the life issue, there wasn't much controversy there. The party stood strong for life while encouraging Republicans who might not share that view to be part of our governing majority, too.

For me, the biggest challenge set out by Governor Bush and Josh was to take the issue of K-12 education, one that had traditionally been way down on the Republican priority list, and elevate it to the very top of the platform, making it the number-one issue on the Republican agenda. Governor Bush had extensive experience with education in Texas, where his reforms were working well in reducing the so-called achievement gap between students from rich and poor communities. It was an issue he was passionate about, and very comfortable with. My initial reaction was that it couldn't be done. Republicans don't believe education is a federal issue, considering it a matter for local control. But through his emissary Bolten, candidate Bush sent the message, "Just get it done." And we did.

We finished our work on the platform two days before the convention. I made sure we dedicated the Republican platform document that year to recently deceased Paul Coverdell—an unprecedented move that met with unanimous support.

The August convention came off without a hitch, and of course, George W. Bush was elected president in November. At the same time, I had been running for re-election back home and won decisively. Democratic nominee Al Gore had lost his home state of Tennessee; if he had won at home, he would have been president of the United States. And in a small way, the Frist campaign played a role. The Bush and Gore teams had monitored how much each was spending on airtime in the media in Tennessee. Both reasoned that staying about even would allow their candidate to win. It was Gore's home state—surely he would win. But the Gore campaign overlooked the fact that the concurrent Frist Senate campaign, even without a viable opponent, had raised several million dollars to spend on TV with a message exactly paralleling the one that Bush was using. Thus, though monitors were reporting equal media spending by the Bush and Gore campaigns, the Bush message was being heavily and daily reinforced in the minds of Tennesseans to the tune of an extra $3 million of impact. Of course, our campaign is not why Bush won Tennessee (and thus the presidency), but the massive message support our under-the-radar Senate campaign purposely and strategically provided didn't hurt either.

So now I had stepped into raw politics at the national level. I'd come to Washington solely to be a policy maker, but now through a series of events beginning with the untimely death of a colleague, I began to see how political elections—not just my own—could affect the direction of the country.

Before the November elections, I'd begun to consider running for the chairmanship of the National Republican Senatorial Committee (NRSC), the campaign arm of the party whose responsibility is to recruit top-quality Senate candidates, convince them to run, and help raise funds to finance their successful campaigns. Of all the positions in Senate leadership, the chair of the NRSC is the one most like an executive position. You have a clearly defined job to do—to win elections. You have total control over the money you raised for all of the candidates, deciding who gets it and who doesn't. You develop the overall strategy and you hire the best campaign people to fulfill your vision and plan. And, more so than in any other Senate leadership position, you are measured in wins and losses. That's accountability.

My chief rival for the post was Senator Spence Abraham, the former head of the Michigan Republican Party and a keen political operative who knew well how to run campaigns. He was also a great colleague, and a close friend, a fellow member of the Senate class of 1994. My work with the platform committee and my own re-election effort had highlighted some issues I thought could be good for Senate Republican candidates around the country. For example, I saw what we'd been able to accomplish in elevating a nontraditional Republican issue like education to the forefront of the Republican national agenda. We needed that sort of change and fresh approach. What about another nontraditional issue—health care?

I went by to talk to our majority leader at the time, Trent Lott, as did Spence, and he encouraged us both to run.

I met with Mitch Bainwol, with whom I had developed a close working relationship on the platform committee. Mitch loved politics and had demonstrated over the years, initially working with Florida senator Connie Mack, strong political and management acumen. I called Mitch and asked if we could discuss the NRSC. To get away from the phone and other distractions, we left my office, walked across Constitution Avenue, and began strolling the large circular driveway on the east side of the Capitol, lined with dark green park benches and a variety of trees planted by members of Congress in honor of their states. (Karyn, the boys, and I had ceremoniously planted a Tennessee tulip poplar there in 1996.) It was a glorious, sunny fall day.

Lap one. Mitch laid out the strategy. "It can't be done in two years. It will take four years to win back the Senate, so just accept the fact that this cycle we will not win but we will smartly build for the next. Thus, you will have to serve as NRSC chair for two two-year cycles."

Mitch explained to me his reasoning. This was all before the election, and we had the majority going in. Winning seats two years later would be virtually impossible if we kept the majority in November, and thus we should frame the assignment as a four-year project to condition public expectations. He explained that if for some reason Republicans were no longer in control after the elections, we would have a much better shot in picking up seats.

Lap two. "You can do this. People will doubt it initially—you are not seen as a political animal—but they doubted you in your first Senate race. I saw how you worked the platform committee. It is a winning style . . . I know." As we were walking, Pennsylvania senator Rick Santorum, our Republican Conference chairman, was passing in the other direction. He glanced at the Congressional Directory in Mitch's hand, a good hint at what we were discussing. He walked by us, smiled, and simply said, "I know what you guys are doing." He did. He understood the game.

Lap three—and by this time I was no longer noticing the people eating their late, brown-bagged lunches on the benches, or kids stopping to be photographed with the majestic Capitol in the background. "I will leave my job and support you if you do it," Mitch said.

That evening I went home and discussed with Karyn whether to run for NRSC chair. I told her it would be the only job in leadership that I would want—it would be like setting up a transplant center from scratch. All would be under my control, so I couldn't be whipsawed by having to please my colleagues or be tempted to bend to the whims of the media. Karyn saw my enthusiasm, but she tempered her encouragement with the thought that I would have to be gone on most weekends recruiting candidates, raising money, and then campaigning state by state. But, knowing that in the long run the real appeal to me was bringing future outstanding leaders into the fold, she said, "You should do it."

While I was honing my ideas and my plans to present to my colleagues in anticipation of what was likely to be an interesting leadership contest between Spence and me, circumstances changed. That November, Spence lost his bid to return to the Senate, and I would become chairman of the Senatorial Committee almost by default, another unexpected turn in my career. No one else was about to run and lead the NRSC when, as Mitch had spelled out so clearly as we walked the circle, Republicans by all accounts were going to get killed in the next cycle—the first midterm election of a Republican president.

Once again, I was reaching out of my comfort zone, a doctor running the major campaign committee for the highest legislative body in the land. It was exhilarating to be entering the national political stage on behalf of my party. But politics-as-usual was about to be interrupted by history in a more shocking fashion than anyone could have anticipated. The world was forever transformed.

10

A Frightening New World

For me, as for most Americans, September 11, 2001, began as a beautiful early fall morning. My staff and I had just completed our ritual "Tennessee Tuesday," a weekly breakfast meeting held on the top floor of the Hart Senate Office Building looking out over the dome of the Capitol for me to personally welcome and interact with all the many constituents from Tennessee who visited Washington each week. I'd left the meeting a bit early to go to Senator Kay Bailey Hutchison's office to lead a 9:00 A.M. discussion on tax policy with a small roundtable group of twelve or so businesspeople she had pulled together.

Shortly after nine o'clock, one of Kay's staff pulled her aside and said a small plane had gotten off course and crashed into the World Trade Center. A few minutes later, word came it was an airliner. As a pilot I knew that airliners didn't get off track. And a minute later, as a TV was being hauled into the room so we could keep up with what was happening, another airliner penetrated the other tower. It was clear we were under attack.

I left and rushed back to my office to talk to our staff and make contingency plans for the day. I tried to call Karyn but there was no answer either at home or on her cell phone. All this was shocking enough, but then before long, we could see ominous, long thick plumes of black smoke rising in the west from the Pentagon just across the Potomac River. This was a large-scale, multiple-target attack. And one of the targets clearly was right where we were sitting. What would be next? Were Karyn and the boys safe? How would we respond? That was up to our federal government . . . but I was the federal government, and at that moment I knew my colleagues and I didn't have a clue what was going on.

Nine days later, with our country still reeling in shock and disbelief, I felt it important to approach President Bush about another area of our national vulnerability and to recommend steps to help prepare for an ominous potential threat—the use of biological weapons by terrorists to harm us. Bioterrorism was not a new issue for me; indeed, because of my scientific background and my transplant experience with infectious diseases, I well understood the horrendous potential of an attack in which lethal bacteria, viruses, or toxins could be released into the air, food, or water supply we all use daily. As far back as 1997, as chairman of the Subcommittee on Public Health, I had called for and then chaired a series of formal hearings and briefings on bioterrorism, including our committee's public health preparedness in the face of an attack or a natural outbreak of an infectious disease.

In a hearing in March 1999, I again expressed my concern, stating bluntly my belief that "as a nation, we are currently more vulnerable to bioweapons than any other traditional means of warfare." And then again in July 2000, in a speech before the Centers for Disease Control and Prevention's International Conference on Emerging Infectious Diseases, I asked, "Is the threat of bioterrorism real? Most experts agree that it is no longer a question of 'if' but 'when.' Today most Americans are aware of the threat of natural infection, especially from new strains of influenza (avian and swine), but remain skeptical of biowarfare. And therein lies the danger. This trusting facet of our nature opens us up to terrorist attack." Little did I know then how prescient these words would be, especially to my audience in Washington.

In biowarfare or bioterrorism, the enemy and its weapons remain invisible, while evidence of their attack may not surface for days after they have left the scene. The effects, however, can be devastating. Ounce for ounce, biological agents such as anthrax or smallpox are among the most lethal weapons of mass destruction known. Inhalation of a millionth of a gram of anthrax may be deadly. Scientists have estimated that as little as 220 pounds of anthrax spores released over Washington, D.C., under the right atmospheric conditions could cause three million deaths—and nobody would know we had been attacked until people started getting sick. For the terrorist, whose goal is to terrify and paralyze, anthrax would be an ideal agent.

Well before the September 11 attacks, Senator Ted Kennedy and I had spearheaded a bipartisan bill providing for emergency preparedness in the face of a bioattack. Kennedy's longstanding commitment on health issues had introduced him to the dangers of emerging resistance of microorganisms to antibiotics and the potential use of infectious organisms as weapons of terrorism and mass destruction. The bill called for preventive measures, as well as upgraded early warning systems at the Centers for Disease Control and Prevention (CDC), improved hospital response capabilities, training, staffing, vaccines, antibiotics, and care for victims of bioterrorism. While that was a good start, in many ways we were still doing too little, too late—a fact that began to become clear in October 2001, when the first reports surfaced of unexplained cases of anthrax appearing in the United States.

Amidst a growing climate of national fear post-9/11, on October 15 I called together a statewide roundtable discussion on bioterrorism at the Tennessee Emergency Management Agency (TEMA) headquarters in Nashville. By then, a Florida man named Robert Stevens had already died of inhalational anthrax, although authorities had initially blamed his illness on natural causes.

Seated at a conference table in Nashville, I listened to one person after another confess how woefully unprepared the various responders might be in the face of a bioterrorism attack. Worse yet, I knew Tennessee was not alone in this regard. Few states, if any, were prepared for bioterrorism threats; most knew the threat existed, but had done little to nothing to prevent it, or to prepare for a worst-case scenario.

Immediately following my meeting at TEMA, I walked into the hallway to respond to reporters' questions on the meeting and what we discussed.

"Dr. Frist," said the first reporter, "what can you tell us about the news this morning that a letter containing anthrax has been delivered to the office of Majority Leader Tom Daschle, an attack aimed specifically at the highest-ranking member of the Senate?" My staff had not had time to brief me on the headline news breaking while we had been in our meeting.

As a doctor I have learned to control my emotions, but the news that a potential act of bioterrorism could hit so close to home—some of my own Public Health Subcommittee staff members were right down the hall from Daschle's suite—stunned me. I replied to the reporter that I had not been briefed on the events, and I tried to minimize the concern. I recalled receiving an anthrax hoax letter three years earlier in my Nashville office. Fortunately, it was much ado about nothing, but we had put in place at our office safer protocols for handling the mail as a result. I hoped this was just a hoax as well.

I went on to my next stop in Nashville, a speech about bioterrorism, this time to the Nashville Rotary Club meeting at a downtown hotel. By the time I arrived, I had been notified that a large amount of a powdery white substance had been found in a letter received and opened by a member of Daschle's staff. The hand-printed envelope, made to look as though sent by a child, had a return address reading, "Fourth Grade, Greendale School, Franklin Park, NJ." Already, health officials in Washington were urging people who might have been exposed to undergo nasal swab testing. A three-day supply of antibiotics had been distributed by the Capitol physician's office to people in the Daschle suite known to have been exposed to the substance in the envelope.

Anthrax is an infectious disease caused by a spore-forming bacterium called *Bacillus anthracis*. It cannot be passed from one person to another, but individuals can come in contact with it in three ways: through the skin, by breathing it into the body, or by eating tainted food. Anthrax can switch back and forth between two states: the active "vegetative" form and a dormant "spore" form. When the bacterium senses a lack of nutrients or water, it has the strange ability to encase itself in a thick, hard shell—a spore—that protects it. These spores can survive in the soil for decades, which explains why anthrax often strikes grass-eating animals such as cattle, sheep, goats, and horses.

The form of anthrax that concerns us most is called *inhalation anthrax*, in which the spores are actually inhaled into the lungs. This is the form that is most likely to be used in biological warfare, and it is by far the most deadly. Inhaling a quantity of spores the size of a tiny speck of dust (possibly less than ten thousand spores) can be fatal.

The initial stage of inhalation anthrax makes a person feel as though he or she has the flu. Indeed, that is one reason the disease can be so deadly; it seems relatively innocuous at first. Within a few days, the anthrax releases a deadly toxin that enters the bloodstream, causing severe shock and often death if left untreated.

If given early after exposure to inhalation anthrax, antibiotics such as ciprofloxacin (Cipro) and doxycycline are usually quite successful in combating the disease. Nasal swab tests can be done relatively quickly and easily to determine whether a person has been exposed to inhalation anthrax. But to do all this, our public health agencies needed to be educated, trained, and prepared. In 2001, our nation's ability to deal with a large-scale bioterrorism attack was woefully inadequate, as we were about to find out.

That afternoon, my communications director, Nick Smith, and I headed straight back to Washington, wondering what we might find upon our return. I knew that we needed to act quickly before panic gripped the nation; the priority had to be disseminating accurate, understandable information, as well as treating those who had been exposed to the anthrax. Much to my surprise, I found the Hart Building—the site of the attack—had remained wide open, with people still working at their desks, even in areas that might have been affected by the anthrax. Fortunately, the ventilation system had been shut down within an hour of the incident to help prevent the tiny particles of anthrax from spreading still further.

Trent Lott and Tom Daschle, the Senate leaders, contacted me and asked me to be the liaison for the senators, who were already being deluged with questions from their staff regarding anthrax, and the medical, law enforcement, and bioterrorism investigation just underway at the Hart Building. I told them that I would help any way I could. The questions from the Senate offices ran the gamut:

"How do I know if I have been exposed?"

"Are my children at risk?"

"Am I going to die?"

"Am I contagious?"

We did our best to answer the questions, advising those who thought they might have been exposed to the anthrax to take the Cipro the Capitol physician's office was offering.

It was late Monday afternoon when investigators finally closed off a section of the Hart Building where the anthrax had been found. By that time, nasal swab testing confirmed that at least twenty-eight people had been directly exposed to the anthrax in or near the Daschle suite. Suddenly, the anxiety level on Capitol Hill soared. People were afraid; they wanted answers from their leaders, and they weren't getting them.

My first move was to get trustworthy information out quickly. That afternoon I posted scientifically accurate anthrax information on my personal official Senate website to educate people on the Hill, including the senators' office staff members, many of whom by then feared for their lives, not knowing whether they had been exposed to the anthrax, or whether the spores in Hart would infect their spouses and children when they went home that night.

On Tuesday morning, Senate staff members who worked on the fifth and sixth floors of Hart were surprised to discover a police barricade barring entrance to their workplaces. Instead, they were instructed to obtain a nasal swab. Hundreds of people lined up in the Hart Building to be tested. Others came from all over Capitol Hill to be tested as well, some out of confusion, many out of fear, including many who had been nowhere near the Hart Building on Monday. The lack of information about anthrax, coupled with rumors running rampant, fed the aura of fear and caused many people to be on the verge of panic—exactly what a terrorist would want to happen.

As the only scientist and doctor in the Senate, I knew the most important thing I personally could do was communicate calmly and accurately to the American people, since the most powerful antidote to panic is reliable, honest, straightforward information. Nick had arranged interviews with major media outlets in Washington, so we started early on Tuesday morning with the *Today Show.* I then conducted a press conference and from there, we went floor-hopping at 400 North Capitol, where many of the networks have facilities to do interviews. I did eight back-to-back television interviews in the same building. Later, I appeared on CNN's *Larry King Live.* At 9:30 P.M., we were still doing radio interviews. I shared with the American people the facts; what I could not do was predict the future.

A command center had been set up in the Secretary of the Senate's office on the third floor of the Capitol. My staff and I worked closely with the new command center as well as the Capitol Physician John Eisold, who demonstrated steady, capable leadership throughout, and other agencies, continually posting updated information on my Senate website. Because of my work on the Public Health Threats legislation in 2000, we already had a section on our website devoted to bioterrorism, biological agents, and public safety. It was a good thing, since the CDC website soon crashed due to the enormous number of requests from all around the country. Our site became a reliable source of information for the country.

On Wednesday, the Hart Building was closed completely, and the testing site was moved to the Russell Senate Office Building. The Senate and House leadership met that morning, and when word was received that even more locations had tested positive for anthrax, the government leaders decided to close their respective office buildings. But when the leaders presented the decision to the full Senate, many senators balked, suggesting that closure of the buildings could be interpreted as a sign that we were giving in to terrorists if we disrupted the country's business because of the attack. Many, if not most, on Capitol Hill, believed the anthrax was the second round of terrorist attacks coming on the heels of 9/11.

The Senate opened for business as usual again on Thursday, and following the official presentations of the facts, I briefly addressed those senators gathered in the Senate dining room on the first floor of the Capitol, offering information and my views on the best way to proceed from a medical standpoint. My comments seemed to reassure many of my colleagues, and I stuck around afterward to more fully answer the questions of particularly anxious or inquisitive members. We decided to close the three Senate office buildings but to continue the normal course of Senate business in the Capitol. The nation's business would continue. The House closed its offices and formally adjourned, creating a bit of an awkward situation in terms of public perception, since the Senate remained in session. (House leadership publicly blamed the Senate leadership for misrepresenting their intentions to stay open.)

When test results confirmed that anthrax contamination had then been detected in the Dirksen Senate Office Building's mailroom, as well as other places in Hart, the decision was made to close all congressional buildings until further tests could be run. This created even more fear and anxiety among the thousands of Capitol Hill workers. Had hundreds of people been infected with the deadly agent?

Along with other members of the command center response team, I participated in two press conferences, six hours apart, in an attempt to answer the many questions in the public's mind, as well as to provide updates. By Friday, it seemed that the anthrax outbreak had been contained. Thousands of people had now been tested. Although several people were extremely sick, as yet nobody had died as a result of the attack. They were being treated, and everything finally seemed under control.

But that was about to change. On Saturday morning, I attended a meeting in the Secretary's office in the Capitol, at which it was reported that an individual who worked and lived several miles away from Capitol Hill had been admitted to a community hospital with acute shortness of breath and flu-like symptoms similar to what one would see with anthrax. But his test results would not be back for another twenty-four hours. Our military labs were shouldering the bulk of the highly specialized anthrax testing being requested. But what caught my ear was the fact that the patient was a postal worker.

I was alarmed.

The importance of this seemingly innocuous bit of information could not be overstated: A person who had not been anywhere near the Hart Building on Monday now had signs of anthrax! It would have been impossible for someone miles away from the location where the letter was actually opened to have inhaled spores from the anthrax-laced envelope. I feared that the news could portend a much larger scenario. *Was this an expansion of terrorist activity? Were there other deadly letters going around the country? Would we now start seeing cases around elsewhere? Were postal workers safe, or would we now have to shut down the mail system in Washington, perhaps even nationally?*

While the questions continued to fly, I got up and went across the room to a telephone and called the White House. I asked to speak to President Bush's recently appointed Homeland Security advisor, former governor Tom Ridge of Pennsylvania. Ridge called back immediately.

"Tom, I've just learned something that you need to know," I said directly. "We may have a potentially national public health emergency on our hands. Something we've never seen. The anthrax we are dealing with here on Capitol Hill may be tied to people all around the country. I am worried we are not prepared. We need a lot more resources on this."

Ridge, sensing my alarm, asked for my suggestions. I asked for a little time to get more information. We agreed to have a conference call in one hour, with the nation's top officials in charge of emergency preparedness and key members of our team at the command center in the Capitol. By the end of our call, the leaders understood the seriousness of the situation. The unspoken question in all of our minds was, *How much of this stuff is out there?*

On Sunday morning, we received word that the patient's test results were in—he had inhalational anthrax. My worst fears had been realized. Immediately the public health command began testing postal employees. But even as the testing began, the first postal worker, fifty-five-year-old Thomas Morris Jr., had died. A short while later, a second postal worker, forty-seven-year-old Joseph Curseen Jr., passed away as a result of anthrax inhalation. We were in big trouble.

We realized then that our understanding of how anthrax could be spread was antiquated. All our assumptions were based on how the anthrax acted in rural, pre-modern settings before centralized air-conditioning and before massive air blowers were used to sort mail. Most of our information on anthrax pertained to how it behaved naturally in rural settings, not how it could be "weaponized" through special engineering to remain in the air for prolonged periods of time, and used by terrorists or others intending to kill people with it. We were working with an inadequate body of knowledge.

Homeland Security took over the dispensing of information to the American public regarding the anthrax alarm, although I continued to answer questions in interviews on national television newscasts. Repeatedly, I emphasized that anthrax was infectious but not contagious (that is, transmissive from person to person), but fear could be paralyzing, debilitating, and dangerous. I did my best to discuss the situation just as I would any medical crisis, as a physician, a counselor, and a reassuring voice to those in need, even though this health issue involved the entire nation. My website received more than forty thousand hits per day during the crisis, as people sought out accurate, reliable information. Over the next three months, I wrote an entire book (*When Every Moment Counts: What You Need to Know about Bioterrorism from the Senate's Only Doctor*) to educate our citizenry regarding the dangers, prevention, and response to biological attacks. Knowledge is power when it comes to fighting terrorism.

I had run for the Senate to help affect a larger group of people than I could in a single hospital, and now here I was dispensing medical information to the nation. In this one event was the convergence of science, security, medicine, policy, diagnosis and treatment, psychological reassurance, and communication. I would never have dreamed that my medical training would be put to use in such a way.

As we dealt with the ramifications of the anthrax-laced letter, those of us interacting with the command center became increasingly concerned about how vulnerable our nation was to such attacks. Think of it: One letter had essentially shut down the legislative branch of our U.S. government and threatened to shut down Washington. Indeed, the Hart Building would remain closed for three months, ousting from their offices for the duration over half the U.S. senators. During that time, another anthrax-laced letter, addressed to Senator Patrick Leahy, chairman of the Judiciary Committee, was intercepted and opened safely by well-protected hazardous-materials personnel inside a laboratory. The handwritten letter matched the one sent to Daschle's office. *Was this a terrorist, or a disgruntled former employee, or someone related to the perpetrators of 9/11? Would we ever find out?*

Postal facilities began passing all mail through radiation machines, since the gamma rays could kill the anthrax. Nearly ten thousand people in the Washington area received Cipro during those first days following the receipt of the anthrax letters. The federal government negotiated with Bayer, the company that produces Cipro, to purchase the antibiotic for less than a dollar per dose, a quarter of the usual price. But the fact that we did not have a ready supply pointed up another area of concern.

As the nation moved into the Thanksgiving and Christmas seasons, fortunately, there were no further confirmed incidents of anthrax or any other biological agents launched against us. Tragically, five people died up and down the East Coast as a result of the 2001 anthrax attack; seventeen others were sickened. It appeared that postal workers were now on the front line of the first "new" war of the twenty-first century.

When the government went back to work, Senator Kennedy and I redoubled our commitment to pass preparedness legislation to better thwart bioterrorism. This time around it no longer took a lot of effort to convince Congress of the need. Meanwhile, the FBI interviewed more than five thousand people in an effort to track down the perpetrators of the attack, but nobody was ever brought to trial. The case has never been solved. In mid-2008, the Justice Department paid Steven Hatfill, a scientist at the Army's biological warfare labs at Fort Detrick, Maryland, $5.8 million in damages for having wrongly accused him of wrongdoing. And in August 2008, Bruce E. Ivins, a brilliant but troubled Army biodefense researcher, who was being aggressively pursued by the FBI as the primary suspect, committed suicide.

It took nearly three years, but in 2004, when I was majority leader, we finally enacted the most comprehensive reform of our intelligence community since 1947. This legislation broke down the barriers to information sharing between the U.S. intelligence agencies and created a National Counter Terrorism Center to coordinate our efforts. We also established a provision for a National Counter Proliferation Center to stop weapons of mass destruction from being made and delivered.

The anthrax scare on the heels of 9/11 was a wake-up call for many in the medical community, as well as Congress. We realized how grossly unprepared our nation's hospitals, clinics, and producers of vaccines and antibiotics were for a major threat of deadly anthrax or other chemical and biological agents. Since then, our government has moved from a precarious position to being more appropriately prepared. But we have a long way to go, and we dare not let down our guard for a moment. We as a nation respond to crisis with determination and courage, but we must also be smart and plan so as to prevent and preempt.

MEANWHILE, DESPITE THE MOOD OF NATIONAL CRISIS CREATED by the 9/11 attacks and anthrax, politics never completely disappeared. And as the 2002 elections neared, my role in running the NRSC campaign committee of the Senate loomed as a major challenge.

The hand we were dealt put us at a huge disadvantage. Twenty Republican Senate seats were up for grabs, but only fourteen Democratic seats. Moreover, as 2001 had unfolded, the mood of the country had turned disconsolate. Our economy had spiraled downward after the 9/11 attacks. Corporate scandals riddled the news, producing even more suspicion on the part of the public. While the awful terrorist attacks provided a brief burst of genuine congressional unity, soon Congress was back to its bickering ways, the Democrats quarreling with the Republican president on seemingly petty issues rather than addressing the economic unease people felt, as war in Afghanistan unfolded and America struggled to recover. Many of my colleagues were concerned that these congressional fissures would reflect badly on Republicans.

Given that the first midterm elections are notoriously bad for the party of a sitting president, no one gave us much chance to gain ground. The American people historically seemed to like balancing the power equation by electing a majority of Congress from the party opposite that of the president. Consequently, as we approached the midterm election, the sense of unease among Republicans was palpable.

Nevertheless, the NRSC executive team we put together over the month after my election operated seamlessly. There was the former Marine, no-holds-barred campaign operative Chris LaCivita; my long-term close friend and finance director from Nashville Linus Catignani; the sophisticated and gracious fundraiser and friend to senators, Ed Rahal; the experienced media director Ginny Wolfe; and the disciplined and detailed legal counselor Alex Vogel. And there was the mastermind of it all, Mitch Bainwol. Mitch had run several statewide campaigns, run the Republican National Committee, managed the platform committee, and been in two different leadership staff director roles. His political experience balanced my policy experience.

We had our humorous moments as well. Alex recalls his first meeting with Linus, our lead fundraiser, who had come with me from Nashville. Alex cautioned him about receiving shady money. "For any new donors over twenty-five thousand dollars, we need to vet them in advance. We just can't have Russian mobsters giving us fifty-thousand-dollar checks," Linus nodded.

Two days later, Alex received an e-mail from Linus: "Exactly what does *vet* in Washington entail?"

Alex, realizing we had a long way to go, recalls thinking, *We're in serious trouble!* Two years later, Linus had raised more money for the NRSC than anyone in its history.

Service in the Senate is serving your constituents. Service as chairman of the NRSC is serving your team of Senate colleagues. The distinction is subtle but important. Effective leaders must clearly identify who they are leading and serving.

Our team faced three main challenges: finding the right candidates to run, formulating a unified message, and then, of course, finding the money. What appealed to me about the NRSC was that it had to be run with an executive style. In many ways running the NRSC was a lot like starting up a business, managing it aggressively for a year or two, and then closing it down. With the NRSC, however, you only find out whether your product is a success in stark win-loss columns after all the work is over—on election day.

My number-one priority was not fundraising—that would come. It was recruiting top candidates to run. It takes a great horse to win a competitive race. So that's where I put in my time and focus. I thought a lot about Dad's old saying, "Good people beget good people." We were recruiting people to serve their country, and I began with the same values Dad wrote about in his letter to future generations: "integrity and high moral standards."

As an unlikely candidate not so long before, I could use my own campaign story to refute just about every preconceived notion I would hear from a potential candidate about the difficulties of a political novice's taking on an incumbent. "If I could do it," I'd say, "so can you." We actively sought candidates to run in Missouri, Tennessee, North Carolina, Georgia, and Minnesota, mostly through face-to-face meetings. Mitch systematically planned out the recruitment process and we began very early, in January and February, almost two years in advance of the election, conducting polls and testing people's names long before they were aware of our interest. Week after week I'd take off to encourage, cajole, and confide. I flew up to Nantucket to meet with Congressman Saxby Chambliss of Georgia and his wife, Julianne, while they vacationed. I did a poll showing Lamar Alexander that Tennessee wanted him to return to public service, that the Senate needed his experience and statesmanship. I met with St. Paul (Minn.) mayor Norm Coleman late one night under a lamppost in D.C. to persuade him that living in Washington could be positive for a family. And I shared with John Cornyn on a drop-in visit to his attorney general office in Austin that the Senate campaign committee would give him full financial support if he ran.

In other cases, we faced the diplomatic challenge of convincing a would-be candidate that he or she was *not* the best choice. There is a lot of ego in politics. For instance, in New Hampshire, we had a sitting senator who we knew could not win the upcoming election. My colleague and friend, Bob Smith, had served in the Senate since 1990; then in January 1999, he launched a whimsical campaign for president. When it appeared certain that George W. Bush would be the nominee, Bob announced that he was leaving the Republican Party to run for president on the Taxpayer's Party ticket. Finally, after dropping out of the race and supporting George Bush, Smith recanted his repudiation of the Republican Party, saying that he'd never really changed his voter's registration. He still had two years to go on his Senate term, but the damage had been done. It wasn't that Bob Smith was not a good man, but he had diminished the respect the people of New Hampshire had for him and it had become impossible for him to win re-election.

To replace Smith, our NRSC team quietly leaned toward John Sununu, a thoughtful young congressman whose father had served as White House chief of staff under President George H. W. Bush. John wanted to do it, but taking on an incumbent senator from the same party is a big hill to climb. John hedged and hesitated until Mitch Bainwol finally forced the issue. "Look me in the eye," Mitch said, "and tell me you're going to run, because if you're not, don't kill us." If the NRSC had supported Sununu and he later pulled out, our credibility would have been severely damaged. Sununu ran and won, serving the people of New Hampshire with distinction for the next six years. Bob Smith stepped aside and eventually moved to Sarasota, Florida, to sell real estate. (In 2004, he flirted with another run for the Senate and endorsed Democrat John Kerry for president.)

As for our message, we chose an edgy tone for our television commercials, emphasizing homeland security and spelling out the defining contrasts between our candidates and the opposition. To get the top quality in message delivery, we interviewed twenty advertising production teams before awarding contracts to five to produce our ads. And their services didn't come cheap: During just the final week of the campaign we spent more than a million dollars per campaign in more than seven states.

Money, of course, is an essential ingredient in contemporary politics. Our new fundraising strategy for the NRSC was based on the ancient adage, "Go where the money is." We aggressively pursued donors in places considered Democratic strongholds, most prominently New York City. I started spending part of every other week on the ground there planting the seeds. And New York was responsive. Under the leadership of Linus, who worked closely with the gracious and experienced Linda Pell, and with the help of the majority of my Senate colleagues, we raised more than $120 million for our candidates over the two-year cycle, substantially more than any previous NRSC, and a record that still stands today. This cycle was the last in which nonfederal or so-called "soft money" could be raised and spent. The magnitude of these resources meant the committee was more heavily involved in advertising compared to more recent times. Indeed we spent more than $50 million on advocacy through the five media teams and spent more than candidates did on their own races in some circumstances.

Throughout the process, Mitch and I had a biweekly breakfast with White House strategist Karl Rove and worked seamlessly with the president's campaign team. We sought to do things differently than had been done before. For instance, we boldly ran television ads featuring President Bush in at least five states where conventional wisdom said that incumbent Democrats were safe, but where we felt our candidates could wage successful challenges. The ads worked, and indeed we won two seats in those Democratic stronghold states.

Despite all this groundwork, most political pundits still gave us little chance of winning as the election drew near. But three significant issues showed the Democratic Party in a negative light and helped us enormously.

First, there was the response to the tragic events of 9/11. In many ways, our nation was still reeling, searching for a renewed sense of security after the massive, brutal act of radical Islamic terrorism on our homeland. Democrats had balked over plans to create a Department of Homeland Security because of concerns over labor union prerogatives, which made their party look weak on national security in the minds of many voters. Americans trust Republicans when it comes to security.

A second negative grew out of another horrible tragedy. One senator that I and many Republicans admired deeply was Minnesota Democrat Paul Wellstone, who argued passionately and with conviction for the interests of the common man.

While Paul was running for re-election, Republican Norm Coleman was running a politically smart race against him and had actually inched ahead. Then, just eleven days before the election, while flying to a campaign event, Paul, his wife and daughter, two pilots, and two campaign staff members died in a plane crash.

The nationally broadcast memorial service was attended by President Clinton, Senator Hillary Clinton, Al Gore, and many Senate colleagues.

Karyn and I went to Minnesota for the service. It was held in a huge convention hall, filled with people who had poured in to pay their respects and honor the great man and his family. There was a huge screen in the hall that showed individual attendees in the crowd. As some of the Republican Senate leadership entered the arena and their faces were shown on the screen, many in the auditorium vocally expressed disdain. After moving tributes by his family, as Karyn and I sat high in the stands of the large hall, you could almost feel the mood begin to shift. The Wellstone service quickly took on the tone of a spirited political rally rather than a solemn tribute to a fallen public servant, as speakers urged that voters should "win the election for Paul." The widely reported booing of Republicans at an hour of grief put many people back on their heels. It didn't reflect Paul's legacy. But it happened, and this politicization of a tragic accident backfired, evoking a negative response from a large segment of the American public, including many Minnesotans.

A third negative image resulted when House Democrats David Bonior and Jim McDermott visited Iraq in 2002 and from Baghdad appeared live on ABC's *This Week* with a message that seemed approving of Saddam Hussein, overly critical of President Bush ("The president of the United States will lie to the American people to get us into this war.") and hostile toward plans for military enforcement of the U.N. mandates concerning Iraq's possible ownership of weapons of mass destruction. Most Americans were disturbed by this apparent effort to undercut the president at a time of international crisis.

These three negative images contrasted with the NRSC-driven direction of the Republican Senate campaigns to stress a security-focused, patriotic agenda. And when the dust settled after the 2002 election, we had not only won our most hotly contested races, but also gained a net total of two Senate seats, enough for a fifty-one-vote majority that wrested control of the Senate from the Democrats—the first time since 1913, when the popular election of senators was mandated by the Seventeenth Amendment, that the president's party had regained majority control of the Senate in a first midterm election.

Washington has a lot of curious traditions, and one quickly emerged: Since I had participated so vigorously, and successfully, in helping the Republicans reclaim the majority in the Senate, pundits and politicians alike assumed I now had much grander ambitions. A previous majority leader, George Mitchell, had reclaimed the Democratic majority as his party's campaign chief in 1986 and subsequently took the majority leader's job in 1988, so many insiders concluded that might happen on our side as well.

Almost immediately my staff was besieged by individuals wanting to know if that was my plan. I had no desire to be majority leader. Over the years I'd actually told Karyn night after night, as we went to bed and watched the majority leader closing down the Senate for the day on C-SPAN, "That has got to be the worst job in the Senate." My plans then were exactly the same as when I announced to run for the Senate in 1994: to serve two terms and then return home to Nashville. So when I turned down another stint as chairman of the NRSC and emphatically stated in an interview before Thanksgiving that I planned to devote my remaining four years in the Senate not to leadership positions but rather legislative issues like Medicare and health care, the soothsayers just jumped to another scenario: They started predicting that my ambitions must be much bigger, that I was planning a presidential bid in 2008. They just couldn't accept the fact that my mission was not to remain inside the Beltway for the rest of my life, but to make a difference for Tennessee and the country simply as one of fifty-one Republican senators for twelve years.

Those were my plans—but life, as we all know, has a way of making plans of its own.

11

Unexpected Storm

Cynics will forever be convinced that I became majority leader of the Senate through collusion with President Bush and his advisors. It wasn't that way, and for those who are fascinated by the "inside baseball" of Capitol Hill, the story reveals the inner workings of our upper legislative body.

The Senate is a different kind of place. The Founders designed it to be one step removed from the passions of the American people, with each senator serving a relatively long term of six years. It determines its own rules of governance every two years and in fact is run by precedent and tradition more than by rigid rules. The very nature of the Senate caucus is to resist outside influences and forces, even those that might come from the White House. And for leadership selection within the body, the complicated personalities, fierce loyalties, and the deferential respect for the institution and its traditions play a much larger role than outsiders might imagine.

I've always had respect for Trent Lott, and still do. Trent had been good to me since my arrival in Washington. He'd honored many of my committee assignment requests, encouraged my run for the chairmanship of the National Republican Senatorial Committee in 2000, and cheered me on in my public appearances (as I'm sure he did for all our Republican colleagues). If I appeared on one of the Sunday morning television shows, Trent usually called afterward. "Great job," he'd tell me, or offer some friendly word of advice about how I could perform better next time.

Trent was also good at giving responsibility to people on our team, putting them in the game, and then letting them play. For example, when the anthrax scare struck in 2001, Trent called me in to handle the issue—with colleagues, the administration, health professionals, and the public. Similarly, in 1998, Trent chose me to serve on the bipartisan Medicare Commission to make recommendations to President Clinton on reform of our health-care system for seniors. The move made sense, since I was the only physician in the Senate. Nevertheless, the option was Tom Daschle's and Trent's, and he invited me to the party, an assignment that I appreciated.

So by the time my tenure as NRSC chair ended, although Trent and I were not close friends, I felt that we had a strong working relationship. I was looking forward to being a part of our Senate Republican team, now back in the majority, ready to tackle some pretty big issues—especially health care.

But then a storm hit.

December 5, 2002, was a snowy Washington evening and the weather made the pre-Christmas mood even more festive as guests crowded into a banquet room in the Dirksen Building to celebrate Strom Thurmond's one hundredth birthday as the South Carolina senator prepared to retire after forty-eight years of service.

The atmosphere that evening was relaxed. The hard-fought midterm elections were over, Congress had recessed until January, and with the incoming Republican majority, Trent was set to reclaim his position as majority leader, a role initially bestowed upon him when then–majority leader Bob Dole left the Senate to run for president in 1996.

The Thurmond birthday event was attended by a wide variety of friends, political colleagues, and prominent members of the news media. It was a celebration and a tribute to a man whose life bridged two centuries, and even those in the room who hadn't been Strom's strongest supporters left their differences at the door.

Bob Dole led off the evening with stories and quips about Strom, cracking up the crowd with his droll, sardonic humor, and ending on a strong note of respectful tribute. Trent followed. He began by speaking kindly of Strom's longevity, but then it seemed he attempted to outdo Dole, even repeating a joke that Bob had just delivered. Abandoning notes prepared by his press aide (as he later acknowledged), Trent began talking off the cuff. Speaking of his home state, Mississippi, Trent said, "When Strom Thurmond ran for president, we voted for him. We're proud of it. And if the rest of the country had followed our lead, we wouldn't have had all these problems over all these years, either."

Trent later said repeatedly that he was merely trying to compliment Senator Thurmond. In truth, the off-the-cuff remark was scarcely noticed by most people in the crowd that night, and it was largely ignored by the mainstream media.

The first small gust blew the next evening. PBS's program *Washington Week* centered on topics such as President Bush's economic team, the Supreme Court's stand on affirmative action, and concerns over the impending war with Iraq. But at the close of the program, moderator Gwen Ifill introduced a brief segment about Strom Thurmond:

As we go tonight, we take note of the 100th birthday of the nation's longest-serving senator, Strom Thurmond. Senator Thurmond has served South Carolina as its Republican senator since 1954. In 1948, he was also the presidential candidate of the segregationist Dixiecrat Party. That career detail brings us to tonight's little history quiz, something we call "What Was He Thinking?" The "he" in this case, Senate Republican leader Trent Lott of Mississippi. He had this to say about his home state at yesterday's Capitol Hill birthday celebration.[1]

PBS then ran a videotaped excerpt of Trent's remark at the party the previous evening. In her parting words, Ifill said, "Drop us an e-mail. Tell us what you think Senator Lott meant."

With that, the trouble began. Internet users responded not simply to PBS, but in various forums throughout the Web. Suddenly the public connected Trent's statement to the fact that one of the primary issues on which Strom Thurmond had run for president in 1948 had been the perpetuation of racial segregation—a position he later renounced. When the *Washington Post* followed up by publishing Trent's comments, a maelstrom of negative publicity struck Lott, with some denouncing his comment as racist.

As the storm gathered intensity and speed, Trent attempted to explain his statement in the national media; over the next several days, he apologized at least four times publicly, but his efforts were mostly futile. Some felt Trent was getting a bum rap, that he was merely attempting an innocent compliment to an old friend. Others, however, thought that Trent's comment dragged out attitudes toward race that should have remained buried.

The controversy was exactly what the Republicans didn't need. President Bush and other party leaders had been working hard to dispel the myth that the Democratic Party was the logical home for minorities, emphasizing that the Republican Party had been a true party of inclusion since the days of Abraham Lincoln. Lott's comment offended not only African Americans, a large percentage of whom were Democrats, but many white Republicans as well.

At first, it seemed that the flap over Trent's statement would melt away with the Washington snows, and had it not taken place during a slow news cycle, it might have. But as sometimes happens in politics, the story developed a life of its own. Trent had gone home to Mississippi, then to southern Florida for a vacation, and was essentially out of contact. As the storm gathered fury, telephone lines burned with members calling back and forth, expressing their concern that the leader's ability to drive the Republican agenda might have been seriously weakened by the incident. Several senators suggested a private, closed-door conference to discuss the issue. While we had just elected Trent as our majority leader right before Thanksgiving, our rules provided that a minimum of five members could request such a conference, calling a special meeting of all fifty-one senators.

It soon became clear that five requests could be gathered within minutes. The question was: To what purpose? If we got everybody together, what would we do?

As the storm clouds darkened, I talked with Trent several times. In response to a reporter's question, I said simply, "The statement was unfortunate, and it was off the cuff and casual. I know Trent Lott, and he's not a racist. It is important that people understand the Republican Party leads on issues of equity and fairness and nondiscrimination. Any implication otherwise would be a disappointment to me."[2] Karyn and I discussed whether we should go down to Florida to demonstrate our support for Trent, but decided against it, thinking it would draw too much media attention. Many of my fellow senators joined in supporting Trent, and most felt he would weather the storm.

Many in Washington assumed that the senator who would most likely replace Trent, should he resign or be removed, was Don Nickles, the well-liked and highly respected senior senator from Oklahoma and second-highest-ranking Republican. Strongly conservative—some said even more so than Trent—Don had genuine aspirations to lead the caucus. He'd been in the Senate since 1981 and had served as assistant leader since 1996. It was no secret that he and Trent didn't always see eye to eye. As the Lott story unfolded, it was easy to imagine Don thinking that his time to step up had finally come. But Don had privately indicated to close associates as early as October 2002 that he planned to leave the Senate at the end of his term. Before the 2002 elections, he had publicly stated that he would not run for majority leader, but would instead serve as chairman of the Senate Budget Committee.

The week after the Thurmond party, Don called me and we talked frankly about his chance of becoming majority leader. "It's not in the cards. I don't have the votes," he said matter-of-factly, "but I am going to write a statement, and I'm thinking of going on one of the Sunday morning shows to express my concerns and that I think Trent should step down."

Then, to my surprise, Don dropped a real bomb. "*You* should be the majority leader," Don said. "You have the support, you don't have any negatives, and you have the positives. You are the kind of image we need right now."

Don's statement was a powerful one, especially coming from someone who had been around the Capitol longer than almost anyone else on our team and was highly respected by his colleagues.

When I hung up the phone, my mind was racing. Don's suggestion was so radical it was hard to fathom. I had no designs on the role of majority leader. And even after I'd spent eight years in the U.S. Senate, a number of Republican senators had much more seniority than I. Some, like my good friends Thad Cochran of Mississippi and Mitch McConnell of Kentucky, had served more than twice as long as I had.

A few days later, when Don and I met face-to-face, Don encouraged me again. "The fact is nobody else has the votes but you. Hang in there, and you will be the majority leader."

I appreciated Don's comments, but I was not at all sure I *wanted* to be majority leader. I had come to Washington to be a policy maker. I stepped into the political realm by leading the Senate campaign committee, but I was ready to end my time in D.C. after a final four years devoted to substantive legislation— that's why I had not run for the leadership position of the NRSC chair again. I knew the gamesmanship that went with the majority leader's position, and dealing with the powerful personalities usually detracted from being a successful legislator. There were just too many people to try to keep happy. Without Don's encouragement, I probably would not have even considered tossing my hat in the ring.

The mood in the capital changed drastically on Thursday, December 12, when President Bush referred to Trent during a

speech in Philadelphia at the White House Conference on Faith-
Based and Community Initiatives. In the audience were Cardi-
nal Anthony Bevilacqua, Reverend Franklin Graham, and other
leaders of organizations providing hope and assistance to people
of every race—"the armies of compassion," as the president referred to them.

The president began his remarks talking about the challenge of
defending our freedoms from terrorism. He then moved quickly
to the Lott affair. "We must also rise to a second challenge facing
our country," said President Bush. "This great and prosperous
land must become a single nation of justice and opportunity. We
must continue our advance toward full equality for every citizen,
which demands the guarantee of civil rights for all." The audience applauded enthusiastically, and then the president honed
in on the issue. "Any suggestion that the segregated past was acceptable or positive is offensive, and it is wrong."[3]

Although the president did not call for Trent to step aside, his
remarks were pointed. "Recent comments by Senator Lott do not
reflect the spirit of our country," the president said. "He has apologized and rightly so. Every day that our nation was segregated
was a day our nation was unfaithful to our founding ideals."[4]

The president's words were greeted with resounding applause
by the audience, and a rush of nervous responses by conservative leaders. Leadership in Washington is often about signals, and
to many, the unequivocal message President Bush was sending
could hardly be missed: "Trent is on his own." But I still wasn't
sure whether the president was merely trying to disassociate the
party from any hint of racism, or had intentionally cut the props
out from under Trent.

The opposition had already latched on to the racial issue,
with everyone from Senate Democratic Leader Tom Daschle and
House Democratic Leader Nancy Pelosi to Senator Hillary Clinton
offering blistering remarks. Members of the Congressional Black
Caucus released a statement calling for a "formal censure of Senator Lott's remarks," as did former Vice President Al Gore. African-
American activist Jesse Jackson was not satisfied with censure,

instead calling for Trent's resignation, as did Democratic senators John Kerry and Russ Feingold.

As I went home that afternoon, I knew I could no longer keep my thoughts to myself. After prayerful reflection, I decided that I needed more minds on this problem than just my own. Karyn and I discussed this constantly. She said simply, "Follow your heart," reminding me of all the late-night conversations in which I'd said that serving as majority leader was not a job I would like.

That same night I had the first of many late-night conference calls with Mitch, Alex, and Ginny Wolfe—all of whom had just spent two exhilarating years with me at the NRSC—and my trusted advisor Emily Reynolds, who had helped shape my political plans since 1994. We initially broached the *possibility* of my becoming majority leader, discussing how it might work, what it would cost me in terms of legislation I hoped to pass regarding Medicare, and how it might affect Karyn and the boys. The more we considered these questions, the more drawbacks our group identified.

Mark Tipps, my former chief of staff, and Gus Puryear, who had served as my legislative director and counsel, came in from Nashville and brought along a stack of files that had been used in the extensive vetting process for President George W. Bush's vice presidential selection committee. I had been under consideration as a possible vice presidential candidate, so the Bush team wanted to meticulously sift through my background to see if there were any skeletons in the closet. Mark still had all the information they had returned to us, so he brought all the boxes to Ginny and Alex and said, "They're going to vet him in ways they never have before, so here are all the files. You better start going through them."

All the while, Trent and his staff were assuring people that he would be returning as majority leader.

Senate Republicans got together on a Friday night conference call organized by Senator Rick Santorum on behalf of the Senate leadership team, hoping to bring the issue to a quick resolution. Unfortunately, the call was inconclusive; some proposed a plan that would keep Trent out of the public eye for several months as the new Congress convened, hoping the storm would eventually blow over, while others feared this would lead to a never-ending siege.

Don Nickles was the first Republican senator to post a less-than-supportive statement on his website late Saturday night, stating what many of his colleagues were thinking: "I am concerned that Senator Lott has been weakened to the point that may jeopardize his ability to enact our agenda and speak to all Americans."

Without naming anyone specifically, Don added, "There are several outstanding senators who are more capable of effective leadership, and I hope we have an opportunity to choose." He reiterated that statement on national television on Sunday, December 15, 2002.

People who didn't know the complete inside story, including Trent, assumed that Nickles was attempting to enhance his own position. But Don had already indicated his personal plans to leave the Senate and had reiterated them to his colleagues. Besides, in my estimation, the most-likely person to replace Trent as majority leader was not Don, but Kentucky senator Mitch McConnell, the incoming Republican whip. Mitch maintained his support for Trent, telling ABC's *This Week*, "I think he's going to continue to lead us, and I think he can be very effective as our leader in the Senate." To *Fox News Sunday*, Mitch was even more emphatic. "Senator Lott was elected to a two-year term, and he's said he's not going to resign, and in my view he shouldn't. We need to stay together and pursue the president's agenda."

Another possible contender also on the leadership team, Pennsylvania senator Rick Santorum, was publicly supportive on *Meet the Press*, emphatically stressing to interviewer Tim Russert, "I know Trent Lott. This is a man of tremendous integrity, [with] a deep faith, someone who believes all men are created equal, not just under the Constitution but more importantly in the eyes of our Creator, and his faith has grown in that commitment." Yet

Rick, sensing what just might happen, began counting his own votes among his closest supporters in the Senate.

Nevertheless, once Nickles opened the possibility of considering senators other than Lott for leader, other senators began to speak openly about the matter as well. Senator John Warner of Virginia, a longtime friend of Trent's, suggested that Senate Republicans should gather together face-to-face to decide what to do. Nebraska senator Chuck Hagel echoed John's sentiments. Both Mitch and Rick, however, remained supportive of Trent, and at least publicly played down the need for a conference, as did Lindsey Graham, the former House member who had just won the South Carolina Senate seat vacated by Strom.

Lindsey remained strongly supportive of Trent and confidently assured his new Senate colleagues that things were not nearly as bad as they seemed. But his certainty was disturbing to many. They explained the sensitive issue was not simply whether Trent would be able to negotiate the negative media blitz and survive as majority leader, but whether the now almost universal interpretation of Lott's comments, however unfair, would paint all Republican senators as racist for the next two years, stymieing any attempts we might make to move the country forward, and especially affecting the discussion of future Supreme Court justice nominations we were anticipating.

I knew from my discussions with other senators that they felt Lindsey's assessment was short-sighted. Things had not been getting better. I spoke in addition to every one of the other new senators just elected, and without exception they felt there was no way this issue was going to disappear. I told Lindsey, "We have to deal with this one way or another. We either have to come out together with an endorsement of Lott, or we need to have new leadership." The newly elected senators—all of whom confided in me because of our relationship through the campaign committee—were disturbed that one of the first things they'd have to fight for was to prove that they were not racists.

From my perspective, the evening Senate Republican conference calls led by Santorum as chairman of the Senate Republican

Conference were pivotal. Most of us hung up the phones feeling that this issue was not going to simply disappear, that sooner or later, we were going to have to deal with it definitively. Trent, of course, was not on those calls.

Meanwhile, on Monday, December 16, Trent appeared on Black Entertainment Television and touted his role as a strong advocate of affirmative-action programs.

On Tuesday evening, Virginia senator George Allen telephoned Trent and told him, in essence, that he should step aside for the good of the team. Trent did not respond positively to such advice. His spokesman, Ron Bonjean, said, "Mr. Lott will be the majority leader in the next Congress." Hinting that there could be reprisals for senators who abandoned ship, the official line coming from the Lott camp continued, "Mr. Lott hopes to persuade some senators he will be a force in the next Congress and will remember with disfavor those who have broken with him."

The Bush administration was under pressure to react to the situation. Wary of giving the impression that the president was attempting to control the Senate, White House Chief of Staff Andy Card gathered the White House staff and told them "not to play." Secretary of State Colin Powell condemned Lott's comment, and the president's brother, Florida governor Jeb Bush, suggested, "Something's going to have to change. This can't be the topic of conversation over the next weekend." White House press secretary Ari Fleischer denied White House involvement in leaks concerning Trent's status, repeatedly offering the same tepid line: "The president doesn't think Trent Lott needs to resign." Ari stuck to his story even though the president offered not a single public word of support for Trent.

People close to Trent later claimed reporters from the nation's largest papers had revealed that Joe Allbaugh, the president's former campaign manager (then at the Federal Emergency Management Agency) and a close advisor in the White House had leaked statements that the president wanted Trent to step down. The White House adamantly disavowed any knowledge of such shenanigans.

Regardless, toward the end of the week, as it became increasingly clear to everyone but Trent that his future as leader was in doubt, I received a phone call from Mitch McConnell about a possible future leader. "Nickles says that he doesn't have the votes," Mitch said. "Santorum says he doesn't have the votes. Most likely, you and I are the only two possibilities for the position. If there is an election between you and me, I don't know how it is going to turn out. I may or may not have the votes. You may win. And I may certainly win. But we should work together."

I wasn't surprised at Mitch's straightforward approach, because I knew how focused he was, how determined he was to move up to the leader's position after Trent. "My goal as a legislator is to someday be the majority leader," Mitch admitted. "I've been here all these years, and the highest position I can attain is leader. Everything I have done in my political career has been moving in that direction. From serving my two stints as chairman of the NRSC, to moving my way up to majority whip, leader is the next step, and that's what I want to someday do." We continued our confidential conversations and made no public statements.

About that same time, Rick Santorum called and told me that he was thinking hard about running for the leader's position. A number of our fellow senators had suggested that he run, since he was reputed to have the strongest conservative voting record. But as we were talking, Ginny pulled out a voting scorecard analyzing every vote since 1994. To my surprise, it clearly showed that I actually voted more conservatively than Rick.

"Wait a minute, Rick," I interrupted him. "According to the rankings I'm looking at, you are the fourteenth-most-conservative senator, and I am number eight."

Rick chuckled, but my comment sent a message to him that I was doing my homework in a tough situation, and that I hadn't ruled anything in or out just yet.

Eventually, it was clear that more and more senators believed a change of leader was the best way to clear the stormy skies. By Thursday evening, even Trent's closest allies let it be known that his support was no longer strong enough to stave off a change.

On Friday morning, little more than two weeks after the fateful celebration in the Dirksen Building, Trent talked to Mitch and to Rick, informing them that he planned to make a statement. Trent's staunchest supporters understood what that meant. When Rick and Mitch talked, McConnell said, "Well, I'm on the Bill Frist team now, and you need to be on the Frist team, too."

But Rick was still running a leader's race, although it would last only about six hours. During that time, Rick and his staff made one last check to see if he might have the votes; they determined that he did not. Rick threw his support in my direction. It was now up to me.

SERVICE IS ALWAYS A COMMITMENT, BUT SOMETIMES CAN BE A calling. I had a lot to think about. After a busy two years at the campaign committee, I was looking forward to Christmas with Karyn and the boys and visiting with my brothers' and sisters' families. Karyn, of course, reminded me of my habitual remark that majority leader must be "the worst job in the Senate." But it was, after all, another opportunity to serve, albeit certainly not in a way I had ever anticipated. The realm of service would expand, no longer to a patient, or to a state, but now more to a country.

Some political crystal ball gazers had begun tossing my name around as a future presidential candidate, but I had not made any overtures in that direction. People, however, were quick to share with me that serving as majority leader would likely be the death knell for any future political aspirations. In modern times, it was considered next to impossible to be elected as president after having led the Senate. Too many compromises had to be made, and too much water had to be carried for the administration. As leader, one becomes the target for the opposition party and the media always hungry for a negative story. I realized from the outset that if I consented to toss my hat in the majority leader's race, doing so would likely cap my national political career. But then again, I had come to Washington to serve as a citizen legislator—and that meant returning to Nashville to the life of a citizen after serving in the Senate.

Helping our Republican conference escape the terrible storm in which we seemed perilously stuck was my immediate goal. Members from throughout the conference—senior, junior, older, and younger—were encouraging me to step forward to run for leader, to help heal the harm our party was suffering.

"Do you think I should call Trent and talk to him?" I asked John Warner, who'd been hovering over the situation and offering me advice in a kindly, almost fatherly fashion since the storm had erupted.

"No, no. I'll handle that," John assured me. "It's too tender."

Trent later implied that I had been disloyal to him—that I should have called him and given him a heads-up. Moreover, he asserted that had I not let it be known that I would accept the job, he might have been able to recapture his position as leader. That is doubtful, although I understand how it might have seemed that way from where Trent was sitting in Mississippi and in Florida. I imagine he truly believed the crisis was dying down, and that by making myself available, I threw gasoline on the smoldering embers of a bonfire. But in reality, the controversy had not died down. It had escalated. Nevertheless, I was very careful to do nothing to undermine Lott in any way, and in fact, had to be persuaded to even allow my name to be considered.

On the eighteenth the calls to my office began to pick up. Norm Coleman and Jim Talent each called with the same message: you have a responsibility to the caucus to make yourself available to lead the Senate. I finally relented on December 19. I issued a public statement: "If a majority of Republicans believe a change in leadership would benefit . . . the United States Senate, I will likely step forward for that role."

When Senator John Warner took that statement public, he removed the "likely." With my permission, he first presented the statement in the Russell Senate Office Building Rotunda, and then clarified it in an interview with Margaret Warner of PBS.

"Yesterday afternoon I was in the office with Bill Frist," he told her. "I had visited with him very quietly throughout the week. I was sort of his blackboard. He would scratch notes and chalk and erase it, and we'd think things through. But once we learned that Senator Nickles was going to withdraw . . . we felt that the caucus, the Republican Conference, as we call it, was entitled to choice, and so Bill made the decision to step up and indicate that he would run. We struck the word 'likely' from the release at the end, but somehow it got out in the beginning. There is no *likely*. He went in it with full force, and did it in a very respectful way."[5]

Exacerbating matters further was the delicate balance of power in the U.S. Senate. Should Trent resign as leader, and then choose not to return to the Senate at all, Ronnie Musgrove, the Democratic governor of Mississippi, would appoint a replacement, presumably a Democrat. That would send us right back to a tied Senate. Still chafing from Vermont senator Jim Jeffords's defection in 2001, many Republican senators were worried about the risk of another colleague's deciding that he no longer wanted to remain part of the team because of the Lott situation.

Furthermore, we'd already experienced a substantial obstruction from Senate Democrats, using their majority status to stop the Bush agenda in its tracks. Since Republicans now had gotten back the majority, we all hoped things would work better, but we needed to be able to count on every one of our members. We could not allow the Lott debacle to divide us. For the long-term benefit of the country, we relished the possibility of replacing one, two, or possibly three Supreme Court justices before President Bush left office. With all that at stake, Trent's return to the Senate was vital, but nobody knew for sure just how Trent would react.

LATE IN THE MORNING OF DECEMBER 20, 2002, TRENT LOTT announced that he would step aside, "in the interest of pursuing the best possible agenda for the future of our country." For all the pain that it had cost him personally, I believed Trent wanted what was best for all of us, because he also announced that he *would* return to the Senate, making sure that our majority agenda had a full chance to succeed. "To all those who offered me their friendship, support, and prayers, I will be eternally grateful," Trent said.

Almost immediately, John Warner went public with his support of me, as did George Allen. Before midday, a large majority of other senators followed suit, including Don Nickles, Mitch McConnell, Rick Santorum, Chuck Hagel, Lamar Alexander, and Kit Bond.

It fell to Rick, as conference chairman, to set up an election. How to do so was the question, given that most senators had vacated Washington until after the first of the year. Nobody wanted to keep Trent and the entire situation dangling in front of the media wolves for another three weeks. After thinking it over, Rick proposed a novel idea: conducting the election by conference call. This had never been done before, but there were no rules against the procedure. Rick set up the conference call for Monday afternoon, December 23, and the plan was in place. The storm was about to pass.

The night before the vote, Karyn and I were not in Washington, but in Nashville, attending a service at Two Rivers Baptist Church. As we had done before my two previous elections, we wanted to pray together, asking for God's direction and wisdom. Near the close of the service, the pastor noticed Karyn and me in the audience and explained to those in attendance the new role I would likely be assuming within a matter of hours. He invited us to come to the front of the church so he and other members of the congregation could pray for us. Many people gathered around Karyn and me as the pastor led us in prayer. The preacher prayed that God would grant us strength, courage, and wisdom. I would need them all in the days ahead.

The following afternoon, I had lunch with Karl VanDevender, the doctor who had assumed my father's medical practice years earlier. We talked about how I might be able to help ease the racial tension opened by Trent's comments, and the resultant ill will. A theologian as well as a physician, Karl was more politically liberal than I was, but I respected his opinions and valued his friendship.

Karl put in a call to Bernard LaFayette, a former associate of Dr. Martin Luther King Jr. When Bernard called back, he had arranged a conference call with Coretta Scott King; former Ambassador to the U.N. Andrew Young; and chair of the NAACP Julian Bond. After some initial conversation, I reiterated my question, this time to the group on the phone: "What specifically can I do to help?"

Each person had suggestions, but Bernard summed up the attitude of the group: "Senator, you can listen when we call. We don't necessarily expect you to do everything we ask, but you can listen when we call."

I had been a good listener all my life; that was not going to change now.

On Monday, December 23, 2002, I picked up the phone in my Nashville Senate office on White Bridge Road and dialed the conference call number. Sitting in the room with me were Karyn, Emily Reynolds, Ginny Wolfe, and Bart VerHulst, who directed my field staff in Tennessee and who had loyally been with me since the day we opened our campaign office in 1994. Within moments, I was on the line with all the other Republican senators, one of whom was Trent Lott.

The responsibility of moderating the call fell to Conference Chairman Rick Santorum, who opened the meeting and read the roll call. But John Warner quickly interrupted, suggesting that due to the gravity of the circumstances, we should pray before going any further. With Rick's permission, John read aloud a prayer that his father, a highly acclaimed obstetrician, had often quoted entitled "A Physician's Prayer." The prayer concluded, the meeting continued.

Trent then gave a brief, gracious statement, apologized to his colleagues for what everyone had had to go through, and then concluded with, "And I'll be talking with all of you when I get back to Washington." He then signed off. The rest of the meeting moved fairly quickly, since all of the other contenders for the position of majority leader had pulled themselves out of the race. Rick opened the floor for nominations, my name was put forth, and a yes or no vote was taken. The vote was unanimous.

Suddenly I was occupying one of the most influential offices in the U.S. government. No longer was I serving a single patient as a doctor, or a state as a senator, but now all Americans as a leader of the Senate.

12

Getting It Done

We all have a day in our lives that is burned in our memories and stands out among all others. For me it was a week. New facets I had never really considered accompanied assuming the role of majority leader. One of those was having a constant Capitol Police security detail assigned to me. On Monday afternoon, even before the election call, a couple of Capitol Police officers flew in to Nashville and drove a large, dark sports utility vehicle to our home on Bowling Avenue. After a few quick introductions at the door, they requested a few minutes in private with Karyn and me to explain their responsibilities. "We'll be with you essentially twenty-four hours a day," they told Karyn and me. "We'll try to be as inconspicuous as possible, but we will never be far from you."

"Never?" Karyn asked.

"Never," said Noel Gleason, the highly professional and passionately committed special agent who would lead my security detail over the next four years. "As majority leader in the 9/11 world, you become a target for terrorists and will receive death threats, which we will monitor daily."

I could sense Karyn's unease. As he recalled the anthrax letter sent to former leader Daschle.

"You can't pilot airplanes anymore," one of them told me. "Too dangerous."

"And we know you like to run marathons, so when you run, we will always run with you."

"And these medical mission trips to Sudan and Congo you do every year will have to stop. And no more free medical clinics as a volunteer in Southeast Washington."

"Listen," I said with a smile, "you're in for a treat. Because I'm still going to fly, and I will also be going to Sudan in a few months. But if you want to run with me, I'd love the company!"

The security agents stared back at me soberly. "Yes, sir," one of them said. But they didn't go away . . . and for the next four years, some assortment of dark-suited Capitol Police dignitary protection agents with wires in their ears were never far away from me, seven days a week. And they flew in small planes with me and ran marathons with me—but they didn't go to Sudan (or elsewhere on my medical trips). Over time they would become like members of our family.

Both members of my security detail that first day were from the East, and neither were familiar with our Tennessee hunting culture. They got their first eye-opener of what to expect the next day. As an avid hunter, I love getting out in the woods with my sons Bryan, Jonathan, and Harrison.

While some people might celebrate being elected majority leader by having a big party, I went home and packed up my guns. One of my best friends and the person who opened the world of hunting to me and my boys, Steve Smith, and I had for weeks planned on going hunting the night before Christmas Eve with our sons, so as soon as I finished my inaugural press conference on the day I was elected majority leader, Steve and I headed off with our sons on a nighttime raccoon hunting trip, led by Marty Warren, Steve's expert farm manager and master backwoods hunter. It was a sight to behold. Steve and Marty were leading the way through the woods, with their powerful flashlights piercing the darkness, up and down the rolling hills on Steve's family property—with my two security agents on their first night of duty with me, slipping and sliding in their black leather dress shoes and dark blue suits! Accompanied by the yelping and baying of some of the best walker and bluetick hounds around, we scored a raccoon, which is still mounted in our home to this day—a fond reminder of my first full day in my new role.

Two days after Christmas, Karyn, Jonathan, Bryan, and I were to fly commercially to Fort Lauderdale, Florida, joining some of our extended family members for our annual "minireunion," a tradition begun by my parents years ago. Early that morning, Special Agent Noel Gleason was running on the treadmill at the Marriott Hotel near Vanderbilt. His sole responsibility was my safety. Across the TV ran a scrolling banner: BREAKING NEWS: WILLIAM HARRISON FRIST IN PLANE CRASH. A picture flashed up on the screen of the crashed plane, upside-down. In shock, he fell off the back of the treadmill. The person he was charged to protect had apparently been in a plane crash!

An hour earlier, our nineteen-year-old son, Harrison, had headed out to John C. Tune Airport, a single-runway facility west of Nashville, a few miles from home. Harrison was flying to Florida in a small, single-engine Cessna airplane, along with my brother-in-law Lee Barfield and his son Cole. All three of them were licensed pilots, and Cole and Lee were instrument-rated. We were *all* planning to meet later that night after the boys' adventure of flying the small plane there.

It was densely foggy that early morning as they taxied to the runway, and there were no air traffic control authorities at the small general aviation airport. As the plane reached the north end of the taxiway, it slipped off the pavement, hurtled across the narrow shoulder of the taxiway, and tumbled down a twenty-five-foot embankment, flipping over as it rolled before finally coming to a stop upside-down. The plane was demolished, but Lee, Cole, and Harrison were able to crawl out of the wreckage safely, suffering only minor injuries, a few cuts and scrapes, and a lot of embarrassment.

Television reports ran the story that William Harrison Frist (my son Harrison's complete name) was in a plane crash, so naturally many people thought I had been involved. All three were taken to Centennial Medical Center. Karyn and I rushed there, as did Noel. Lee and Cole were treated and released; Harrison did not even require treatment. Thankful all were safe and sound, we picked right up and all of us flew that night commercially to Florida. Material things come and go, but that Christmas season provided a poignant reminder that we must always be grateful for the gift of life.

And the week wasn't over.

We received another graphic reminder on New Year's Day when the boys and I—and our around-the-clock, two-person Capitol Police security detail—were traveling back toward Fort Lauderdale on "Alligator Alley," the long stretch of Interstate 75 that runs from Naples across Florida to Fort Lauderdale through Big Cypress National Preserve, a protected swampland hedged in by high aquatic weeds on both sides of the road. We'd spent the morning hunting and sightseeing at Billie Swamp Safari in the Everglades. It was a beautiful sunny day, and traffic was racing by on the straight, flat highway. At about four in the afternoon, a short distance in front of our vehicle, the right rear tire of a red Isuzu Rodeo sports utility vehicle blew out, flipping the SUV and ejecting the passengers—a family of five and a friend—who were strewn over distances of nearly 150 feet up the highway.

Traffic came screeching to a halt. As they were trained to do, the officers in the front seats of our vehicle were already devising a way to keep moving to get around the traffic jam. They started to pull our vehicle across the wide median strip, to do whatever was necessary to get us to safety, when I called out from the back passenger's-side seat—my new official position for the next four years assigned by the security detail—"No, wait! There's an accident. We have to stop to help. Call 911 and get as close as you can."

Jumping out of our vehicle and telling the boys to stay put, I ran toward the accident, my two security agents racing right behind me. It was devastating. At least three of the victims were children, their contorted bodies tossed up and down the highway like rag dolls. I ran from child to child, trying to assess who needed the most immediate help. I began the typical resuscitative maneuvers, but had to await the arrival of paramedics and their equipment for intubation and intravenous line placement from the Broward County Fire Rescue squad twenty miles away. Meanwhile, several other people with some degree of medical training had run to the scene from their stopped vehicles and were pitching in to help. Three were firefighters, and at least one, Lara Spalding, was a nurse. Lara, who attended college in Tennessee and had been on staff at Vanderbilt Medical Center, threw herself into helping the injured, working in dress clothes and high heels to save lives along the highway. There were a lot of volunteer heroes in action.

When the first helicopter arrived on the scene, I ran over to the paramedics getting off the chopper and triaged them to the patients, letting them know which needs were most critical. "Start there," I said, pointing to the bodies lying motionless on the grass, "you go to one and two, and I'll go to three." The challenge was magnified because the victims were so spread out.

Captain Ken Kronheim of Broward County Fire Rescue started toward one of the patients, a little girl who looked to be about ten years old. I didn't want to tell him that the little girl's body had been severely crushed, that there was nothing he could do for her. "No, that one!" I waved him toward one of the other victims. I took some bags of fluids and intravenous catheters from the EMTs and ran to stabilize another, thirty yards away.

At one point, I noticed Captain Jeffrey Andrews struggling to insert a breathing tube in one of the victims, a woman who had severe trauma to her face and neck. I offered to help and worked alongside Captain Andrews to open the airway and get the endotracheal tube in place.

After the patients had been loaded onto the chopper and into the ambulances, a paramedic turned to me and asked, "Have you had some medical training somewhere?"

"A little," I responded. I hopped back in our SUV to join my sons and we drove the thirty miles back to Fort Lauderdale.

That night I slipped by the hospital to see the victims' families. Sadly, two children, an eleven-year-old girl and a fourteen-year-old boy, died as a result of the crash. A twenty-year-old sister would die a few days later. The mother and father, and the family friend, though injured severely, survived the crash. Life is fragile.

It came out the next day that the new majority leader of the Senate—who also happened to be a surgeon—had stopped and assisted the victims. Later the press asked me whether I was concerned about stopping to help at the scene of an accident, nowadays, with trial lawyers' bringing lawsuits for malpractice against Good Samaritans. I well understood their concern. Sadly, even dedicated doctors nowadays will sometimes not identify themselves in an emergency situation for fear of a lawsuit, should the worst-case scenario happen in trying to help. I could only respond for me: "As a doctor, my first instincts are to help, and I was privileged to offer my assistance today at the scene of this horrible accident. My heart goes out to this family, which must face the start of a New Year with this terrible tragedy. My thoughts and prayers are with them."

We are sometimes called to serve when we least expect it. And sometimes there is a limit to what we can do.

I was elected to serve as majority leader on the Monday before Christmas. It was a mad dash to put together a complete, up-and-running leadership office and staff in addition to the team that directly served my constituents in Tennessee. Since I had not anticipated my rise to leader even a month earlier, I had no list of readily available people in mind. Fortunately, fifteen extremely talented individuals—including Mitch, Ginny, and Alex, who came with me from the NRSC—changed their career plans on the spur of the moment to join me in working at the majority leader's office. Mitch went into high gear in assembling this team; by New Year's Day, the potential team members had been identified. The only thing that had to happen was persuasion.

Mitch had four pockets of potential staff to draw from—the NRSC campaign committee staff, my existing Senate office staff, a loyal and experienced group from Senator Pete Domenici's office, and the new recruits. Emily Reynolds joined me again, this time to serve as secretary of the Senate. Ramona Lessen, who served as my first-class assistant through all twelve years in Washington and remains a dear friend, summed up the attitude of many on our staff; when she looked around our conference room, and she said, "All right, this is really scary. Who's supposed to be the adult here?" Most of the staff entrusted that responsibility to Ramona!

As had been the case when I first set up my D.C. office in 1994, our goal was to get the best available people on board quickly. Bob Stevenson, a gifted communications director and an icon on Capitol Hill, moved from the Senate Budget Committee to take the reins of our press operation. Bill Hoagland, a Senate veteran and one of the sharpest budget experts ever to walk the halls of the Capitol, had worked with Pete Domenici and the Senate Budget Committee since its inception. Bill worked with us the entire time I served as majority leader. Similarly, Dave Schiappa had served as secretary for the minority, then secretary for the majority, during the tenure of Senators Dole and Lott. Dave knew more about how the Senate business actually got done than most senators, and I was thrilled when he agreed to stay on with us. Having Dave in place allowed us to breathe a lot easier, just knowing that we had somebody experienced on the Senate floor every day to guide the processes.

Marty Gold was one of the most brilliant and highly respected experts on congressional procedures. He loves and respects the institution and knows Senate parliamentary procedure inside out, which would prove invaluable during my tenure as leader. Marty had worked through the 1970s with Senator Mark Hatfield and then he joined the staff of Republican Leader Howard Baker, where he served as the procedural specialist from 1979 to 1982. For years Marty had been offered the position of Senate parliamentarian but had declined. But just maybe he would respond to my invitation—to return to the majority leader's office now that it was again occupied by a Tennessean. I called him on Christmas Eve and asked him to help, and he willingly put his career as a partner in Covington & Burling law firm on hold to help serve the country. Steve Biegun, whom I'd known when he was chief of staff of the Foreign Relations Committee and who had enormously impressed me with his work on the platform committee, came to work with us as our foreign policy advisor and proved to be another extraordinarily skilled team member.

Dean Rosen came on board as my chief advisor on health-care issues. Dean was so knowledgeable about health care that many people actually thought he was a doctor. He had the useful experience of having served in and out of government—as counsel for the Health Insurance Association of America and before that as counsel to both the House Ways and Means Committee and the Senate Labor and Human Resources Committee. Mitch Bainwol agreed to serve as chief of staff during the transition period but was anxious to return to the private sector. Lee Rawls came over from the FBI to serve as our chief of staff. Lee had been with me previously in my Senate office after Mark Tipps had returned to Nashville. Lee, who had formerly been chief of staff with Pete Domenici and had worked closely with Howard Baker at Howard's law firm, provided maturity and keen insights into almost every issue we faced. I relied heavily on his wisdom. Everyone who came to work for us from the private sector took a big cut in pay to do so, but signed on nonetheless, a demonstration of their commitment to public service.

The intensity of those days reminded me of setting up the Transplant Center at Vanderbilt. Then, I had more than six months to put together a smooth working operation to give people hope through transplantation, but after becoming majority leader on December 23, we had only fifteen days before the Senate reconvened to address the nation's business. I will always be appreciative of those who sacrificed what they were doing to come on board, on the spur of the moment.

The Republican leader's office, S-230, was a majestic suite of high-ceilinged rooms in the Capitol building, facing west toward the Washington Monument and the Lincoln Memorial—the view that Bob Dole often quipped was the "second-best view in Washington." Even the physical aspect of moving into the suite was made more difficult because most people had left D.C. for the holidays.

With such a transition, there is a complete turnover of staff. The Lott staff, many still reeling from shock at the events that had transpired after the Thurmond incident, were unable to vacate the offices until the night before the new session of Congress began. Alex described a poignant moment when he first walked through the empty, vacated offices. There in the middle of the floor was a large trash can, full of discarded paper and personal effects. Sitting atop the bin was a huge framed painting of the White House, the glass shattered in dozens of pieces.

Under the awkward circumstances, we didn't want to seem overly aggressive or obnoxiously forward. Even changing the nameplate outside the office door was a sensitive issue. So Ramona asked the Capitol maintenance staff to wait until the building was closed to the public, and all the reporters had cleared out, before taking Trent's name down and putting mine up. We did not have so much as a single desk in place or a telephone assigned the evening before the opening gavel of the first session of the 108th Congress. We had to start from scratch, and we had to do it fast. Fortunately, we discovered that the competent Capitol maintenance staff can, amazingly, empty, paint, and refurnish a suite of offices overnight.

Exacerbating matters still further, all of the major television networks were vying for early-morning interviews featuring our first day on the job. We agreed to an exclusive interview with Diane Sawyer of ABC's *Good Morning America*. The interview was to be done at 7:00 A.M. from my new office. We moved what little furniture we had in front of a large fireplace in the office, making it appear on television that we were comfortably moved in and operating.

Later that morning, Mitch McConnell introduced me as the new leader, saying, "In a remarkably short period of time, Bill Frist has reached the pinnacle of two very demanding professions, one, heart surgery, the other in politics. He has become the majority leader in less time than any other leader in either the House of Representatives or the U.S. Senate."

I opened the Senate floor as I would almost every day for the next four years, following the Pledge of Allegiance and prayer by Lloyd Ogilvie, the Chaplain of the Senate. We began as usual, negotiating all the organizing resolutions and delineating how things would run in the new session. The rules defining how the Senate will operate have to be passed anew at the beginning of each two-year Congress. All of the negotiations had been done ahead of time, so the first day of the new session was typically more formality than action. But in the early hours of the new session, as we were still going through the rules pro forma, Senator Hillary Clinton came to the floor, offering a partisan, Democratic-sponsored new bill on workman's compensation. We interpreted this as a provocative shot being fired by the minority party on a day customarily reserved for the swearing-in of the new senators. Was the minority party simply attempting to throw a wrench into my first day as majority leader? It was a bit of political gamesmanship—and a statement of what was to come.

At the January 7, 2003, swearing-in of the ten new senators, nine of whom were Republicans, CNN congressional reporter Jonathan Karl related what he thought an interesting observation to his audience. Apparently, I had been standing in the center aisle of the Senate floor, along with the now minority leader, Tom Daschle. Trent had joined his fellow Mississippian, Thad Cochran, as Thad took the oath of office in the Senate well, at the front of the chamber. Jonathan Karl reported Trent's actions after Thad was sworn in by Vice President Dick Cheney:

> As he [Lott] walked back, Daschle was standing next to Frist, to shake everybody's hands. Senator Lott went over to Tom Daschle. They shook hands, they embraced, they shared a laugh, and then Senator Lott walked right by Bill Frist without giving him so much as a handshake. It was a very chilly moment. You could actually feel the chill up in the spectators' galleries in the Senate.[1]

Ironically, if that happened, I never noticed. Trent and I were on the same team, and I was glad he was there. He may have experienced some awkwardness coming back to work, but I would routinely call on him for advice and opinions. Rick Santorum had been supportive of Trent all the way to the end. In the post-Lott shuffle, Rick was in line to be the chairman of the powerful Senate Rules Committee. But Rick felt so bad about the way events had devolved that he graciously gave up his committee chairmanship to Trent.

Trent Lott was not a visionary sort of leader who comes up with innovative transforming ideas, but he relished the political maneuvering required of an effective leader and was outstanding at it. He was by nature not a risk taker; he hesitated taking legislation to the Senate floor unless he had the support to pass it. He knew how to count votes. Trent playfully continued to command attention, a trait that may trace back to his cheerleading days at Ole Miss. For instance, for the first several months of my tenure, Trent consistently showed up about fifteen minutes late at our weekly caucus policy lunches in the dark-paneled Mansfield Room of the Capitol. The lunches took place immediately following a small prayer group that he, Rick, and several other senators held every Tuesday. Trent had a way of making a dramatic entrance, talking as he entered the back door, flicking various senators' ears as he passed behind his seated colleagues, and finally sitting at the far side of the room. This was all in good fun but sometimes a little distracting to his Senate colleagues when they were in the middle of a presentation.

From our majority leader's office budget, we quietly extended courtesies that reflected the body's appreciation for Trent's service, including extension of his official car and driver for a couple of years and provision of an additional staff person. Trent was a very good leader. I had admired him for coming back after his resignation amidst all the controversy. He worked hard and eventually re-entered leadership when he defeated Lamar Alexander for Senate minority whip. He served until December 2007, when he resigned from the Senate to become a lobbyist.

DURING THE DECEMBER 22 CONFERENCE CALL WITH CORETTA Scott King, Andrew Young, and Julian Bond, the group invited me to speak at the Congress of Racial Equality (CORE) dinner in

New York City on January 20, less than two weeks into my new role as majority leader. Of course, I accepted the invitation.

The attendees at the CORE dinner that evening received me warmly, and perhaps it was fitting that one of my first speeches as Senate majority leader should be before that particular group.

I opened my message with Martin Luther King Jr.'s *Letter from a Birmingham Jail.* In it, King wrote, "Like a boil that can never be cured so long as it is covered up, but must be opened with all its ugliness to the natural medicines of air and light, injustice must be exposed, with all the tension its exposure creates to the light of human conscience and the air of national opinion."

I then told the crowd about a man who had come for treatment to a hospital in Sudan during one of my medical mission visits:

Several villagers were carrying a man who was deathly sick—pained, feverish, and stick thin. Except his leg. It was huge—inflamed and swollen enormously with what to my eye was a deep-seated abscess. A boil buried deep and covered up by muscle and skin. The infection would bring certain death if not opened and drained. The tribal medicine man did not have the experience to cure such an ugly wound.

So I took a scalpel and folded it in the man's hand. I then held his hand and together we incised the skin, pushed deep into the wound—through the swollen underlying tissue, then through the muscle. Sensing his hesitancy, I assured him it was okay. We were doing it together—hand grasped over hand.

Carefully, respectfully, steadily, we pushed deeper. The patient's pain was intense. But suddenly we struck the pocket of infection. All its ugliness gushed forth and was exposed to the air and light. At that instant the hurt flowed out and the healing began. And I saw, in the eyes of a patient facing death, the hope that shines with new life.

I paused long enough for the audience to fully grasp the picture I had described—a true story—and then I continued:

Like the boil deep in that man's leg, America's wounds of division run deep. They have festered long. Too long. And we as a people have paid a terrible price throughout our history. Nearly thirty-five years ago, Martin Luther King paid with his life. Tonight we honor his sacrifice. And celebrate his bold commitment to lifting up the less fortunate among us. But we also have a duty—a duty to act.

My title is majority leader of the United States Senate. It is not a position I sought. It is not a position for which I ran. And of course no one wished for the event that led to my ascension. But I do feel deep inside—just like in Africa—that my hand can now be grasped by others to seize an unprecedented opportunity. To dig deep into America's soul and lift up our dialogue to a higher and more robust level. This may cause tension. But by letting air and light into our dialogue, I believe we will find a new optimism to help heal our wounds of division.

As I finished my talk to the members of CORE that evening, the crowd rose to their feet in appreciation and agreement. The nation had been through a difficult two months, reminding us of our ugly past. But as I headed back to Washington that night, I felt as though we had started anew, and we had a great future ahead.

LEARNING THE MYRIAD PROCEDURAL INTRICACIES OF RUNNING THE U.S. Senate was a daunting task, and one that had to be done virtually overnight. I couldn't have done it without the expert group of people around me, especially Marty Gold and Dave Schiappa. We really were baptized under fire—especially from the Democratic opposition—but we surged forward, achieving some major victories in a relatively short time.

Adding a significant moral impetus was President Bush's stunning announcement during the January 2003 State of the Union message that he would seek an astounding $15 billion over five years to combat HIV/AIDS in the world's poorest and most heavily AIDS-burdened countries. This sum was more than any other country in history had committed to fight a single disease outside its borders. While liberal voices loved to talk about the problem of HIV and AIDS in the developing world, it took the conservative President Bush to actually move the country from rhetoric to action. The President's Emergency Plan for AIDS Relief (PEPFAR) is, I believe, among the president's top two or three defining legacies of his tenure in office. And no other initiative better illustrates how one man's passions to bring health, hope, and healing to the world can alter the course of history.

Amazingly, when the president made his announcement, only a handful of people were in the loop. Particularly surprising were the people *not* in the loop, including Health and Human Services Secretary Tommy Thompson, the senior budget watchers at the Office of Management and Budget, and the many global health experts at the government's beck and call. The idea for PEPFAR seems to have originated with Condoleezza Rice, deputy chief of staff Josh Bolten, and Mike Gerson, the president's brilliant head speech writer and conservative social voice. Bolten instructed a very small group of people in the White House, which included Gary Edson, a deputy national security advisor, to develop a major global AIDS initiative that would be built around providing life-saving antiretroviral drugs as well as prevention measures. Bolten encouraged his small group to "think big." Tony Fauci, the long-standing director of National Institutes of Allergy and Infectious Disease at the National Institutes of Health, was the chief scientist charged with developing the policy: he was dispatched to Africa by the president specifically to determine if a truly bold initiative could have an impact in saving lives. His conclusion: it could!

The president was personally involved. In private meetings, he asked pointed questions about what specific outcomes could be achieved, how the program could work, and what risks might be involved. He was most interested in tangible results. His view seemed to echo the sentiments of Gerson, "If we can do this and don't, it will be a source of shame."

The decision had been a long time in coming. Many people think that AIDS developed in the early 1980s, when the syndrome was first observed in the United States, but actually the disease had been around for a long time—we just didn't know it. Perhaps as early as the 1940s, a condition that later came to be called Slim Disease had been decimating populations in West and Central Africa, causing drastic weight loss, diarrhea, and overall physical decline leading to early death. No one knew what caused it or how to treat it, and most of its victims died horrible deaths. We may never know for sure, but it was most likely AIDS.

A number of researchers have concluded from DNA evidence that HIV—the Human Immunodeficiency Virus—may have arrived on American shores as early as 1969, coming in first from Haiti.

I was a third-year surgical resident in Boston when the first reports appeared in the medical literature. On June 5, 1981, the *Morbidity and Mortality Weekly Report*, a widely read publication of the Centers for Disease Control and Prevention, published the first report of five mysterious cases of Pneumocystis carinii pneumonia among previously healthy young men in Los Angeles, two of whom had already died. Within just eighteen months, epidemiologists identified the major risk factors, and in March 1983 the CDC issued recommendations for prevention of sexual, drug-related, and occupational transmission of AIDS even before the cause of the new, unexplained illness was known.

It was natural that I, as majority leader, take on this issue in the legislative branch. What other senator had researched and published scientific papers on immune suppressed patients, and held the hands of patients dying of HIV? During the mid-1980s, in response to the sudden emergence of the mysterious and deadly HIV virus, we in surgery radically altered how we carried out our daily procedures. Before, blood was always considered relatively sterile, but now it could contain a deadly, toxic agent. We began to double-glove while performing surgery and wear eye protection. In the early days when I operated on a patient with HIV, I would not require my assistants to scrub in—if they accidentally got stuck with a needle and got infected, we had no treatment to cure them. Early on, some surgeons even refused to do heart surgery on HIV patients because life expectancy from the disease was so poor.

Why did it take so long for America to wake up to the global crisis created by this virus? Not until the death of the famous movie star Rock Hudson in 1985 and a local school district's decision to bar from class Ryan White, a thirteen-year-old hemophiliac with AIDS, did most people in the United States pay much attention to the disease. Eventually, substantial funding was made available to deal with the problem in the United States, but unfortunately no similar response was made for Africa, where the invisible killer had been making death rounds for years, undetected and undeterred. It was not until the mid-to-late 1980s and early 1990s that the world at last began to recognize that parts of Africa were at far greater risk than was America.

President Ronald Reagan first spoke publicly about AIDS, not in a formal statement, but in response to a question at a press conference in 1985. The first help for battling AIDS in Africa came a year later—$1 million, obviously just a drop in the bucket compared to what was needed. The following year Congress authorized a special appropriation for global AIDS, and by the end of Reagan's second term, the United States was spending $40 million annually.

Many Americans could not understand why our government was getting involved in the battle against AIDS, a disease that was so obviously behavior related. After all, the groups known to be most vulnerable to the disease were homosexual men and injection drug users. Most Americans did not initially perceive the disease as a threat to themselves or to society, nor did they see fighting the disease as a legitimate spending priority for our government.

Furthermore, U.S. government officials were predicting that a vaccine for AIDS would be available within a few years. That did not happen. Today, more than twenty-five years later, almost no one in government, science, or medicine believes we are within ten years of a vaccine. There are currently no promising clinical trials in the making; all that have been tried have failed.

In 1988, tennis champion Arthur Ashe rocked the world when it became known that he'd contracted HIV through a blood transfusion he was given during one of two heart operations. Ashe had not engaged in risky behavior but had contracted the disease by merely going to the hospital for health care. Ashe died of complications due to AIDS in 1993.

In an incident equally shocking, though less widely known, the daughter-in-law of the former president of the Southern Baptist Convention, then the world's largest Protestant denomination, contracted AIDS through a blood transfusion. Unaware that she had AIDS, she passed on the disease to her two baby boys at birth. The mother and both sons died of AIDS, but not before the Southern Baptist Church realized that it had a responsibility to minister to those with the disease, young or old, sick or well.

Then in 1991, the sports world was shocked again when Ervin "Magic" Johnson, who had said he had hundreds of heterosexual partners, announced that he was HIV-positive and retired from professional basketball. Gradually, the world began to realize that AIDS was a disease that could infect all sexually active people and others who received blood products. Heterosexuals could contract and were contracting the disease; children were dying from it. And the numbers affected were growing rapidly.

During the administration of George H. W. Bush, America's funding of the global fight against AIDS tripled to $120 million, focusing primarily on education and condom distribution. That's all we knew to do at that time.

Under the first six years of Bill Clinton's presidency, spending for fighting global HIV/AIDS increased from $120 million to $140 million, barely keeping pace with inflation. It is difficult to explain such a major moral and political failure. Some of it, no doubt, was due to ignorance; some was lingering indifference; much was due to politics. During the end of the Clinton administration there was an internal battle between the president's director of the Office of National AIDS Policy (ONAP) and the staff of the National Security Council (NSC). The NSC, at the urging of Vice President Gore, wanted to dramatically ramp up planning and funding for international HIV/AIDs assistance. In nearly a year of counterproductive stalling by ONAP, the NSC gave up and the end result was a lack of progress and no significant initiative for the president to promote. Leadership and lives were lost in classic Washington infighting. Whatever the reason, while there was much speech-making, there was no serious call to action by either the president or Congress.

Nor was there any bipartisan political consensus to move forward aggressively in the fight against AIDS. AIDS activists were calling for more money to fight the disease in America. They called for the government to finance expensive new drug treatments for Americans who were HIV-positive. Their priority was not universally embraced. Many people, especially those who did not yet understand the nature of the disease, thought the idea tantamount to saying, "I refuse to change my risky behavior, and I want you to pay for it." Some vocal AIDS activists here at home feared that American assistance to Africa would take away limited resources that could be used to treat HIV patients in the United States. In the midst of the wrangling, no one including the president stepped up to fill the leadership vacuum.

Congress plays a major role in deciding where to spend our tax dollars, and during the Clinton years, those in Congress, too, waffled on the AIDS issue. But, it is the president who sets the priorities and leads the country to new places. Since leaving office, President Clinton has repeatedly said he regrets that he did not adequately lead on this issue during his administration. Since leaving office he has joined the fight against the disease in a significant way. The Clinton Foundation HIV/AIDS Initiative reports that it has helped bring AIDS care and treatment to over eight hundred thousand people around the world and has partnered with more than twenty-two governments to make treatment more affordable. I do know that America's failure to act in the 1990s, along with the willing negligence of other wealthy countries, will plague our collective conscience, and our checkbooks, for generations.

In the last two years of the Clinton presidency, AIDS spending finally started to climb, topping out at $460 million spread among dozens of initiatives. None of this money, however, was designated to provide drugs that could slow the effects of the disease in people who had already contracted HIV/AIDS. A drug treatment program for a person was incorrectly thought to be too expensive and too complicated to be implemented in poor communities in Africa.

Global AIDS activists challenged the lack of bold initiatives by Western governments, especially that of the United States. Our nation's editorial pages, both conservative and liberal, began to call for action. Despite early skepticism, conservative Christians were among the first to awaken to the fact that turning a blind eye to suffering people—regardless of how they had contracted AIDS—was inconsistent with their faith.

What most people don't know is that we in Congress had begun pushing the White House much earlier. Years before President Bush's 2003 unprecedented commitment I was ahead of the curve on the magnitude of the crisis because of my personal experiences as a physician. I had treated and operated on HIV patients. As a transplant doctor I had daily managed patients whose immune systems were similarly suppressed. And I'd seen the ravages of the disease in Africa during my medical mission trips to Tanzania, Kenya, Sudan, and the Democratic Republic of Congo. Two years before the president's announcement, early in 2001, I'd proposed a budget amendment to allow for more than doubling AIDS spending up to $1 billion a year.

The origins and subsequent history of this doubling amendment provide a useful illustration of how important Senate staff are to producing transformative change. First, senators try to hire the very best staff we can find and then we give them guidance as to our priorities. With them we develop plans of action, and we rely on them to help us implement the decisions we make. My priority was to commit substantially more to combating HIV; it was morally the right thing to do. I instructed my new legislative director, Allen Moore, a seasoned professional who had previously worked in the Senate, the executive branch, and the private sector, to generate bold ideas consistent with my interest in Africa's unique health challenges. At the time I was chairman of the subcommittee on African affairs. Allen worked side by side with another new staff member—a medical doctor—Dr. Ken Bernard, who had been highly recommended to me by Donna Shalala, the former Secretary of Health and Human Services. Ken was an assistant surgeon general and rear admiral in the U.S. Public Health Service who had previously fought, without much success, in the Clinton White House for the expansion of the U.S. global HIV/AIDS program. He knew the science, he had fought the battle once and lost, and now was ready to fight again.

As the Senate began the arduous process of working on the 2002 budget, Allen and Ken proposed to me a bold global AIDS amendment to the budget resolution, the annual act of Congress that establishes spending totals for the upcoming year. Allen asked Ken about the need and capacity of poor African countries to spend more than the $460 million we were then spending on AIDS globally: "Could we spend twice as much—$900 million—and have the money used well?"

"Absolutely," responded Ken.

"How about a billion dollars? Could we spend that?" Allen asked.

"Yes," Ken replied. "The need is overwhelming and we have the treatments and know-how."

"Okay," Allen said, "let's write up the arguments and present the idea to the senator."

"Can you just *do* that in the Senate?" Ken, with long executive-branch experience but new to the halls of Congress, asked disbelievingly.

"In the Senate, you can do almost anything," Allen replied, "if you have the votes."

Ken became ebullient discovering he had found an ear in another branch of government that could finally move the talks to action by appropriating the large sums needed to get the job done. He had the plan that included treatment from his former NSC days and Allen knew that I would be receptive.

When the amendment came to the Senate floor, it passed overwhelmingly, allowing me to extract assurances from my Budget Committee colleagues that they would fight to maintain the Senate's position in negotiations with their counterparts from the House of Representatives. Our amendment was the first step that would help lead to a $900 million increase in global AIDS spending for 2002. More important, such a large sum demonstrated that official Washington was beginning to understand the magnitude of the emerging tragedy.

Later that year, United Nations Secretary General Kofi Annan and President Bush proposed the creation of a new, multilateral Global Fund to fight the big three diseases in the developing world: AIDS, tuberculosis, and malaria. Bush made a lead gift of $200 million to the Global Fund. Other countries joined in, but to this day the United States continues to be the largest single donor, providing about 30 percent of the Global Fund's resources. Although wealthy nations may never be willing or able to do all that is necessary, America is doing far more than any other nation on earth.

But it takes a lot more than budgetary action to create a transformative movement. It was during 2000 that I met and became friends with the U2 front man Bono. Born into an Irish Catholic home in Dublin as Paul David Hewson, Bono and his U2 band members had become involved in an informal Bible study group known as Shalom. Out of those Christian roots, Bono later parlayed his fame as an international rock star into a voice for social activism, especially raising awareness of the African AIDS crisis. Bono was committed to the issues. He was sincere and he was smart. Unlike many celebrity advocates, he invested the time to study the problems, to learn how to talk convincingly to policy makers, to ask for things that were doable, and to seek out personal meetings with the president, senior administration officials, influential senators and congressmen to discuss the issues. In the late 1990s he had started making what would become regular visits to Washington to talk about canceling Third World debt, improving trading opportunities for poorer countries, and increasing the resources to fight HIV/AIDS, especially in Africa.

And Bono is a man of action. We had met many times on the

issues in Washington, but what surprised me was the extra steps he would take.

"Can you take a call from Bono?" asked his assistant Lucy Matthew, calling me in Florida just prior to Christmas in 2000. "He wants to see if you can meet him in Africa."

"Sure," I politely replied, a bit skeptical.

"Senator Frist, can you meet me in Africa next month—doesn't matter where—but I need you as a doctor and a senator to go with me so we can determine if the money we are spending there is making a difference?" Bono asked.

Bono knew I went to Africa each year on medical mission trips, and indeed I told him I'd be going in January to Kenya and Sudan.

Bono seized the moment: "Let's meet in Kampala and quietly and without fanfare travel throughout rural Uganda to see the medical clinics, the HIV programs, and new wells dug with the aid we are making available."

And that's what we did. No press, no security—just a couple of guys trying to serve others.

SUBSTANTIVE PROGRESS IN WASHINGTON REQUIRES BIPARTISANSHIP. And I found my Democrat partner in Senator John Kerry of Massachusetts. John and I, both members of the Foreign Relations Committee, began working together on the first truly comprehensive global HIV/AIDS bill in 2000. The following year, he and I served as cochairman of a pioneering new AIDS policy task force funded by the Bill and Melinda Gates Foundation at the esteemed nonpartisan think tank, the Center for Strategic and International Studies (CSIS). We shared a commitment to finding innovative, bipartisan ways to address this scourge, and worked closely on this groundbreaking initiative, which pulled together all the stakeholders interested in global HIV.

In 2001 and 2002, Kerry and I partnered on two seminal bills that ultimately became fundamental elements of the legislation that authorized President Bush's 2003 PEPFAR initiative.

The first was introduced on June 13, 2001. I went to the floor with Senator Kerry to introduce our legislation, cosponsored by Senators Jesse Helms and Richard Durbin, "to expand assistance to countries seriously affected by HIV/AIDS, malaria, and tuberculosis." The bill, formally called the International Infectious Diseases Control Act of 2001, went beyond what the House was considering by including money to combat tuberculosis and malaria and by including the U.S. contribution to the Global Fund. Altogether, the bill proposed spending $2.3 billion to battle the three deadly diseases through a "science-based approach that includes prevention of new infections and the treatment and care of infected individuals, public-private partnerships, and good governance."

In my speech on the floor that day, I laid the foundations of a philosophy that I had been articulating with increasing frequency over the past several years. The key theme: that "investment in global public health activities to reduce HIV/AIDS, malaria, and tuberculosis not only is a humanitarian imperative, it also helps bolster the economic and social development necessary to build political and trade alliances." Years later in the post-9/11 world, this would translate into global health efforts as a kind of currency for development and peace—a way of strengthening the social, political, and economic bonds among peoples and nations, as well as alleviating human suffering.

In July, the House of Representatives passed a global AIDS bill that proposed to spend $1.4 billion per year and would authorize the first large-scale AIDS treatment programs in the developing world. Our bill passed the Senate, but there wasn't time or inclination to work out the major differences between the House and Senate bills. In spite of our efforts, the elected congressional leaders weren't clamoring for it (in fact, some held it in great disdain), nor at the time was the president.

The second bill on which I collaborated with Kerry was formally called the U.S. Leadership Against HIV/AIDS, TB, and Malaria Act of 2002. More commonly known as the Kerry-Frist Global AIDS Bill, this legislation represented the first coordinated effort by U.S. leadership to respond to the global AIDS pandemic. We kept up the pressure. The bill never passed but dramatically raised the aspirational goals for Congress; it proposed to double global HIV funding to $2 billion and required a five-year comprehensive plan to reduce the global spread of HIV. It became the framework for what was to follow.

And, finally, transformative change is much likely to occur if the issue attracts well-recognized converts. During my early Senate years, I served on the Senate Foreign Relations Committee, where I developed a close working relationship with Senator Jesse Helms of North Carolina, the committee's highest ranking Republican. Jesse and I talked often about our need to do more on the AIDS issue, especially in the area of HIV orphans and mother-to-child transmission. This was a tough road for Jesse and he was resistant at first. He had been rather famously unsympathetic early on about AIDS.

It wasn't until Bono came along with a combination of facts, Irish charm, and Biblical passages about the Christian's responsibility to care for the hurting, especially the widows and orphans, that Jesse began to change his tune. Bono knew the real power lay not with the HIV activists and sympathizers—they were already supportive. It lay with those like Jesse who controlled the purse strings and the leadership. If you could get Jesse on board, there was a good chance that the Senate leadership would go along.

Jesse Helms and Bono became the odd couple of AIDS relief. The media loved it. And it was a genuine friendship, felt by both. I will never forget when Jesse and his wife Dorothy joined Karyn and me in the front row of a U2 concert in Washington. Jesse removed his hearing aids, and Dorothy pulled some big balls of cotton from her purse that both used to stuff their ears. The Helms grandchildren were there and loved every minute.

But it was fellow North Carolinian Franklin Graham who probably had the greatest impact on Jesse's views of HIV. He explained to Jesse the Christian and evangelical basis of combating global HIV. They prayed together, and Jesse respected Franklin's leadership and activism of rallying evangelicals around the world to support prevention of the spread of AIDS. In 2001, well before most were paying much attention, Franklin began planning a "Prescription for Hope." The Washington-based gathering that would bring together more than seven hundred emergency relief workers, along with government, medical, and church workers from around the world, to help mobilize Christians in the fight against the pandemic. Sharing the podium with Franklin were the remarkable first lady of Uganda, Janet Museveni; Andrew Natsios, of the U.S. Agency for International Development (USAID); my good friend Dr. Angelo D'Agostino, a colorful and endearing American Jesuit who ran an HIV-related orphanage I visited often in Nairobi; and me. The evangelical Christian community was becoming energized in the global fight against HIV.

Jesse Helms made a surprise appearance at the conference. Inspiring the crowd by his very presence, he rose to say that he was ashamed that he had not done more to fight AIDS in the developing world. He later wrote a remarkable op-ed piece in the *Washington Post* echoing and expanding that statement. We announced at the conference that he and I together would be seeking a special $500 million appropriation to initiate a program to prevent mother-to-child transmission of HIV. No one in the White House or in the global AIDS advocacy community knew anything about our intentions at the time.

Jesse had already announced that he would not seek a sixth term in the Senate, and when he complained of feeling tired and weak around the time of his op-ed, I encouraged him to check into Bethesda Naval Medical Center. Shortly thereafter, on April 25, 2002, Senator Helms underwent open-heart surgery by a surgical colleague of mine at Inova Fairfax Hospital to replace a failing valve. I pursued our proposal in Jesse's absence. The White House knew that we had more than enough votes to pass it in the Senate, especially with Jesse's support in absentia, so we struck a deal that would make the idea a presidential initiative if we agreed to restructure the spending. With the president's support, a new $500 million program was assured, even in the face of a far-less-enthusiastic House of Representatives. Our mother-to-child initiative got off the ground quickly and helped lay the groundwork for what was to follow.

Jesse Helms retired as he said he would, but he did more to help suffering people during his last months in office than most legislators do in a lifetime. I will always admire him as a man big enough to say, "I was wrong about AIDS," and then do something to make amends.

IN EARLY 2002 THE WHITE HOUSE WAS BEGINNING TO SECRETLY put together its historic AIDS initiative. As a member of the Senate leadership team, first as chairman of the NRSC campaign committee and later as majority leader, I began in 2000 to attend regular leadership meetings at the White House. They provided the opportunity to talk freely about a variety of topics, including global AIDS.

I vividly recall one time in the Roosevelt Room at the White House in a small meeting with the Republican leadership when President Bush surprised me with his detailed knowledge about HIV and its ravages in societies around the world. At the end of a wide-ranging political discussion, I asked the president if there was any chance that the administration might be willing to do more on global AIDS.

"I'm willing to do more," he replied, "but only if I am absolutely assured that the new spending will produce tangible results." Then he discussed Niverapine, the inexpensive drug used to help prevent an HIV-infected mother from passing on the disease to her newborn child. *How did the president know so much about Niverapine?* Most of the political figures in the room—not to mention most of the president's own aides—had never heard of Niverapine. The president's obvious knowledge of the entire issue of African AIDS and the passion he displayed caught most everyone by surprise. It was clear to me he had been studying the topic.

Soon he would be ready to take action. In mid-January 2003, about a week before the State of the Union address, the president and first lady invited Karyn and me to dinner. When we showed up at the White House, we were ushered not to the customary state dining room, but to the Red Room, a room rarely used for dinners. It was a special night. Also in attendance were United Nations Secretary General Kofi Annan and his wife, the pastor of the president's church in Washington, National Security Advisor Condoleezza Rice, and one or two others.

The conversation covered the waterfront, but halfway through the evening HIV became the topic. The president told us, "In a few days, I'm going to make an announcement that you all are going to be proud of. Keep it confidential for now. It will change the course of history for those people with HIV/AIDS all around the world, but most significantly in African countries. Our country will lead the world in the fight against HIV."

Indeed when several days later the president unveiled his $15 billion proposal for PEPFAR, it stunned the world. It also created an important challenge for Congress. The chairman of the International Relations Committee Henry Hyde quickly pushed a bill through the House of Representatives with the help of his Democratic colleague Tom Lantos. The bill had a lot of support in the Senate because it drew heavily from the original Kerry-Frist bill.

The White House sent a senior advisor to "negotiate" the bill through Congress. I sent Allen and two other highly capable staff members, Andy Olsen and Shana Christup. Back and forth we went with the White House, working with a small team of Senate Republicans over a period of weeks to craft the final wording of the bill. The time pressure resulted from the president's desire to have a signed piece of legislation before going to the G-8 meeting that June. And it was already May.

Facing the deadline of the G-8 meetings, I made a tough decision as majority leader: we would pass the House bill without amendments. It was a controversial decision. It meant that I was asking my Republican senate colleagues to refrain from making any changes to a bill that was imperfect and to oppose any and all changes proposed by Democrats, regardless of the merits. It was far from the ideal way to proceed, but it was the only way I could guarantee passage of the bill.

The strategy worked and the bill passed overwhelmingly in late

May 2003, just four months after the president's surprise pledge in the State of the Union. After years of foot-dragging in Congress and a decade of disappointing leadership from the White House, President Bush's PEPFAR program had come to pass in near record time.

The impact has been remarkable, but even today, more than six years later, we are losing ground to the virus. Even with the massive amounts of money we are spending—more than $6 billion per year now—there will still be well over 2 million new HIV infections this year. Though the cost of treatment with antiretroviral drugs (ARVs) has plummeted, the world still does not have enough resources to treat its way out of the problem. Today, for every person that we place on ARVs, there are three newly infected patients. And more successful prevention programs will require cultural change, which takes time. The problem has been with us for more than a generation, and it may take a generation or two more before we see the change for which so many of us are hoping.

In the meantime, we dare not back off from the battle. In 2008, in an effort led by then-senator Joe Biden and supported by then-senator Barack Obama, Congress reaffirmed its commitment to fighting global infectious disease by passing legislation that authorized an additional investment of up to $48 billion over five years. It's a big step in the right direction—but the road ahead remains long. In the current domestic and global economic environment, it is unlikely that all the resources authorized will be funded.

Nevertheless, one of the greatest—maybe *the* greatest—foreign policy legacies of the Bush administration was PEPFAR—its rapid passage; its unprecedented size; and then its five years of spending nearly $19 billion to fight AIDS, tuberculosis, and malaria. In addition to the 2.1 million people who have received life-saving anti-retroviral therapy, over 60 million people have been reached through PEPFAR-supported community outreach programs, over 16 million women have been involved in mother-to-child transmission programs, and over 2.2 billion condoms (more than provided by all other countries in the world combined) have been distributed. This is a gift to humanity of which all Americans can be justly proud.

Readers of *Time* magazine were probably surprised to see a February 2008 column praising President Bush by former musician and antipoverty legend Bob Geldof, whose song "Do They Know It's Christmas" helped spawn a global outpouring of aid during the mid-1980s famine in Ethiopia. After listing the generous support of the Bush administration for many efforts to alleviate disease and poverty in Africa, Geldof concluded, "The Bush regime has been divisive—but not in Africa. I read it has been incompetent—but not in Africa. It has created bitterness—but not here in Africa. Here, his administration has saved millions of lives." In time, this little-recognized side of George Bush's presidency working closely with the leaders in Congress will get the recognition it deserves.

IN MARCH 2003, WE ALSO TOOK ON ONE OF AMERICA'S MOST heinous and egregious "legal" medical procedures—partial birth abortion. In 1996, Congress had spoken loud and clear by passing legislation outlawing this brutal practice, but President Clinton had vetoed the bill, not once but twice. Now, with a Republican president and a Republican majority in the House and Senate, we had a golden opportunity to stop the barbaric, government-condoned slaughter of preborn babies.

I never regarded partial birth abortion as a political issue. To me, it was a medical atrocity. Although I was not trained as an obstetrician, I had delivered babies and shared every parent's awe at the miracle of newborn life. As a surgeon, I know there are ethical boundaries that should never be crossed, and partial birth abortion, which requires a physician to kill a living fetus on the verge of being delivered into the world, is one of them.

The procedure begins by turning the living baby around in a mother's womb, partially pulling the baby out of the uterus feet-first, and then forcibly penetrating the base of its skull with eight-inch-long scissors. The scissors are then opened wide inside the baby's skull, creating a hole large enough to evacuate the brain and the contents of the head. Once the skull is collapsed, the now-dead infant is pulled from the mother's uterus through the birth canal. That is the procedure that some were defending on the floor of Congress.

This procedure is most commonly performed in the second trimester of pregnancy, when the baby is from twenty to twenty-seven weeks old. How developed is the child at that point? Let's put it this way: If those premature babies were born at twenty-three weeks, they would have almost a 50 percent chance of surviving on their own. For babies born at twenty-five weeks, the survival rate jumps to between 60 and 90 percent. Yet for years, our nation turned the other way while these babies were purposely destroyed.

As the only physician in the Senate, I sought to dispel the myths about partial birth abortions and discuss the facts from a medical perspective. For instance, proponents of this procedure generally claimed that it was most often used to preserve the health of the mother. That was simply not true. Moreover, partial birth abortion is not the only procedure or the best procedure available in a true medical emergency. It is a fringe procedure generally performed by doctors who specialized in optional late-term abortions and who were not board-certified surgeons.

As a physician, and as the majority leader who brought this bill to the floor, I am proud that the Senate voted to ban this morally offensive procedure in America. President Bush signed the bill, and it remains law today—a victory not for one party but for all those who value the sanctity of life.

I'M FREQUENTLY ASKED WHAT SINGLE PIECE OF LEGISLATION PASSED during my four years as majority leader will have the most lasting impact on everyday Americans.

The answer, hands down, is the bill that today guarantees seniors affordable access to life-saving prescription drugs. We passed the Medicare Prescription Drug Improvement and Modernization Act in 2003. Historically, Republicans seldom led on health-care reform and had earned the reputation of obstructing meaningful reform in the early 1990s. As the new majority leader, and as a doctor, I was determined to elevate health as an issue. The Medicare program, which provides health care to seniors and individuals with disabilities, had become seriously outdated since it was created in the 1960s. I was committed to making improvements to Medicare a defining issue for Republicans and for the Congress. Prescription drugs were included in most private health insurance plans, which served more than 180 million people. Why should they specifically be excluded from the coverage Congress has given to America's 40 million seniors—Medicare? The Medicare program simply had not kept up with the times.

Medicare was originally designed to help seniors four decades ago, when much of the American medical system was focused on treating acute, episodic illnesses rather than chronic disease. In Dad's medical practice, he had only a handful of useful, curative drugs available. In my generation, I used hundreds of life-saving drugs to prevent disease and return people to good health. In the 1960s, prescription drugs were just not that important in the overall scheme of things for most patients. Today, they are the single most powerful weapon in the doctor's arsenal to fight disease and to promote health. Yet they were not covered for seniors in Medicare. So the time had come to act.

Shortly after President Clinton was elected, he proposed a massive government program to provide health insurance to every American. While his "managed competition" model was intended as a compromise between liberals who preferred a single-payer government-run approach to health-care reform and conservatives who favored a more market-based approach, it was nonetheless rejected soundly by the American people. A broad coalition formed against his plans, branding them a dangerous intrusion of the federal government into individual choice and a vast expansion of bureaucracy.

But the call for health-care reform was still alive, and most of us who had studied health-care programs knew that reforms to the Medicare program had to be near the top of the list. The 1997 Balanced Budget Act created the National Bipartisan Commission on the Future of Medicare to "make recommendations regarding a comprehensive approach to preserve the program." Meeting in 1998 and 1999, this program included seventeen members, representing eleven Democrats and Republicans in both houses of Congress, and experts from academia and the private sector.

The commission was chaired by John Breaux, a senior member of the Senate Finance Committee and a centrist Democrat highly respected for his ability to build bipartisan coalitions, and Bill Thomas, Republican chairman of the powerful Ways and Means Health Subcommittee in the House of Representatives. I was appointed to the commission as well. The group broadly supported the Breaux-Thomas model developed by the commission; it was based on the popular Federal Employees Health Benefit Plan (FEHBP), which covered all federal workers. Seniors would be able to choose from a menu of comprehensive health plans, which would compete one with the other under strict federal guidelines. The Breaux-Thomas plan also would begin to update Medicare's outdated benefit package, adding prescription drugs and new preventive services. These private health plans would compete on value by offering the most attractive package of health benefits at the lowest possible price. And, over time, this competition would help make the Medicare program sustainable.

But our model was not supported by President Clinton, who had meanwhile fashioned his own plan, and when it came to a final vote in the committee, two of the Clinton appointees voted against it, leaving us one vote short and therefore unable to issue a final report or recommendation. (The final report required approval by eleven of the seventeen members.) But the wheels had been set in motion; a bipartisan group of reformers had started to coalesce around a plan that held promise for improving the Medicare program, and the relationship between Bill Thomas, John Breaux, and me would resurface four years later as we developed the Medicare Modernization Act of 2003.

Shortly after I became leader, I went to see Chuck Grassley and

Max Baucus, chairman and ranking member of the powerful Senate Finance Committee, which was responsible for Medicare. They were both eager and ready to engage in modernizing Medicare and making prescription drugs affordable to seniors. Moreover, the two had a history of working together, and I knew that Medicare prescription drug legislation would have to have bipartisan support to surpass the sixty-vote threshold required to pass in the Senate. Bill Thomas, now chairman of the full Ways and Means Committee, took the lead, supported by Speaker Denny Hastert and Majority Leader Tom DeLay. The White House was strongly supportive as well. President Bush campaigned on a promise to provide prescription drug benefits to seniors. He knew that both health care and Social Security needed to be modernized and that the solvency of both of these programs had to be addressed. Although the president always seemed to make Social Security a higher priority than Medicare, Medicare's problems were far more urgent and far more challenging to address.

As a government, we have overpromised to the next generation. I argued that Medicare was the problem we should tackle first. Why? Because the actuaries told us that the gap between Medicare's promised benefits and what the government could afford was about $35 trillion over the next seventy-five years, whereas the problem with Social Security amounted to only about a sixth of that. Furthermore, Medicare was predicted to go bankrupt about nineteen years sooner than Social Security.

As leader, I had one very important power—the power to decide which bills come to the floor of the Senate. And as a physician, I was personally committed to addressing the problems with Medicare and prescription drugs. Although the White House never submitted a specific bill to us—merely a list of general principles—in the end it was the administration's wholehearted enthusiasm and the president's $400 billion budget commitment that helped push the bill through.

At the time Republicans had a narrow 51-49 majority over Senate Democrats. I also knew that in the previous congressional session, Democrats had been in the majority by the same margin

(51–49), and they failed in their attempt to pass a prescription drug bill. Passing a bipartisan bill would be a challenge—and a test for the new Senate leadership.

I deliberately chose not to use a budgetary loophole called reconciliation, which would limit the time allowed for Senate floor debate and lower the threshold required for passage to fifty votes. That would have been wrong, because substantive legislation that will ultimately affect every American should be bipartisan and not subject to limited debate and amendment. Reconciliation injects blatant partisanship into the process.

Bill Thomas put together a strong bill in the House that had conservative backing from the House Republican caucus, in large part because he had significantly expanded consumer-oriented health savings accounts and included a central feature of the Breaux-Thomas approach that would require Medicare to compete directly over time with private-sector health plans. In the Senate we crafted—in accordance with long-standing Senate tradition—a much more bipartisan bill, reflecting both Republican and Democratic principles. Whereas the majority rules absolutely in the House, bills in the Senate require a sixty-vote supermajority to pass, which demands bipartisan cooperation. In the background throughout the debate was Senator Ted Kennedy, a superb legislator who had been committed to health-care reform for some forty years. (My first experience listening to Ted Kennedy on health-care issues was in his office in 1972, when he graciously took the time to speak to a handful of us college students interning in Washington for the summer.) Ted supported the Senate bill and voted for it when it passed the Senate. In the end, however, he did not vote for the final bill, largely because he felt we were not spending enough to subsidize employers, and he distrusted the competition we had injected into the final bill (a major step toward the original Breaux-Thomas plan crafted by Medicare Commission four years earlier).

The Senate bill passed with bipartisan support, seventy-six to twenty-one.

And now the hard part started—marrying the House and Senate versions of the legislation into a single bill to be voted on by both bodies. This process, too, had its share of controversy and drama. Congressman Bill Thomas chaired the Conference Committee, the joint House-Senate committee that fashions the final bill. Because I felt so strongly about the bill, I took the highly unusual step of putting myself on the bill-writing conference committee, a role that the elected leader doesn't usually play.

Thomas ruled with a heavy hand, and he excluded House Democrats from the active negotiations—not in itself a terribly unusual step since the House rules by strict majority control—but he also went further and eliminated my counterpart, the Democratic leader Tom Daschle, from a seat in the conference, arguing that Max Baucus, the vice chair of the Finance Committee that had written the bill, should represent the Senate Democrats at the table instead because Daschle did not support the bill in the first place. Not unexpectedly, this caused some hard feelings among the Senate Democrats. This exclusion understandably strained my relationship with Tom during consideration of the Medicare bill.

We met several days a week for weeks in Chairman Thomas's small hideaway office deep in the basement of the Capitol, a location chosen in part to minimize the chance of leaks to the press or to lobbyists. For the same reason, we all agreed not to carry even a single piece of paper out of the room. Over bowls of pistachio nuts and occasional Chinese or Mexican food brought into the crowded room, conference members Don Nickles, Jon Kyl, Chuck Grassley, Billy Tauzin, Mike Bilirakis, and Nancy Johnson, all Republicans, debated and negotiated with Max Baucus and John Breaux, both Senate Democrats committed to a balanced bill that would provide affordable drug coverage for seniors. Baucus was the lead Democrat negotiator, but Breaux played a pivotal role in both the design and ultimate passage of the bill on the Senate floor. Officials from the Bush administration attended each meeting, offering not only the president's perspective on the bill but also their valuable knowledge of the detailed operational workings of the Medicare program.

The conference was at times contentious, as much over personalities as substance. Disagreements between Thomas and the chairman of the Senate Finance Committee Chuck Grassley, were frequent, including Grassley's staff temporarily boycotting meetings. And then there were occasions when Thomas made proposals that ignored weeks of careful negotiations. In the end I had to leave my position as just another member of the conference committee to assume my majority leader status; House Speaker Dennis Hastert and I, as leaders of our respective bodies, stepped in to personally negotiate the final settlement. Thomas was smart; this was all part of his strategic plan.

I worked hard to pull the many outside voices together on this issue, going to meet with the leaders of the influential seniors' group the American Association of Retired Persons (AARP), to seek their counsel and, I hoped, to secure their endorsement of the program. Republicans rarely successfully enlisted the support of the AARP, which almost always leaned to the left in Washington matters. It boasted more than thirty-five million seniors in its membership. I knew that without their support, the bill wouldn't pass. It simply made sense to me to consult with the representatives for the people who would benefit from the bill's passage. After many negotiations behind closed doors in my Capitol office, Speaker Hastert and I reached agreement with the leadership of AARP. That organization's support and political muscle were critical not only to help pass the bill but also to make sure it would be broadly supported by the American people during implementation. My staff, under the able leadership of health policy advisor Dean Rosen, worked tirelessly to secure the political support of other organizations representing doctors, hospitals, patients, and others. This behind-the-scenes staff work was invaluable in getting this big bill over the finish line.

Rank-and-file Republican congressmen and many conservative groups had major problems with the bill. Complaints ranged from fiscal conservatives outraged by the expansion of a new entitlement, to those concerned that the government was forbidden from directly negotiating for lower prices, to those concerned the plan would not pay to reimport cheaper drugs from abroad. The

Heritage Foundation and the National Taxpayer Union were two of the loudest and most prominent critics.

The passage of the final bill in the House and Senate was a compelling minidrama in itself. The House vote began late at night. I remember lying in bed, watching the vote on C-SPAN, until Karyn complained, "Bill, how can you come home and watch C-SPAN after spending all day on Capitol Hill? Turn out the lights and go to sleep!"

I did—only to wake up two hours later. Burning with curiosity about the final result, I slipped into my office and turned on the TV there, and discovered that the House vote was still going on! The legislation negotiated in the House-Senate conference had moved to a more centrist bill than the original House version conservatives were backing. Speaker Hastert was holding the vote open . . . and open . . . and open, while he and Tom DeLay were encouraging, prodding, and even twisting a few arms to get the votes needed to pass the bill. Hastert had toiled on health care for years as leader of GOP House Health Care Task Force; he knew this legislation was a good bill and it was a personal priority for him.

The bill did finally pass at 3:00 A.M., and for the next two days the headlines focused on how Denny Hastert had "abused" his privileges as House leader by strong-arming his colleagues into voting for the bill. Such is life in Washington.

Two days later came the final vote on the Senate side—or rather, on a significant test vote in which we needed sixty votes to force cloture and thereby, in effect, assure passage of the final bill. The test vote occurred late in the afternoon. The senators submitted their votes one by one, and, as was the norm, I planned to cut off the voting after twenty minutes. Senator Kennedy had turned against the bill by this time, and he'd taken with him several Democrat votes. Still, I hoped and believed that we would reach the critical sixty-vote threshold we needed.

But as the twenty-minute cutoff time approached, I saw that we had just fifty-nine votes—and that two senators had not yet voted. *Who were they? Why were they holding out?* I had to find out. I walked up to the front desk where the parliamentarian sits and looked at the long white card where individual votes were recorded to see which names did not have either an aye or a nay checked. The two blank names belonged to Democratic Senator Ron Wyden—long committed to a centrist approach to health-care reform—and to Trent Lott.

I looked around. Trent was in the back of the room, surrounded as usual by a small audience. The clock was ticking, and everyone's attention was focused on him. Ron, holding out because Daschle and the Democratic leadership had urged their caucus to defeat the bill, was watching to see what Trent did—if Trent voted no, so would he, since the bill would fail in any case. For the moment, the future of the entire Medicare bill was in Trent's hands.

I wondered what Trent was thinking. Health-care issues had never been his cup of tea. He didn't like the increased spending in the bill, estimated to be some $400 billion over five years. I knew Trent blamed me for his loss of the majority leader's seat, as indicated by the jibes he'd directed toward me in public and private in the months since his fall. Would this be about payback?

As the time to cut off voting approached, I hesitated about how I should act. I didn't want to keep the vote open and incur the same criticism Hastert had received. But I also didn't want to go over to Trent and beg for his vote. He knew what I needed, and what his colleagues needed, too. He knew what seniors deserved.

Finally, with seconds to spare, Trent strolled toward the parliamentarian's desk. He'd have to pass me to get there. As he did so, he leaned toward me, paused for a moment, and whispered just for my benefit, "This is the worst vote I have ever cast." Then he stepped up to the parliamentarian and cast his vote.

As Trent turned and stalked out of the chamber, the parliamentarian called his vote out loud: "Mr. Lott—yea!"

Trent had voted for me—for the seniors—and for the good of the country. And that, to me, is Trent Lott. At the end of the day— in this case a long, suspenseful day—he proved himself the ultimate team player, even if he might not like every single player on the team.

After this vote to overcome a filibuster, the vote on final Senate passage was close, but not nearly as close as in the House. The final bill passed 54–44.

As soon as the bill passed it was lambasted by Democrats and the left for its limited coverage and alleged concessions to big health-care companies. The right was equally uneasy with the expansion of an entitlement, and budget hawks from both parties complained about the long-term impact on the federal budget. Even moderates were upset by the irregular process implemented in the House and Senate to accomplish passage.

In the weeks following passage, the initial response was disappointing. The president's Office of Management and Budget revealed that its estimated cost of the bill was $534 billion, 35 percent more than previous estimates. A few months later, the chief actuary of the Centers for Medicare & Medicaid Services (CMS) alleged that his office had projected much higher costs, but the CMS administrator Tom Scully had pressured him to keep these estimates from Congress. Several members of Congress said they would not have supported the bill had they known these cost estimates at the time. Due to these embarrassments, many initially saw the drug bill as more of a liability than an achievement in the upcoming 2004 election. The mainstream press reinforced the initial dissatisfaction with the legislation on grounds of process. And even the AARP ran TV ads stating how confusing the bill was for seniors.

The new law made major changes to Medicare, the largest being the new prescription drug benefit for seniors to be administered entirely by private insurance plans. Congress mandated the drug benefit, including an annual premium, deductible, and varying coinsurance, including the infamous "doughnut hole" where at a certain level benefits ran out until catastrophic levels were reached. Why did we create the doughnut hole? We ran out of available money. Private insurers were paid based on a standard benefit, though they were given the flexibility to offer any plan they wanted that was actuarially equivalent. They also were required to offer minimum formularies—a preapproved list of prescription drugs. We made the private insurers the primary bearers of risk, a radical change in their Medicare role. Shifting risk from government to the private plans, we reasoned, would introduce incentives to lower cost and thus spending. This was revolutionary for an entitlement program.

The government was forbidden from directly negotiating prices with drug companies. We knew this wouldn't last more than a few years, but without this restriction it would be unlikely that any of the private insurers would come to the table to participate because government would always undercut them. In addition, we paid the private plans more than traditional fee-for-service—again, a provision that we knew would not be tolerated for long but that would allow them upfront resources to establish new systems necessary to adapt to the new markets of integrated care for seniors. I jokingly say we had to bribe the private sector to come to the table because of an inherent distrust of big government. But they came, and the results have surpassed anyone's expectations in terms of improved quality of care and lower-than-expected costs.

The law also made changes to the so-called "Hatch-Waxman" law to make it easier for cheaper generic drugs to reach seniors and required pharmacists to notify beneficiaries if there was a less expensive option. The plan relied on the power of private insurers to negotiate the best prices based on market mechanics.

Despite the improvements it provided to traditional Medicare and the new health-care choices for seniors, many people panned the Medicare Act. Conservative talk show hosts, with whom I held much in common, adamantly opposed the prescription drug benefit, fretting aloud on radio and television that it was a giant step toward socialized medicine. This reflected either a less-than-accurate understanding of the features of the senior prescription program or an inadequate understanding of how socialized medicine works—or both. Republicans way too often cry "socialized medicine" in response to even reasonable health reform proposals.

The most socialized system in the world exists right here in the United States. It is the Veterans Administration (VA) health-care system, which is available to all men and women who have served our country in the military. I spent ten years operating every week in the VA system. The current VA system far surpasses the private sector in systems management, the implementation of information technology, and adherence to evidence-based standards. It is the model for current plans to enhance information technology throughout our health-care system.

Sadly, this has not always been the case. Indeed, when I was in medical training, the VA was regarded as an antiquated, run-down system where only average doctors (or worse) would want to practice. The lines were horribly long and the waiting rooms overcrowded. The contrast reflects to me the advantages and disadvantages of a purely socialized system. With a centralized, command-and-control, top-down structure and generous budgeting, quality and access and costs can all be maximized for the patient—in the case of the VA by a massive commitment to electronic medical records and information technology. But with poor leadership at the top or limited central budgets (as is frequently the case overseas, where a few bureaucrats in the central government are making all the rationing decisions), the system falls apart, quality diminishes, and patients are hurt. When central budgets decline, patient care and innovation suffer.

Medicare, with or without prescription drugs for seniors, is *not* a socialized system, and the rhetoric to the contrary that comes from the mouths of uninformed politicians and talk show hosts—unfortunately Republicans much more often than Democrats, conservatives as well as liberals—is just flat-out wrong.

The Medicare prescription drug bill significantly expanded private health plan options in Medicare and dramatically increased enrollment in these private plans, which integrated health-care delivery for seniors, a marked improvement over the traditional fragmented fee-for-service care. Reimbursement in Medicare is determined by federally set fees, but the care itself is delivered entirely through the private system in private and public hospitals, nonprofit and for-profit alike, all across America. Doctors and nurses are not employed by the government. Medicare has been wisely structured as a public-private partnership that is flexible, maximizes patients' choices, and keeps administrative costs relatively low.

Medicare Part D—the official name for the prescription drug program we added in 2003—was set up to maximize participation by the private sector. There is no *government* prescription drug plan. It is entirely administered by the private sector. It is competitive and prices are determined by the marketplace, not by government fiat. The private-sector firms compete against one another to get the lower prices for their patients. And this competition is working!

And Part D, for the first time in Medicare, is "means tested," in the sense that the very wealthy get fewer benefits (unless they pay for them), and the poor get more. The benefit was structured to lean heavily in the favor of the poor and near-poor. And for the first time it began asking seniors with higher incomes to pay higher premiums for their physician services as well. To me it seems inevitable that this policy will have to be adopted broadly in future Medicare reform efforts.

The concept of prevention has historically been absent in Medicare. With the new law, for the first time a complete physical exam is provided by Medicare on entry to the program. And the inclusion of prescription drug benefits for seniors means expensive diseases can be averted. A pill to treat high blood pressure, available now through the new law, can prevent a heart attack or a stroke that would otherwise occur. The cost of the pill is a lot less than that of cardiac and stroke intensive care units. Maybe, just maybe, a large portion of the heart disease I operated on every day as a surgeon will be erased by the prevention we made possible for the first time in this new law.

The Medicare drug story illustrates how major reforms can be led by the congressional branch. It's a lesson that the Obama administration is likely to follow, when it comes to health-care reform. While President Bush supported prescription drug coverage, the White House's main contribution was its help pushing the bill to passage, not crafting the specifics of the legislation. The Bush administration had not made health care a major priority, and thus was comfortable having Congress lead. Moreover, the Bush team was well aware of the Clinton administration's mistake in attempting to foist specific health legislation on an unwilling Congress.

So how has the 2003 law fared? Better than anyone expected.

Seniors have flocked to the new program. By 2009 over 26.7 million seniors had enrolled in the new drug plans, 59 percent of the Medicare population.

And costs have each year come in much less than predicted (which explains the about-face of fiscal hawks and conservatives who today embrace the results of the program). Competition works. The marketplace works: Seniors are prudent shoppers and the financial incentives have resulted in a massive move toward generic drugs, away from the more expensive brand drugs. In 2007 the five-year cost of the prescription drug plan was revised downward by 26 percent from 2003 predictions! In 2009 the CBO announced an additional $86 billion reduction in projected Medicare outlays, due mainly to lower-than-expected prescription drug outlays.

Lawmakers originally worried that some regions of the country would have trouble attracting at least two competing plans from which a senior could choose, but there are currently several dozen plans offered in each enrollment area. Choice is guaranteed for seniors.

And the program is popular and well-liked. The percentage of seniors with a favorable view of the program has jumped from 17 percent at the beginning of 2004 to 42 percent in 2006 to 83 percent in 2009.

The prescription drug law represented a huge political shift for the United States. The social safety net of health-care security for seniors was strengthened with the addition of drug coverage. Ironically, the most conservative government in recent times had pushed through the largest increase in entitlements, including generous subsidies for low-income beneficiaries, since Lyndon Johnson. Private plans for the first time became major players in an entitlement program. Political alliances were transformed with the historically Democratic-leaning AARP strongly supporting a Republican-led initiative and market-driven, private health-care interests backing expansions in Medicare. The law was transformative.

In 1994, I left the practice of heart surgery, dreaming that I could play a role through public service in healing more than one patient at a time. I never envisioned, however, that I would be in a position to help pass a bill that over time will contribute to the health, hope, and healing of every American.

13

When Push Comes to Shove

We all make mistakes in life. Some play out in private, and some play out in public. Many consider my biggest mistake as majority leader was to act on the case of an incapacitated woman in Florida, Terri Schiavo. Looking back, politically and publicly, it may have been advantageous to have never addressed the issue. But morally? Let me share the full story of what happened, and you can be the judge.

The Terri Schiavo story was difficult and heartrending. As a physician who has focused on preserving life and who spent my medical career in transplantation, a field that requires the certification of brain death before doing a heart transplant, I suppose it was almost inevitable that I would become involved, especially because of its implications for future sanctity-of-life issues. And in addition to the oath every senator takes to protect the country and support the Constitution, I had also taken another professional oath, the Hippocratic Oath, promising to "do no harm" and to protect life.

Moreover, I knew something about disability policy at the federal level. I had strongly advocated and legislated for the rights of those with physical and mental disabilities—yes, even severe disabilities like those of Terri Schiavo. In fact, in the mid-1990s I served as chairman of the Subcommittee on Disability Policy, that focused on the rights of individuals with disabilities.

288

The saga involving Terri Schiavo's parents, Bob and Mary Schindler, and Terri's husband, Michael Schiavo, had been going on for nearly fifteen years before I first learned of the case. On February 25, 1990, Terri collapsed in the couple's St. Petersburg, Florida, apartment. She was twenty-six years of age. According to reports, paramedics who responded to Michael's 911 call found Terri lying facedown and unconscious, not breathing and with no pulse. The emergency workers attempted to resuscitate her and rushed her to the hospital. The period without oxygen caused severe brain damage. The cause of her collapse has never been determined, though at the time, she was considered to have suffered a cardiac arrest, possibly caused by a potassium imbalance or a lack of electrolytes in her blood.

In the months before her collapse, Terri had been striving to keep her weight down by dieting and drinking megadoses of iced tea to cause fluid loss. Terri remained comatose for two and a half months. When she came out of this coma, she was fed through a tube inserted through her abdominal wall.

Though severely brain damaged, Terri was breathing under her own power, she maintained a strong heartbeat, and her blood pressure was stable. Her vision was impaired, but she seemed to be able to follow objects with her eyes. When Terri's condition did not improve after nearly a year, the doctors who treated her in St. Petersburg diagnosed her as being in a "persistent vegetative state" (PVS), indicating that it was highly unlikely that Terri would ever get better. Michael Schiavo filed and won a malpractice suit against one of Terri's fertility doctors, for failing to diagnose bulimia in Terri. He sought $20 million to cover the cost of her future medical care. The jury awarded $1.4 million to be used for Terri's future care, and $600,000 to Michael for the loss of Terri's companionship.

In November 1990, Michael took Terri to the University of California in San Francisco in hopes that an experimental procedure involving the implanting of a thalamic stimulator in her brain might help. It didn't, and in January 1991, Michael admitted Terri to Mediplex Rehabilitation Center in Bradenton, Florida. In July, she was transferred to Sabal Palms Skilled Care Facility, a nursing home, where she received neurological testing and therapy.

Early on, Michael and the Schindler family worked together, doing everything possible to help Terri. But after the financial award in mid-1993, when Terri contracted a urinary tract infection, her husband halted treatment and entered a "Do Not Resuscitate" order. Terri's mother and father and the nursing home protested, and Michael rescinded the order. Apparently, by this time, he had lost hope of Terri's ever recovering.

In May 1998, Michael filed a petition to disconnect his wife's feeding tube. In response, Terri's parents again took legal steps to block such actions against their daughter. Terri had no living will indicating her desires should she become incapacitated, so the family remained embroiled in a legal battle for years over whether Terri would want to remain alive in her current condition. Michael claimed that she had made statements to the effect that she would not, saying, "If I ever have to be a burden to anybody, I don't want to live like that." Terri's parents disputed those remarks, unheard by anyone else, on the basis that as a devout Roman Catholic, Terri believed in the Church's position on sanctity of life and would not agree to euthanasia by refusing food and water. The Schindler family insisted that despite her difficulties, Terri demonstrated a strong will to live. Her parents and siblings all wanted her to live; her husband felt otherwise.

A trial was held in January 2000 to determine Terri's wishes, and Judge George Greer of Florida's Sixth Circuit Court in Clearwater, Florida, ruled that there was "clear and convincing evidence" that Terri would not want to be kept alive by artificial means. Based on Greer's ruling, Terri's feeding tube was disconnected for three days in April 2001 before a series of legal appeals halted the intentional starvation and dehydration. Michael Schiavo had not divorced his wife; he eventually fathered the child of another woman while Terri remained in various care facilities. The Schindlers questioned Michael Schiavo's motives for wanting Terri's feeding tube removed.

Following the 2000 trial, the Schindlers gathered opinions

from thirty-three medical experts who signed affidavits contesting the diagnosis that Terri's condition was beyond hope of recovery. A three-judge panel of the Second District Court of Appeals ordered that five doctors—two chosen by Michael Schiavo, two chosen by the Schindlers, and one chosen by Judge Greer—conduct tests on Terri.

Exact determination of the diagnosis was critical—the difference between Terri's life or death—since the law would allow food and water to be withheld if so directed by her husband if she was definitely in a *persistent vegetative state*, a specific syndrome that must be distinguished from *coma* and *minimally conscious state*. Under Florida law, Terri's next of kin—her husband and not her mother and father—could make the decision to withhold food and water, so it was essential to be absolutely accurate on the diagnosis.

Dr. Ronald Cranford was one of the two neurologists solicited by Michael Schiavo's attorney, George Felos. A neurologist, bioethicist, and known proponent of euthanasia, Cranford was a familiar face at "right to die" trials across America. He sometimes referred to himself as "Dr. Humane Death." Dr. Cranford was also a member of the board of directors of the "Choice in Dying Society," which supported doctor-assisted suicide. In addition to Cranford, Michael Schiavo chose neurologist Dr. Melvin Greer. The Schindlers selected Dr. William Maxfield, a radiologist, and Dr. William Hammesfahr, a neurologist. The judge chose Dr. Peter Bambakidis, also a neurologist.

As part of the court-ordered exam, Terri was videotaped for nearly six hours. The five doctors studied the tape and Terri's medical records and examined Terri as well. Michael Schiavo's two doctors concurred that Terri was in a persistent vegetative state, as did the doctor appointed by Judge Greer. But both Dr. Maxfield and Dr. Hammesfahr testified that Terri was *not* in persistent vegetative state, but rather was in a minimally conscious state. Maxfield testified that Terri had shown improvements in brain tissue and would benefit from treatments increasing blood flow and oxygen to the brain.

Neurologist Dr. Hammesfahr testified that Terri showed cognitive function and could benefit by treatment. In an interview, the doctor later told CNN, "I spent about ten hours across about three months [examining Terri], and the woman is very aware of her surroundings. She's very aware. She's alert. She's not in a coma. She's not in PVS." Dr. Hammesfahr went on to say, "With proper therapy, she will have a tremendous improvement. I think, personally, that she'll be able to walk, eventually, and she will be able to use at least one of her arms."

Video of Dr. Hammesfahr's examination of Terri was shown to the court during the evidentiary hearing. In the court-ordered video, Terri seemed to interact with her mother. Reacting with smiles, she seemed to follow commands to open and shut her eyes and lift her limbs. At several points, she turned her head toward the person speaking.

Dr. Cranford and Michael Schiavo's attorney described Terri's movements as nothing more than "involuntary reflexes."

Appearing on the *Oprah Winfrey Show* by satellite, Terri's sister, Suzanne Vitadamo, said, "When you go in and say 'hi' to Terri, Terri will in a sense do her best to say 'hi' to you. Or there's a lot of times where if you tell Terri you're going to leave, she'll cry. She doesn't want you to leave. So her reactions are very purposeful." In the same broadcast, Mary Schindler described Terri's actions for Oprah and her audience, "She cries, she laughs, and she follows me around the room. She laughs at her dad's jokes. Each day is different." Terri's brother and sister, her mother and father—all her immediate blood relatives—loved her and did not want her life terminated.

Sarah Green Mele, a speech-language pathologist at the highly regarded Rehabilitative Institute of Chicago, studied Terri's medical records, audiotapes of Terri and her dad, and the videotape presented at the evidentiary hearing. In a nine-page sworn statement Mele declared that Terri Schiavo was definitely not in a persistent vegetative state.

Despite the conflicting testimony, in November 2002 Judge George Greer reaffirmed his original decision and ordered that

Terri's feeding tube be removed on January 3. Court appeals delayed the action until October 15, 2003, when for the second time the feeding tube was removed. For six days Terri Schiavo hung on even as she was denied food and water, but a groundswell of support arose in Florida, prompting the Florida legislature to pass what was called "Terri's Law," empowering Governor Jeb Bush to intercede and order Terri's feeding tube be reinserted.

In a public statement, Governor Bush said, "I understand the limitations cited by the judges who have declined to hear the later stages of this case. However, any life-or-death decision should be made only after careful consideration of all related facts and conditions."

Michael's lawyers immediately appealed the ruling, calling it unconstitutional on the basis of the separation of powers, charging that Governor Bush had overreached his executive powers. The American Civil Liberties Union joined the fracas as co-counsel on the side of Michael Schiavo. Terri's Law was subsequently declared unconstitutional by Circuit Court Judge Douglas Baird. Upon appeal, the Florida Supreme Court struck down the law by a 7–0 decision, opening the door for the third time so that Terri could be legally and intentionally starved to death.

The case continued to draw national attention, with Michael and his attorney appearing on *Larry King Live*, and members of the Schindler family taking their case public on Fox News Channel's *Hannity & Colmes*. Meanwhile, Judge Greer continued to reject scores of motions brought by the Schindler family, including tests to see whether Terri could swallow food and water and more modern functional radiological studies.

Because of the lingering doubts and questions regarding personal agendas and conflicts of interest swirling around the case, calls to save Terri's life came from a wide variety of people—from the Vatican after Pope John Paul II stated that health-care providers are morally bound to provide food and water to patients, including those in persistent vegetative state, to Focus on the Family founder Dr. James Dobson, wheelchair-bound Christian author, artist, and singer Joni Eareckson Tada, actor Mel Gibson, and thousands of others. Many Americans could not understand why the young woman could be forced to die when both her parents, her brother, and her sister all clearly wanted her to live and were willing to take care of her. She was not brain-dead or on mechanical artificial life support; how could our legal system allow one individual—her husband—to terminate her life when her parents and siblings objected?

A California businessman offered Michael $1 million to leave Terri in the care of her family and walk away. Schiavo rejected the offer, stating that he had received other similar offers—for even more money. Talk show host Glenn Beck set up a pledge fund with over $6 million in hopes that Schiavo would back away from the decision to remove Terri's feeding tube.

Knowing my strong support of sanctity-of-life issues and my familiarity in dealing almost daily with the issues of brain death in the transplant field, constituents and colleagues alike repeatedly asked me about the various ethical and medical issues involved in the Schiavo case. But it was an interfamily issue, to be decided most appropriately locally—or so I first thought. *But does government have the right to terminate life when a family objects?*

The questions intensified when Judge Greer continued to deny the Schindler family's motions to nourish Terri orally, rather than through the tube. Instead Greer ordered Terri's feeding tube to be removed at 1:00 P.M. on Friday, March 18, 2005.

When I first heard about the situation facing Terri, I was curious to know more details from a medical standpoint. From my transplant work, I was well aware that for the diagnosis of persistent vegetative state the spouse can ultimately decide the fate of the patient. So the critical issue from a legal standpoint is to make absolutely certain the diagnosis is solid. Simply watching the continuous stream of news stories and reading the deluge of conflicting media reports raised the question in my mind, *Is she definitely in a persistent vegetative state?* It can be a difficult diagnosis to make, and according to a 1996 British medical journal article, even experts are wrong nearly half the time.

As a transplant surgeon whose work centers on the definition of death of the donor, I had spent many years studying and working through the various issues surrounding brain death, defined in a 1968 landmark article in the *Journal of the American Medical Association*. I knew the standardized clinical exams for the differing stages of incapacitation: coma, minimally conscious state, persistent vegetative state, and brain death. Making the diagnosis was often a tough call, and one that should never be made cavalierly. In addition, I knew from the medical literature that in the early weeks after injury (which Terri was not) there may be a progressively improving continuum from coma to persistent vegetative state and then to minimally conscious state.

I was surprised that a judge had made the decision to remove the feeding tube from a woman who everyone agreed did not meet the criteria for brain death—a decision that would essentially lead to death by starvation—when her family objected. As a transplant surgeon, I would never remove the heart from an individual—even to give life to another—when both parents and all immediate blood relatives objected. Yes, the law says I could do so with consent of the spouse, but I wouldn't. Although the parallel is not perfect, it's close enough. How could I support active termination of a young woman's life when her parents objected? The answer: I couldn't.

My next question was: If indeed Terri Schiavo clearly had no hope of being rehabilitated, did she have a living will, a written directive describing her wishes? I discovered that she did not. My interest piqued, I asked my staff to pull all of the court documents so that I could review them. I also called Dr. Hammesfahr, who had been the last neurologist to examine her, and he reiterated his expert opinion that Terri was definitely not in a persistent vegetative state. I talked with Terri's family members and met personally with her brother, and they told me of her reactions when they were with her. They told me that despite their willingness to care for Terri, physically and financially, their efforts had been blocked by the courts, thus leaving them no more options.

As the clock ticked toward the time when Terri's feeding tube would be removed, I consulted with Senators Mitch McConnell, Rick Santorum, and Democratic senators Harry Reid, Tom Harkin, and Kent Conrad. House Majority Leader Tom DeLay and his leadership team had led on bringing the Schiavo case to the level of congressional consideration. A bipartisan group of senators agreed the case warranted Senate consideration. Senator Conrad of North Dakota said of Schiavo, "Her parents want to give her a chance. I think of my own daughter. We ought to give her a chance." Democratic senator Bill Nelson said he supported the Senate bill "so that this case can be reviewed and decided in a timely manner." And Democratic senator Tom Harkin, an advocate for the rights of people with disabilities and the author of the original American with Disabilities Act, said, "It is my belief that people with disabilities and those who are incapacitated deserve the utmost dignity and respect. I plan to work with my Senate colleagues on both sides of the aisle to give cases like this an opportunity for further review in federal courts."

On Wednesday evening, March 16, I spent more than an hour in my Capitol office reviewing copies of the videotapes—the same ones that the court and doctors who evaluated Terri had seen, and *not* the clips shown again and again on the cable networks. These were not Schiavo or Schindler family home movies; the portions of video I watched included a neurologist conducting clinical tests to determine Terri's condition. After reviewing the video footage and after talking with the neurologist who had carefully examined her and concluded the diagnosis of persistent vegetative state was wrong, I was unconvinced that Terri was definitely in a persistent vegetative state. When the data is unclear, you err on the side of life.

On Thursday morning, I opened the Senate for business and made a statement regarding Terri. The members of the House of Representatives had for several days been considering a bill that would allow the case to be heard by a federal court, thus paving the way for Terri to be re-evaluated clinically by independent neurologists using modern structural imaging techniques. This would answer the questions raised in my mind. I knew that the Senate could pass something similar. Speaking to my colleagues about the fast-track debate regarding the Schiavo issue, I said:

> As most people know, this is coming to the floor very quickly, and the real, fundamental reason is, if we do not act, there is a good chance that a living human being would be starved to death in a matter of days. That is why the action now. That is why we are not rushing things, but deliberating quickly, so we can get it to the House of Representatives.
>
> She will be starved to death next Friday. I had the opportunity to look at the video footage upon which the initial facts of this case were based. And from my standpoint as a physician—I would be very careful before I would come to the floor and say this—that the facts upon which this case were based are inadequate. To be able to make a diagnosis of *persistent vegetative state*—which is not brain-dead; it is not coma; it is a specific diagnosis and typically takes multiple examinations over a period of time, because you are looking for responsiveness. I have looked at the video footage. Based on the footage provided to me, which was part of the facts of the case, she does respond.
>
> That being the case, and also recognizing she has not had a complete neurological exam by today's standards—allegedly, she has not had a PET scan or MRI scan; not that those are definitive, but before you let somebody die, before you starve somebody to death, you want a complete exam and a good set of facts of the case upon which to make that decision. All we are saying today is, do not starve her to death now—forever, I would argue—but establish the facts based on medical science today, and then make a determination in the future. That is what we will accomplish with [the] passage of this bill.

Fully aware that the U.S. Senate should rarely if ever get involved in private-action cases, I pondered what we might do. Florida senator Mel Martinez and Pennsylvania senator Rick Santorum worked to design a narrow bill, aimed specifically at the Schiavo case, which would allow Terri to be evaluated by independent neurologists with modern imaging techniques before a final decision was made. Essentially the bill said, "Let's make absolutely sure the diagnosis is correct before terminating her existence." This approach was rejected by the House, where the call for action was growing to a fevered pitch.

Later that night, I returned to the Senate floor as usual to close the business day. As leaders often do in the Senate, I took the opportunity to make remarks of my own. I quickly pointed out that I was speaking more as a physician than as a senator, as I outlined the Terri Schiavo saga as I understood it. At several points in the speech, I raised the question of whether we were sure she was in a persistent vegetative state. And then, in a portion of the speech that would be quoted, paraphrased, and distorted, I said:

> Persistent vegetative state, which is what the court has ruled—I say that I question it, and I question it based on a review of the video footage which I spent an hour or so looking at last night in my office here in the Capitol. And that footage, to me, depicted something very different than persistent vegetative state.
>
> One of the classic textbooks we use in medicine today is called *Harrison's Principles of Internal Medicine.* In the sixteenth edition, which was published just this year, 2005, on page 1625, it reads: "The vegetative state signifies an awake but unresponsive state. These patients have emerged from coma after a period of days or weeks to an unresponsive state in which the eyelids are open, giving the appearance of wakefulness." This is from *Harrison's Principles of Internal Medicine.* This "unresponsive state in which the eyelids are open"—I quote that only because on the video footage, which is the actual exam by the neurologist, when the neurologist said, "Look up," there is no question in the video that she actually looks up. That would not be an "unresponsive state in which the eyelids are open."

Skipping on down to what the Harrison's textbook says about vegetative state, I quote: "There are always accompanying signs that indicate extensive damage in both cerebral hemispheres, e.g. decerebrate or decorticate limb posturing and absent responses to visual stimuli." And then, let me just comment, because it says: "absent responses to visual stimuli," once again, in the video footage—which you can actually see on the website today—she certainly seems to respond to visual stimuli that the neurologist puts forth.

And lastly—I'll stop quoting from the classic internal medicine—one other sentence: "In the closely related, *minimally conscious state*, the patient may make intermittent, rudimentary vocal and motor responses."

I would simply ask, maybe she is not in this vegetative state and she is in this minimally conscious state, in which case the diagnosis upon which this whole case has been based would be incorrect. Fifteen neurologists have signed affidavits that Terri should have additional testing by unbiased, independent neurologists. I am told that Terri never had an MRI or a PET scan of her head, and that disturbs me only because it suggests that she hasn't been fully evaluated by today's standards. You don't have to have an MRI scan or a PET scan to make a diagnosis of persistent vegetative state, but if you are going to allow somebody to die, starve them to death, I would think you would want to complete a neurological exam. She has not had an MRI or PET scan, which suggests she has not had a full neurological exam.

I continued by quoting the British medical journal article concluding there was a 43 percent chance of error in diagnosing persistent vegetative state. "If you are going to be causing somebody to die with purposeful action, like withdrawal of the feeding tube, you are not going to want to make a mistake in terms of the diagnosis. At this juncture, I don't see any justification in removing hydration and nutrition. Prudence and caution and respect for the dignity of life must be the undergirding principles in this case."

The extraordinary measure of the U.S. Congress intervening

in a private case was controversial even among some of my own staff members. As we discussed it, I emphasized, "Let's find a way to give Terri's parents one more shot to keep their daughter; that's all we're saying. We are not dictating the results; we are simply saying 'Let's be sure of the diagnosis.'"

On March 20, I spoke again on the Senate floor about the bill intended to give Terri another chance at life. The bill we passed centered on the sanctity of human life. It was bipartisan and bicameral legislation, passing by unanimous voice vote in the Senate and by a vote of 203 to 58 in the House. President Bush was in Texas at the time, so he flew back to Washington and signed the bill at 1:11 A.M.

The decision evoked a lot of discussion because the bill forced Terri's case to be heard in a federal court. This legislation simply permitted a federal district judge to consider a claim on behalf of Terri for alleged violations of constitutional rights or federal laws relating to the withholding of food, water, or medical treatment necessary to sustain her life.

While the bill guaranteed a process to help Terri, it did not guarantee a particular outcome. Once the new case was filed, a federal district judge could issue a stay at any time, allowing Terri to be fed once again. The judge had discretion on this decision. I fully expected a federal judge would grant a stay of the state court's order to remove the feeding tube under these circumstances because for the court to even consider the case Terri had to be alive. If the new suit went forward, the federal judge would have to conduct a *de novo* review of the case, which means the judge could look at the case anew, not relying on the decisions of previous judges. The judge could also make new findings. Practically, this meant that in a new case, the judge could re-evaluate and reassess Terri's medical condition.

Almost immediately after my statements on the Senate floor, my office was inundated with responses from the public, mostly positive, but some scathingly hostile. Nick Smith, in my communications office, was dogged by perverse e-mails, showing ludicrous photos and taunting, "Senator Frist, diagnose this!" Others accused us of pandering to conservative right-to-life groups: "It's just a Bush play to consolidate the Republican base," some cynically declared.

In the midst of passing this legislation, an unsigned memo was circulated to a number of Republican lawmakers describing the Schiavo affair as "a great political issue" for our party to exploit. I publicly condemned the content of the memo and reaffirmed that my interest in the case, and that of the many Democratic and Republican Senate members who supported action, was to assure that the woman be given every chance to live—not to score political points.

Several aspects of this bill are worth noting. First, it was a unique bill passed under highly unusual circumstances, and it was not intended to, and should not, serve as a precedent for future legislation. Second, the bill did not impede any state's existing laws regarding assisted suicide. Third, the bill recognized that an accurate diagnosis, using current behavioral testing with structural imaging and neurophysiological findings to measure accurately a patient's level of consciousness, had not been performed in this case. Finally, in this bill, Congress acknowledged that we should take a closer look at the legal rights of incapacitated individuals in the future. Should we as a society always allow next-of-kin decisions to prevail when parents object?

The level of cooperation and thoughtful consideration surrounding this legislative effort was remarkable. Harry Reid and I remained in contact during the process. A few senators, including my close friend John Warner and Michigan senator Carl Levin expressed reservations but allowed us to move forward without opposition nonetheless. A strongly bipartisan group of senators—Republicans Mel Martinez and Rick Santorum, and Democrats Tom Harkin and Kent Conrad—shepherded the legislation through the Senate quickly.

But it was all for naught.

In the federal courts, the Schindlers' petitions and appeals were denied, and the U.S. Supreme Court declined to review the lower court's decision. Terri Schiavo and her family members who loved her had run out of options. The feeding tube was removed, and the world sat back to wait as Terri Schiavo died after fourteen days of no water and no food.

In June, Terri's autopsy report came back showing that she had, as expected, extensive, anatomic brain damage. This added nothing new. We'd already known she had a severe brain injury (the diagnosis of persistent vegetative state is not an anatomic diagnosis but rather a clinical one). Almost gloating over the pathologist's conclusions, some members of the media excoriated me following the release of Terri's autopsy report, saying that I had tried to diagnose her condition based on the television videotape of Terri, as some put it "from the floor of the U.S. Senate." That, of course, was totally false; I never made a diagnosis. I did want an accurate diagnosis confirmed. But the media was on a roll, fed aggressively by the partisan left, who saw an opening to challenge the credibility of the Senate majority leader of the opposite party. By undermining my credibility as a doctor, they thought they could destroy my credibility as Republican leader. And they threw arrows where it hurt—at my profession of medicine.

Many friends, physician colleagues, and critics said that Congress's involvement in the Schiavo case was a mistake. They thought that we should never have gotten involved, that I should never have stuck my neck out and worked with the House to bring this case to a resolution. Some went so far as to label it as the worst decision during my tenure as majority leader.

In retrospect, it's obvious that the Schiavo case was not a public relations victory for the Republican political cause or right-to-life values. Many Americans accepted the Democratic spin on the case—that the Republicans rushed for political reasons to interfere in a situation that should have remained purely a family matter. Our actions reflected the sometimes necessary conflict and tension between the rule of law (under which, in this case, the husband would have sole power over the woman's life) and the considerations of ethics and morality. The press conferences and other acts of political "grandstanding" around the Schiavo matter were principally on the House side, where frankly I think things got way out of hand. (I held no press conferences on the matter.) Emotions on the issue ran high and probably overwhelmed reason at times. The Schiavo case was a lot more complicated and nuanced than most people realize.

Still, I can't bring myself to believe that, knowing what we knew at the time, the actions we took in the case were inappropriate. Politically it might have been wise to ignore the plight of the innocent woman and the cry for help from her parents and family. But what about that Hippocratic Oath to protect life and to do no harm? To this day, morally, I believe it was the right thing to do.

THE MOST PAINFUL EPISODE DURING MY TIME SERVING IN THE Senate was one that was even more personal. It struck at my family, tore at my spirit, and even caused me for a time to lose faith in our legal system. Lasting for more than eighteen months, it cost me and my family personally more than we will ever admit. And it explains why many successful people today don't even consider spending a part of their life serving in Washington, D.C.

Hurricane Katrina hit on August 29, 2005. The levies were topped, and three days later I chartered a small twin-engine plane to New Orleans to offer my medical expertise in the chaotic, overwhelmed airport, then housing more than a thousand stranded individuals. Two weeks later, I returned to New Orleans for three days, this time with Franklin Graham and a relief team from Samaritan's Purse. And a week later I returned with a delegation of U.S. senators. Besides addressing the myriad problems raised by that natural disaster and the need for immediate relief funding, we were also monitoring the Senate Judiciary Committee hearing for the Supreme Court chief justice nominee, John Roberts. With all that going on, I wasn't surprised when Amy Call, my tenacious and thorough communications director, came into my office wearing an expression of consternation on her face. But I was surprised when she explained the reason for her concern.

"Senator, a writer for the *Congressional Quarterly*, was hanging around the office the other day, wanting to ask you some questions about a sale of some of your HCA stock. He missed you, so he approached me. He said that he had seen the financial disclosure information on file in the Senate Ethics Committee office."

I removed my glasses, leaned back in my chair a bit, and looked at Amy. A petite woman with an enormous passion for the truth and a keen ability to cut through fluff, Amy's eyes drilled into mine as she continued.

"I talked with him, and it seems he had some questions about why you would sell now, at this particular time, after putting up with all the critics' complaints of supposed conflict of interest all these years."

"Yes, that's right, Amy," I said. "Back in April, I initiated actions so the trustees of my stock could sell any final amounts of HCA stock remaining in the blind trust accounts they manage for me. Years ago when we set the trust up, the trustees were instructed to diversify me out of HCA, and I want to make sure they get me all the way out as we look to the future. The Senate Ethics Committee automatically receives notice of the final sale. It's all public information."

Amy nodded and moved on to other more pressing topics. But a few days later, she was back in my office again with that same worried look.

"A Tennessee reporter was looking into the price of your HCA stock when you sold it, and apparently, the stock price fell shortly afterward. The Associated Press is running with an article out on the wire that implies that you might have had inside information from your family or somebody at HCA before the stock price dropped. He's hinting that's the reason you sold your stock."

I was astounded: "You've got to be kidding me."

The gravity of Amy's statement stunned me at first. Although I was generally aware that the stock price had gone down by a few points recently, I had initiated the final sale of my remaining stock months before the price had slipped. Moreover, I had always sought both outside legal counsel and the written internal approval of the Senate Ethics Committee before making any moves related to the HCA stock, even though I was in no way expected or required to do so.

This was an issue I was sensitive to, given past criticism. Since my first day in office, I had been dogged by my opponents' accusations that my investments in medical-related businesses somehow would compromise my independence on issues relating to health care. It was a specious charge at best, and one I'd gone overboard to dispel through complete transparency and honesty. But in the heated, accusatory post-Katrina Washington atmosphere and with my heightened visibility as the Republican leader, I was not surprised that some members of the media might try to make a name for themselves by looking for some hint of scandal in my personal finances. In Washington, scandal sells.

Amy cut to the heart of the matter with her next question. "Did you talk to your brother before you sold the stock?" she asked point-blank. "Or anyone else regarding the timing of the sale?"

Since my older brother Tommy was a founder, board member, and former chairman of HCA, the implication was obvious—that I might have somehow received inside information that the stock was likely to fall.

"No, Amy. Absolutely not," I said. "Ever since the trust was set up years ago, they've been diversifying out of HCA and out of health stocks entirely. I'm tired of having to explain myself over and over to the critics who insist on seeing a potential conflict of interest. And as you know, during my last few years in the Senate, I want to focus more attention on health reform. The only surefire way to avoid more criticism is to own no health stocks. That's why I instructed the trust to sell any remaining health stocks in my portfolio. That should put an end to the criticism once and for all."

Amy nodded in understanding. "Okay. Sorry. Just had to ask."

"I know, Amy," I said with a smile. "You're doing your job. But I've been really careful about this. Every step of the way, we've gone way beyond what we need to in order to dot all the i's and cross all the t's. There's nothing to worry about."

Nothing, that is, if you don't worry about rumor, innuendo, and false reporting.

SURE ENOUGH, ON SEPTEMBER 21, 2005, THE ASSOCIATED PRESS story ran under the headline, "Senator Sold Stock Before Price Dropped; Shares Fell Two Weeks Later." The very first sentence contained misleading statements:

> Senate Majority Leader Bill Frist, a potential presidential candidate in 2008, sold all his stock in his family's hospital corporation about two weeks before it issued a disappointing earnings report and the price fell 15 percent.[1]

I wasn't a presidential candidate, HCA was a publicly held company and not "my family's" company, and the stock price had fallen less than 10 percent, which, of course, was bad enough for stockholders. But the glaring misinformation suggested to me that the reporter wasn't interested in facts so much as allegations and insinuations. The story's opener, "a potential presidential candidate," probably explained the increased media scrutiny. To me it also suggested that the false accusations could have been politically motivated.

The following day, the *Washington Post* followed suit with an article: "Frist Stock Sell Raises Questions on Timing," as well as another piece on the editorial page, "Mr. Frist's Curious Timing," with the latter suggesting that the Securities and Exchange Commission (SEC) should investigate "this case."

Not surprisingly, the following day, the SEC picked up on the story. Allen Hicks, my chief legal counsel in the majority leader's office, first learned of an inquiry into the sale of my personal stock in Hospital Corporation of America when an SEC representative called my office asking for information. Allen came to me immediately and said, "I know these allegations are baseless, but I think we better secure some outside counsel."

The SEC's involvement was appropriate given the media's unfounded allegations. The SEC investigates any accusation of suspicious trading circumstances. I was not offended by that. I can't say that I was happy, however, when I learned that the Department of Justice was also looking into the matter. I had no concern that they would find anything inappropriate, but U.S. Attorney Michael J. Garcia's office in the Southern District of New York was known for its prosecution of major drug cases and terrorist cases. Was something beyond a stock sale pushing this story? Just to be investigated by such an office lent some credibility to the allegations. I knew that some people, even my closest friends who believed in my integrity, might raise their eyebrows and say, "Well, they must have *some* reason for looking into this matter."

Truth is, the SEC and the U.S. attorney's office would be remiss not to explore the facts once allegations were made, however false they might be. I understood that, respected their positions, and of course promised immediately to cooperate completely with their efforts. Little did I know at the time, however, that the SEC and Justice investigations would drag on for eighteen months, costing the government and me enormous sums of money. If only the millions of dollars spent by the American taxpayers and me personally on this baseless inquiry had been spent investigating the Bernie Madoffs of the world, maybe the public would have been much better off.

Meanwhile, for nearly a month following the initial flurry of articles, the press continued to cast doubts upon my integrity. This was killing me. Almost daily I would open my packet of news clips and read articles questioning my honesty. The *New York Times* asked, "What Did Bill Frist Know and How?"[2] and even my hometown newspaper, *The Tennessean*, ran articles with headlines such as, "Insider Trading Notoriously Hard to Prove."[3] The not-so-subtle implication of such articles was that I was guilty of wrongdoing, but it might be difficult to prove.

To understand how all this came about, a bit of background is necessary.

Before serving in the Senate, while working as a practicing physician, I invested in many companies, including HCA. After being elected, I decided to put part of my personal stock portfolio into a "blind trust," allowing professional asset managers to handle the accounts while I was in office. I was not required to do this by the Senate rules and most senators did not set up blind trusts. I took that extra step to quell any questions about possible conflicts of interest between my personal finances and my public service, especially since the largest portion of my holdings were in HCA.

During my first term in office, I became increasingly involved in health issues. As I rose in the senatorial ranks, so did the number of aspersions cast by the Democratic opposition regarding my stock holdings in HCA. By the time I ran for a second term in 2000, some Democrats went so far as to say that I should not even vote on any health-related legislation.

Keep in mind that I had never been part of HCA. The company had been the brainchild of my brother Tommy, and together with my father and entrepreneur Jack Massey, Tommy had nurtured the business to phenomenal success. They had every reason to be proud of their achievements, as was I. Yet my life had taken an entirely different course. I was never involved with HCA's operations, I had never worked as a physician in an HCA-owned hospital, and in one sense, could have been regarded as a competitor when I helped develop the transplant center at Vanderbilt, which was not an HCA facility.

Despite not being required to do so, on two separate occasions I requested and obtained Senate Ethics Committee opinions acknowledging that my ownership of HCA stock complied with Senate rules and did not present a conflict of interest. Once I had placed my stock holdings in the blind trust, however, I was not permitted to be actively involved in the everyday details of buying or selling the stock. In fact I did not know what specific stocks were being bought or sold by the trustee. For any stock I put in the trust, I could instruct total sale out of it, but nothing more. Senate rules required reports by the trustees to senators who owned assets in the blind trust when any major activity—such as a large sale or purchase of stock—took place in the accounts. These same reports were sent simultaneously to the Senate Ethics Committee and became public information. A few other senators, including Ted Kennedy and John Kerry, also had holdings in blind trusts, and there rarely seemed to be any concerns.

The allegations of possible wrongdoing bubbled to the surface in 2005 when the media, the Democrats, and a number of my Republican colleagues began bandying my name about as a potential 2008 presidential candidate. Actually, I had begun to think about liquidating any remaining HCA stock that might still be in my trust soon after I became majority leader. Although I did not intend to run for president, I did want to keep all options for further public service open. Consequently, in April 2005, as I looked ahead to my final twenty months in the Senate, I decided after consultation with my advisors to make sure I would have no HCA stock by the time I retired from the Senate.

As it happened, at the time I was initiating this process, HCA was doing well. I had no economic reason to sell at the time. I asked Allen to determine whether Senate rules and relevant laws would allow me to direct my trustees to sell any remaining HCA stock in my blind trusts.

Although I was not required to request written judgments by the Senate Ethics Committee on whether I could sell my stock, I did so anyhow on May 20 and waited until I received formal approval before taking any action. It took several weeks before the Ethics Committee came back with their approval, so it wasn't until June 13 that I issued a letter directing the trustees to sell any remaining HCA stock in my family's trusts. The specific timing of the sale of the stock was up to the trustees, who had been diversifying out of the stock for years. Some of the stock was liquidated by July 1 and the remainder was sold over the next seven days. I was certain that I had handled the matter properly all the way along because we had gone to such extraordinary lengths, consulting with the attorneys and getting Ethics Committee pre-approval in writing.

On July 13, HCA issued an earnings warning that due to treating a higher number of uninsured patients and fewer insured patients, the number of patients reneging on payments was higher, and therefore profits were lower than expected. The stock price dropped 9 percent.

When the *Washington Post*, the Associated Press, and liberal watchdog groups caught wind of the stock price dropping after I had issued my instructions, they smelled blood. Although I didn't believe then (and still don't) that the allegations against me were purely politically inspired, Democratic National Committee Chairman Howard Dean wasted no time in urging the government to "fully and vigorously investigate Frist's suspicious stock trade."[4] The House Democratic campaign committee chairman Rahm Emanuel caustically commented, "Bill Frist has this all upside down. He thought Terri Schiavo could see and his trust was blind."[5] The war room of the Senate Democrats set up in the U.S. Capitol by Harry Reid stirred up the pot of controversy every way they could. The liberal left jumped on board because they saw this as a way to take down the Republican leader.

Exacerbating matters further, on September 29, Republican House Majority Leader Tom DeLay was indicted by a Texas grand jury for criminal conspiracy and money laundering. To have *both* Republican majority leaders under investigation at the same time was too good to be true as far as the Democrats were concerned. Although there was absolutely no connection whatsoever between the two, the Democrats hit the airwaves around the country deploring the Republican "culture of corruption," and attempting to spatter my reputation with a "guilt by association" tie-in with DeLay's indictment. More than a few liberal commentators took this opportunity to remind the public that Martha Stewart had been convicted for insider trading with far less money involved, and she had been sentenced to prison.

I had issued two press releases through my communications

office on September 22 and 23. Then, on September 26, I made my first public statement to the media about the inquiry. With a throng of reporters gathered around, and microphones, cameras, and tape recorders thrust toward me from every angle, I briefly explained that I had initiated the sale of my stock months before, in April, not June; that I had requested preapproval from the Senate Ethics Committee in May; and that I had received that full approval in June, before issuing the letter to my trustees with instructions to sell any remaining stock.

"An examination of the facts will demonstrate that I acted properly," I said. "I will cooperate with the Securities and Exchange Commission and the U.S. attorney for the Southern District of New York to provide the information they need as quickly as possible. My only objective in selling the stock was to eliminate the appearance of a conflict of interest. I had no information about HCA or its performance that was not publicly available when I directed the trustees to sell the stock." I glanced at the reporters, most of whom I knew on a first-name basis. "Now, I'm going to get back to work."

After that, I made a few more public statements about the matter, but for the most part, I simply let the inquiry run its drawn-out course. My lawyers advised me early on not to say too much. In retrospect, I don't know whether that was the best way to handle the matter, since in Washington lack of response to allegations is routinely interpreted as a sign of guilt. But I took their advice. We had a lot of serious issues to tackle in the Senate, so I attempted to focus my attention there. Most of my friends on both sides of the aisle in the Senate expressed support for my predicament.

Even Democratic leader Harry Reid was generally very kind to my face, stating privately as well as publicly that he was certain I would never do anything wrong or unethical. Then Harry went out on the Senate floor and made a statement questioning my integrity. Of course, I heard about it, so I immediately left my office, walked to the Senate floor, and told him that I thought that his comment was unfair and politically driven. Harry apologized and never repeated his derogatory comment in public again—although at political fundraisers, Harry repeatedly sought to elicit a crowd response by panning me: "He came in like Jimmy Stewart and is leaving like Martha Stewart." (One of my staff members later discovered that the line wasn't original with Harry but had originated with American University professor James Thurber. Nevertheless, Harry adopted it as his own out on the fundraising trail for the next eighteen months.)

I understand political hardball. But I think my opponents crossed a line or two on this matter. Unfortunately, character assassination is a sport in Washington.

Meanwhile on September 30, an editorial in the *Wall Street Journal* adroitly described the allegations against me:

> The way to understand the recent charges against Senate Majority Leader Bill Frist is as a case of no good deed going unpunished.
>
> The SEC is investigating Mr. Frist for unloading his shares of hospital chain HCA prior to a July earnings warning. Democrats are suggesting that an HCA insider gave Mr. Frist a call to tip him off. Mr. Frist denies it, and to date, there is zero evidence—nada, zilch, nunca—to support the allegation. And nothing in Mr. Frist's past or character suggests he's the kind of politician who'd try to scam the system to save a few bucks.[6]

The *Journal* emphasized that I had first sought legal advice about selling my HCA stock back in April 2005:

> This would have been before even HCA would have foreseen earnings trouble. April would also have been a smart time to sell, with the company's stock up 40% for the year. The irony is that Mr. Frist was never required either to establish a blind trust or to sell his shares. In both cases he did so to insulate himself from the appearance of any conflict. Instead, in doing both he has only made himself a bigger target for those who'd suggest he has something to hide.[7]

Then on Saturday, October 1, I was pleasantly surprised when Carrie Johnson, a staff writer for the *Washington Post*, presented a fair and mostly positive article with the headline, "Frist Sale of Stock Launched in April; Senator and Advisers Discussed It in E-Mail." In her article, Johnson stated forthrightly:

> Private e-mail between Senate Majority Leader Bill Frist and his advisers reflects that Frist began discussing the sale of his HCA Inc. stock in April, months before it became clear that the hospital firm's shares would decline in value, according to documents reviewed by the Washington Post.
>
> An April 29 message from G. Allen Hicks, chief counsel to the majority leader, informs the senator that they can discuss his "blind trust question sometime today." Frist also exchanged e-mail with his accountant, Deborah Kolarich, in Nashville, the same day in what he called an effort to "dispose of all hospital stocks in all accounts that I have control of." [8]

As much as I tried to move on to matters more important to our country, in almost every interview, the subject of the HCA stock sale came up. "Why liquidate?" interviewers wanted to know. "Why now?"

But my Democratic colleagues focused on the stock issue. They continued to make patently offensive statements about the matter as long as the investigations remained open. Months and months went by. The media followed their lead and kept hammering away, as well. For instance, when I appeared on NBC's *Meet the Press* on Sunday, January 29, 2006, nearly four full months after the *Washington Post* and *Wall Street Journal* had run articles revealing the e-mail trail that existed months in advance of my stock sale, the advertised subjects on the table that morning were the war in Iraq, national-security-related eavesdropping, Katrina, Hamas, and the upcoming presidential election campaigns. But the host, the late Tim Russert, a family friend and highly respected journalist, spent a major chunk of time drilling me about the HCA inquiry—even though there was really no news to report.

The questions continued for more than a year until April 19, 2007, when the U.S. attorney for the Southern District of New York notified my lawyers that they were closing their investigation. They had found nothing awry. The following day, the SEC issued a similar statement. It had all been much ado about nothing.

Why the SEC and U.S. Attorney's Office investigations took so long, especially after the discovery of the paper trail proving the time line when I had initiated the actions, I'll never know. The consensus was that they wanted to do a thorough job, leaving no stone unturned, and they wanted to avoid any suggestion that I was getting special treatment because I was a "high-profile" figure. There were concurrent inquiries going on with a number of HCA employees and we were told my case would not be dropped until all others had been settled. I didn't expect special treatment; I just wanted fair treatment. This dark cloud hung over me and Karyn daily. That the inquiry took nearly eighteen months was a travesty. And while the investigation dragged on, the financial cost to defend myself against baseless charges kept adding up. Law firms don't give you a refund when the government closes its investigation after finding nothing amiss. The government doesn't pay these legal bills—Karyn and I do. And the legal fees were huge. In fact, I am still paying off the loans from those bills today. Ethical public service can be expensive . . . very expensive.

Along those same lines, exoneration doesn't receive the same play in the media as an accusation. When the news hit that an inquiry was under way, the *Washington Post*, the *New York Times*, and the Associated Press ran story after story with bold headlines, often above the fold on page one. But when I was totally exonerated, the articles were few and buried deep inside the papers. The headlines in *The Tennessean* sounded almost disappointed: "Frist Won't Be Charged With Insider Trading."[9] In today's media climate, being innocent does not sell papers.

Throughout the eighteen-month ordeal, I was appalled by the

enormously wasteful inquiry. I'd like to say that I couldn't believe it, but after serving in the U.S. Senate for twelve years, I had learned not to be surprised by political or personal smear tactics. Moreover, the allegations were even more painful because HCA was the business embodiment of Dad's values and of my brother's commitment to serving others. It hurt me deeply that my family's integrity was on the line, that innocent family members were investigated, and that my family's reputation for honesty that my father and his father before him had built into a legacy could be so maliciously impugned—and for no reason whatsoever other than political shenanigans and manipulation.

Saddest of all, perhaps, an inquiry like this one, involving unrestrained celebration of false allegations by media and pundits, discourages good people from entering public service. Who wants to run for office if your reputation can so easily be twisted and sullied? Freedom of speech and freedom of the press are two of our most cherished rights in America, but it bothers me to this day that there is no accountability for those who make baseless accusations. As someone who worked diligently to recruit the best and brightest into elective politics, I know our nation is repeatedly robbed of excellent public servants and has fewer qualified, accomplished, noble men and women from whom to choose come election day as a result.

THE PHONY SCANDAL SURROUNDING MY STOCK IS LINKED TO A broader problem with our current political system—the erosion of civility. It's a problem that, perhaps, I saw with special clarity because I came to politics only after a long career as a physician.

As my dad taught me—and, more important, demonstrated daily by his own example—being a physician is about tolerance and understanding, not judging or condemning others. A doctor's task is to alleviate suffering and improve quality of life, regardless of whether a patient's personal choices may have worsened or even caused his or her problems in the first place. Naturally, we try to educate our patients and encourage them to make wiser choices in the future. But our first responsibility is always, simply, to care for others, no matter their background or station in life. That is service.

Coming from this culture of healing, adjusting to the world of politics was a shock for me. Debate is one thing—I fully expected to encounter clashes of opinions and even value systems in politics. But what I experienced, too often, was outright combat. Worse still, it was often combat not in the service of higher ideals but simply for its own sake—as if winning the latest battle for political power was the highest good.

This attitude hasn't always been the rule in Washington. Howard Baker, among others, told me in no uncertain terms how the atmosphere had deteriorated during his years on the scene. Over time, the notion of politics-as-combat has become increasingly institutionalized, with the two major parties growing more and more insular, narrow-minded, and extreme. Nowadays in the Senate, fewer and fewer meetings—even informal lunches or hallway conversations—include members of both parties. Fewer and fewer members of Congress take the time to develop true friendships or even strong working relationships with their counterparts across the aisle. More often than not, legislative discussions center not on what is best for the country or the world but rather on how one party can outmaneuver the opposition, score political points, and improve its chances of gaining seats in the next election. This has got to change.

This approach has infected the broader political culture as well. The news media are increasingly dominated by self-anointed pundits who seem to prefer shouting one another down to engaging in thoughtful discussion of issues. During my years in the Senate, I sat in the green room of many a television studio, preparing for an appearance to discuss some current topic, usually opposite a Democratic spokesperson or liberal commentator. The producer would generally urge us to "mix it up," hoping for personal attacks, inflammatory accusations, and slanted, exaggerated arguments. Flying sparks evidently make for "good TV," even if they do nothing to inform or educate the public.

This simply wasn't my style—either in heart surgery (Dr. Shumway taught us not to throw our surgical instruments) or in political discourse—which meant I probably ended up appearing on the cable stations less often than some of my more combative colleagues. That was fine—my goal was to serve the public good rather than promote myself. In retrospect, I should not have listened quite so much to my advisors, who discouraged me from responding early and more completely to my critics over matters like the HCA inquiry and the Schiavo affair.

In 2008 we elected a new president who ran, in part, on a promise to change the tone in Washington. He has his work cut out for him! Ironically, our previous president made exactly the same pledge—which he proved unable to keep. Like the overwhelming majority of Americans, I hope President Obama will succeed in the effort. But restoring civility to Washington won't be an easy task. It will surely require a genuine commitment by all of us, both inside and outside government. I would love to see it happen—for the good of the country.

14

A Promise Kept

One afternoon in late October 2006, when the Capitol building was relatively empty and the Senate chamber was quiet, I pushed open the back doors and slipped onto the floor of the U.S. Senate. I made my way to the front of the chamber and sat down at my majority leader's desk to carry out a time-honored tradition almost as old as the institution itself. I opened the drawer and began carving my name where previous Senate leaders had left theirs: Robert Taft, Hugh Scott, Everett Dirksen, Howard Baker, and Bob Dole.

Each of today's one hundred senators has a similar desk, forty-eight of which date back to 1819, when they were purchased after a fire had badly damaged the Capitol's furnishings. Years ago, before members of Congress had their own office suites, the chamber desk served as a senator's main work area. Today, the desks are a convenience and a constant, awe-inspiring reminder of the Americans from previous and present generations who have served in the Senate chamber.

As I pored over my handiwork, it struck me that a name carved into the bottom of the old, oak drawer is the only thing of permanence that anyone leaves in the place, that my time there, as for all the senators, was but a season. We were there to occupy a seat for a short time, not to possess it, never to own it. And that's as it should be.

I had pledged to serve two terms and return home; I'd do that. But should I also consider running for the presidency? Pondering all of this caused me to consider the future.

One night, Karyn and I hosted some friends for dinner at our home in Washington, partly to thank them for their service and support, but also to talk through some of the pros and cons of tossing my name into the presidential race. The conversation was lively as my loyal communications director Amy Call, insightful and smart chief of staff Eric Ueland, pollster Dave Winston, national fundraiser Linus Catignani, former counsel Alex Vogel, best friend from Nashville (and strongest, most dedicated supporter of all) Steve Smith, and longstanding confidante Emily Reynolds bantered over the issues. Later that evening, reflecting on the conversation, I told Karyn, "Our passions have always been to bring hope and healing to others, and I don't think running for president is the best way for us to do that. Nothing feels right about it."

In the back of my mind, I kept thinking about a series of confidential conversations that I had had long before with the politically savvy and realistic Mitch Bainwol. Just after the 2004 elections and then a few months later at a planning retreat at an inn on the Chesapeake, Mitch in no uncertain terms said that the combination of being leader and the electoral realities of trying to follow a two-term Republican presidency was just too much of a lift. A few months later Mitch came by and suggested that I formally announce that I would definitely not run, and then focus all my energies on the leader role. Mitch said it wasn't a lack of faith in me (though maybe he was just saying this to be nice!) so much as a sense that the stars just weren't aligned right. I listened carefully and the words sank in—but then again, never in my life had I closed doors to future opportunities. My chemistry professor at Princeton had instructed always take the road less traveled. I often wonder how the last two years of my tenure would have been different if I had taken Mitch's sage advice to publicly close the option of ever seeking higher office.

Just before Thanksgiving 2006, Karyn and I went to Nantucket for a two-day getaway and to make a final decision about whether to throw our hat into the ring to seek the Republican nomination for the presidency. It was exactly two years before the 2008 election—now was the time to take the plunge, if I was going to do it. I had a conference call set up with about thirty of my strongest supporters.

All the necessary groundwork had been laid. We had a strong core of supporters who were primed and ready to go. We had cultivated a nationwide network of fundraisers over the past four years, many of whom I had gotten to know personally through my chairmanship of the Senate campaign committee. Steve Smith had led, with Nashville-based Linus Catignani, our Tennessee-based leadership political action committee, Volpac. Over the years Volpac had attracted over fifty thousand contributors from around the country who believed in conservative principles; we in turn used those resources to support political candidates at all levels of government, concentrating on the Senate races. Steve, with his wife Denise, had systematically explored the possibility of raising sufficient funds with donors nationwide through a series of one-on-one meetings (staged as a monthly cookout at his breathtakingly beautiful farm outside Nashville). He concluded that sufficient money could indeed be raised for the primary. Barry and Jean Ann Banker had spent countless hours traveling around the country over the previous two years building support for my political endeavors.

I knew that my consistently conservative principles were in line with the Republican values of the day. And I felt that my own brand of conservatism, characterized by a style of inclusiveness and a focus on personal issues like health and education, not generally associated with Republicans of the day, would connect strongly with the everyday concerns of American families and workers.

I had crafted strong relationships with numerous leaders of foreign countries. I had met both our allies and our potential adversaries, and I had traveled to most of the hot spots of the world. America wanted action, not just words. My annual medical mission trips to personally deliver needed care to the people of Sudan and other distant parts of Africa, my multiple trips to New

Orleans post Katrina, and my early journey to Sri Lanka just days after the devastating tsunami hit demonstrated a genuine caring that were extensions of my life as a healer.

The political climate was another matter. Two weeks earlier, Republicans had been soundly defeated in the 2006 midterm elections, losing thirty seats in the House and six in the Senate. Only 29 percent of Americans thought the country was on the right track, and President Bush's popularity was in the tank, his approval rating hovering in the upper thirties.

But it wasn't the president alone with whom the American people were disgusted. Congress's poll ratings were abysmal, too. Only 16 percent of Americans approved the performance of Congress in the last poll before the 2006 election. Exacerbating matters still further, on the day that Congress was to leave for the October break to gear up for the elections, the Mark Foley scandal—regarding the congressman's inappropriate contact with a House page—hit the news and from there it was all downhill.

The event played right into the Democrats' theme that corruption was rampant in Congress—especially among Republicans. To be sure, both parties had egg on their faces. Congressmen Randy Cunningham and Bob Ney had resigned after pleading guilty to corruption charges, and U.S. Representative Curt Weldon was under investigation for alleged unethical conduct. Republican House Majority Leader Tom DeLay, who had earlier been indicted by a Texas grand jury on charges of violating campaign finance laws, resigned after two former aides were convicted of playing roles in the corrupt lobbying activities of Jack Abramoff (the same scandal that had taken down Congressman Ney). The FBI had raided the Capitol Hill office of Louisiana Democrat U.S. Representative William Jefferson, as they conducted an investigation into allegations he had accepted bribes in return for political favors. Yes, corruption existed within both parties, but it was we Republicans who were running the show, and it all fell on our watch.

Sitting with my notes spread out before me in Nantucket, I listened as Steve opened the 11:00 A.M. call and then turned it over to me. I presented a review of the elections and what the outcomes implied for the party. It was hard to be optimistic, because the results spoke so emphatically for themselves: Americans demanded change. I quickly moved into the pluses and minuses of my running. Now, as I spoke to my key supporters, the negatives seemed to loom larger in my mind.

First, I was tired. For the past four years, I had served as majority leader, chosen by my colleagues to represent their interests in the Senate. Putting the interests of fifty-four other senators before my own oftentimes meant making difficult compromises and reaching decisions that created short-term frustration for me. And I was tired of investigations and I was tired of false accusations.

For the eight years before becoming leader, my focus had been on the more than six million people in Tennessee. I had regularly visited each of the ninety-five counties in the state, not to merely pass through and check it off my list, but to visit and listen to the ideas, concerns, and needs of Tennesseans. That meant traveling almost every weekend of the year, being away from Karyn and missing the boys' weekend sports events that every father wants to attend. I loved connecting with the people across the state, but there is a family sacrifice to politics that most don't see. The toll public service exacted on my family life was heavy. So I asked myself, *Do I honestly want to spend the next ten years of my life with a schedule that is even more demanding in terms of time spent away from my family and friends?*

Furthermore, America wanted change. Americans did not want someone so closely associated with President Bush following him in the White House, and they certainly didn't want the status quo in Congress. And as the leader of the Senate, I would have a hard time saying I wasn't part of the status quo, no matter how forward-leaning my ideas and plans.

Moreover, I supported President Bush (and still do), and I was not about to betray or forsake that friendship—nor the respect I had for his values, his leadership, or his boldness. Maybe it was just the loyalty that Dad believed to be so fundamental to one's character. Though he never voiced it directly to them, I knew it deeply hurt Dad when young colleagues left his medical practice to join another because of a better deal. A campaign in the existing political climate would demand a repudiation of the Bush presidency—and I knew that was not for me.

Finally, perhaps most important was the fact that I really am a citizen legislator. I had pledged in 1994 that I would go to Washington to serve two terms in the U.S. Senate, then return to Tennessee to live under the laws that I had helped pass. And I was determined to do just that.

Karyn and I were ready to go home and live in the home on Bowling I grew up in.

As difficult as it was for many to understand—even some of my closest colleagues—my goal in life had never been to become president of the United States. That is not why I ran for the Senate and not why I became majority leader. I wasn't there to climb a political ladder to the top; I was there to serve. And the more I considered it, the more I recognized the fire in the belly required to run for president was simply not there for either me or Karyn.

After a long discussion during the conference call, I sealed my decision. "I will not be running for president in 2008," I said, as I closed the call. I knew that I was disappointing many of my closest friends, men and women who had spent hundreds, even thousands of hours working on my behalf, and I sorely wished, for their sakes, it could have been otherwise. But when I considered the matter carefully, the choice was obvious. It was right for me, right for Karyn and my sons, and right for the country.

On December 7, 2006, after the usual flurry of late-night legislative bargaining that occurs near the end of every session of Congress, I stood at my majority leader's desk—my name now indelibly carved in the drawer—to give my farewell address to the Senate. The chamber was full that day, as most senators tend to honor the tradition of a departing majority leader's final formal address.

The galleries were lined with spectators as well. One entire section was given over to my family members and close friends who made the trip to Washington to share in these special mo-ments. Karyn, of course, was there, as were Harrison and Bryan (Jonathan was attending classes at Vanderbilt); so were my brother Tommy, Trisha, and my sister Mary, and her husband Lee. Barry and Jean Ann Banker and Steve and Denise Smith made the trip as well. It was an emotional, bittersweet day, to say the least, as we all had special memories of why I ran for office in the first place, what it took to get here, then to have risen to be the leader of the Senate in such a short time. And now I was preparing to leave.

The audience in the Senate was quiet and respectful as I spoke of some of the successes and challenges of which I had been a part over the preceding twelve years. I thanked my fellow sena-tors, the people of Tennessee, my staff and family. My voice thick-ened and I nearly choked up as I said:

> The two people who won't hear me thank them today directly are two who were here at my swearing-in, but who have since passed on—my parents, Dorothy and Tommy Frist. They left a great legacy of honesty, civility, fairness, hard work, and ser-vice. They passed that legacy to my own brothers and sisters, Mary, Bobby, Dottie, and Tommy, who all in their own way, with their children and grandchildren, live lives of service to others.
>
> I've spent a lot of time these past few weeks reflecting, but I've also spent a great deal of time thinking about the future of this institution. As I prepare to leave here and return to my home, many people have asked me if I regret the promise I made to serve two terms. "If you knew then what you know today, would you have made that same promise?" they ask.
>
> And my answer is "Yes."
>
> I believe today, as I believed when I came here, in the ideal of a citizen legislator. And bittersweet though it might seem today, it is right.
>
> I hope that my service, that the example of someone who had never served before, spent his life pursuing another pro-fession, coming here and rising from one hundredth in se-niority to majority leader, the example of a committed doctor

who has been able to find purpose and fulfillment in serving others through public service, through elected office, will inspire others to seek office. And those that come to serve after me as true citizen legislators will bring fresh perspective and ideas that will in ways small and large make this country and this institution better.

I closed with a word of hope: "I have spent a lifetime learning, 'To everything there is a season.' And today, my season in the Senate draws to a close. Tomorrow is a time for new rhythms."

I paused briefly, looked up toward the Senate chamber ceiling, and said:

And under the dome, it is a time for fresh faces and fresh resolve. Change is good. Change is constructive. The Senate changes, the people who serve change, but what doesn't change is that every one of us who serves believes deeply in the genius of the American democracy.

So, it is with the deepest appreciation that Karyn and I thank you all for twelve wonderful years. There are no words to describe the honor it has been.

My Senate colleagues and the audience in the gallery rose in what seemed a single motion into a somewhat overwhelming standing ovation. I looked up at Karyn and my other family members and friends in the gallery. Many of them had tears in their eyes, as did many of my staff members. It had truly been the time of our lives.

Harry Reid was one of the first to come across the aisle to wish me well, as did Ted Kennedy, and many others. For a few moments, anyhow, we were all on the same team.

IT WOULD HAVE BEEN GLORIOUS TO HAVE LEFT ON THAT NOTE, BUT technically, I still had three weeks in office, and more important, we had a lot of work to hammer out before everyone left town during the Christmas break. We worked late the last two days of the session, fashioning last-minute compromises until nearly 2:00 A.M. each day. When I finally adjourned the Senate for the last time, I was joined by several of my staff members, who as usual had stayed late with me until the wee hours of the morning. I showed them my name carved in the Senate desk, and Amy and Allen took turns in further deepening the carving of my signature. We laughed and cried and reminisced about the good times. We went back to the majority leader's office for the last time as colleagues.

In the office somebody broke out a bottle of champagne, and we toasted our tenure in the Senate—especially our four years as majority leader. Many nice comments and compliments were shared. My brief words centered on what I felt at the time, a verse from the Twenty-third Psalm, "He restores my soul," something many expressed when reflecting on the experience of working together in service to the Senate and the country. It was a memorable evening. Close to 3:00 A.M. I raised a final toast in honor of my staff. After a few final farewell hugs, we quietly slipped out of the Capitol into the chilly December morning. Life would never be the same. When we returned in January for the swearing in of the 110th Congress, we would no longer be the majority. Harry Reid would be the majority leader, and I would be an ordinary citizen.

DURING MY LAST FEW WEEKS IN OFFICE, I HAD MANY REQUESTS for favors—some people wanted job recommendations, others needed last-minute medical advice—but perhaps the most unusual and most poignant request came from Robert (Bob) Ritchie, or as most know him, Kid Rock. Kid is a phenomenal performer who crosses musical genres from hip-hop to southern rock. He grew up in a small town north of Detroit, but for a while he had a condo just around the corner from our Bowling Avenue home in Nashville. Karyn and I had spent some time with him a few years earlier when he was in D.C. for the Kennedy Center Honors. Kid knows how to touch people. When he performed at a Republican convention party in 2004, his incredible musical range and his intense, fever-pitched energy whipped the crowd of a couple thousand young Republicans hanging from the rafters of a converted church into a near frenzy, forever putting to rest the myth that Republicans are stiff-necked, stuffed shirts.

Often characterized as one of rock's rowdiest characters, off-stage Kid Rock is a humble, deeply caring man, especially when it comes to his family. And he has got heart. Maybe that's why we connected so easily.

On December 16, 2006, I was at my Capitol office trying to clean up some last-minute work, when Ramona called and said, "Kid Rock's on the phone. He says it's urgent."

"Bill, I need some help," Kid Rock said. "I'm having a hard time going through my divorce, and I want to do something meaningful for my son."

I had been working night and day on last-minute legislation, so I hadn't been paying close attention to Kid's troubles, but I soon learned that he was going through a highly publicized, tumultuous divorce from actress Pamela Anderson. He began to share some of the details of his life with me on the phone, and then said, "The thing that bothers me most is that I have a teenage son in Detroit. As a single father, I've raised him with the help of my family back home, and then when Pam and I married, I uprooted him and moved to Malibu. He got close to Pam's boys, and now that we are broken up, my son is taking it really hard, because he knows it's been hard on me. I'm looking for some meaningful ways to spend more time with him."

We talked a bit, and he reminded me that we had talked in the past about how much it had meant for me and my boys to take medical mission trips to Africa together. I'd take one son at a time to maximize the experiences we could have together. Kid got excited about the concept of taking his son overseas on some sort of mission trip. I told him this would be impossible to pull off in the short term, but that maybe we could arrange something in the future.

"Well, in the short term," he said, "I want to serve others. Could you arrange for me to get to Afghanistan or Iraq to demonstrate my support, all my fans' support, and America's support for the soldiers who are fighting for us every day? I want to tell them they are great Americans. I want to do something for others."

"Great idea," I replied, knowing from personal experience that trips like this help put life in perspective. "When do you want to go?"

"How about next week?" Kid responded. "Who is going to Iraq to do shows for the troops this Christmas?"

"I'm not sure," I said.

"Well, I'd like to show my son that Christmas is really about being unselfish. Not presents. I want to go be with the soldiers who can't be with their families. I want to spend Christmas with the troops. And I'd like to take my son."

"Kid, it will be next to impossible to get you over there on this late notice, let alone your son. It's not exactly an easy thing to do. But let me see what I can work out."

"Please do whatever you can," Kid begged.

I hung up the phone and stepped into Ramona's office next door to mine. Over the years, Ramona had learned that I liked to take on the quirky, out-of-the box challenges that occasionally make it to the desk of the majority leader. "Ramona," I said, "Kid Rock is down in the dumps and has made a personal request. Who can we contact to see about getting him over to Afghanistan or Iraq to perform for the troops . . . during Christmas?"

"Christmas! That's less than ten days away," Ramona reminded me.

"Yes, but let's see what we can do."

Ramona went to work on it, and I called some people at the White House, as well as former staffer and then legislative affairs director at the Pentagon David Broome, always game for the tough-to-crack problem. David magically made it happen, and a few days later, Kid Rock was performing—just him and his guitar—for thousands of American soldiers in the middle of the war zone.

On Christmas Day an IED hit a convoy, so Kid went to the hospital to visit the men who had been wounded. It was a profoundly moving experience for him, which he later described to Larry King on national television.

I went to the hospital and, I mean, to see Marines crying, grown men crying, first of all, and then to see—just go into a room where these kids have been hit and they are shell shocked . . . to watch the chaplain run upstairs and read last rites or whatever it is to a kid who is dying . . . and to imagine, who wants to call these kids' parents on Christmas Day and say he's gone. It makes every day so appreciative.

When I heard about the way the men in women in uniform received Kid Rock, I just smiled. He went there to serve, to give something to the troops, but he came back having received much more than he gave. That's what happens when a person has the heart to serve; it's a strange paradox, but you always get back more than you give.

"Tomorrow is a time for new rhythms." These are the words I used to close my final remarks on the Senate floor. So what are these new rhythms for me?

I left the Senate with no clearly defined plans for the immediate future, which as far as I can tell is rather unusual. Karyn and I sold our home in Washington, a warm home that had watched our three boys mature from young kids through their frenetic high school years to become strong young men. We moved back to Nashville, where the final renovations were being made on the family home on Bowling. We became empty nesters with the move. Our youngest son, Bryan, was off to Princeton, where he is majoring in history with plans to go to medical school (my dad would be proud of him for continuing the tradition in the "greatest of all professions"). Middle son Jonathan, the one who always took the more adventuresome road and likely will proudly serve in the military, was attending Vanderbilt in Nashville; he'd thought he was "going away to school" when he left Washington, not realizing Karyn and I would be following him there for his junior and senior years. And Harrison, who confidently led the way for the other boys through their high school years, graduated from Princeton and was off to work at Goldman Sachs in New York for a couple of years, and then back to Washington to work in private equity.

When I look back on my life so far, a definite pattern emerges—a series of segmented blocks of about ten years devoted to service in some shape or form. I spent ten years training to be a surgeon in a cutting-edge field; ten years building and running a new type of heart transplant center that brought multiple specialties together; and twelve years serving Tennesseans in the U.S. Senate. Now, God willing, I have another ten to twelve years of productive professional life to look forward to. I've learned that there are many ways to serve; pursuing one's passions has a way of busting open those doors of opportunities to serve.

When people ask me what I'm doing these days, I explain that my time and energy outside of family are divided into three buckets. All three continue the common thread of a lifelong commitment to health, hope, and healing.

The first bucket grows, in part, out of my years in politics. It's focused on reform of America's dysfunctional health-care system.

As I've explained, health-care issues were the major policy concern of mine during my two terms in the Senate—a somewhat unusual choice for a conservative Republican, but a natural one for me. The most significant legislation that I helped develop and bring to fruition was the Medicare prescription drug bill, which brought affordable coverage of life-saving drugs to millions of older Americans. This bill introduced many reforms, but it represented just a first step in the more comprehensive overhaul that our national health-care-delivery system needs. True reform has been on the national agenda for the past fifty years, but it has not yet been accomplished. It will take a huge public-private partnership and commitment, even after legislation passes.

I'm often asked to describe my blueprint for an improved U.S. health-care system. Naturally, I don't have all the answers—no one person does—and this book is not the place for a detailed discussion of health-care policy. But there are a handful of guiding principles that I've come to focus on, both as a physician in the field and as a policy maker shaping the landscape, principles that I hope will be in the forefront of any plans to be developed by the new administration and Congress.

For me, a twenty-first-century American health-care system should be *patient-centered, consumer-driven,* and *provider-friendly. Patient-centered,* in that the well-being and needs of individuals must be at the heart of every decision we make. *Consumer-driven,* in that individuals should make decisions that drive value and quality. Those who receive care should retain the ultimate control and authority over their treatments, rather than ceding that control to government bureaucrats, insurance companies, or professional organizations that may have their own agendas. And *provider-friendly,* in that the system must make medical professions for nurses and doctors rewarding and fulfilling, limiting the impact of problems like excessive paperwork, intrusive regulation, and out-of-control malpractice suits that too often drive good people away.

That 46 million people are uninsured is wrong. The uninsured die earlier. They represent a major moral and economic challenge for our country—a moral challenge because it's simply unconscionable that citizens of the richest nation on earth can't afford routine medical checkups, preventive care, and essential treatments for curable diseases; an economic challenge because the cost of emergency care for the uninsured represents an unrecognized burden on taxpayers and health-care providers that drags down the efficiency and effectiveness of the entire system.

Most agree today that somehow the millions of hare-core uninsured Americans must be brought into the health-care system. But doing so without creating costly additional layers of bureaucracy, or a gigantic new entitlement program that we simply can't afford in this time of economic recession, represents a genuine challenge. It's not easy to do responsibly. The whole TennCare story in Tennessee demonstrates that the system will implode if you try to insure everyone without intelligently and realistically addressing rising costs. Only by reducing the upward slope of health-care spending—rising almost twice as fast as inflation every single year—will we be able to provide all Americans with a decent, basic level of care over a sustained period of time. So I would advise: Don't legislate universal coverage without simultaneously putting in place a framework to slow the growth of spending. To do otherwise at a time of estimated doubling of our national debt and insolvency of Medicare in just eight years could be devastating to our country.

Fortunately, there are some practical steps that can help us achieve these goals. Implementing twenty-first-century information technologies across the entire health sector will improve efficiencies, reduce errors, make it easier to prevent fraud and abuse, and eliminate countless hours of work by physicians and other professionals who now wastefully reduplicate patient information that has already been gathered and recorded. The legislation on health information technology I introduced with Senator Hillary Clinton in 2005 took a first crack at this. And President Obama's first stimulus package has heavily invested in adoption of electronic medical records. Now it's up to doctors and hospitals to adopt information technology and take full advantage of the promising potential benefits produced by connectivity, data mining, and decision support.

Funding objective comparative effectiveness studies of alternative health-care strategies for particular conditions and treatments and then making the resulting data widely available to both providers and patients will encourage wiser and more efficient choices that will produce better outcomes while saving time and money. Such information empowers consumers to maximize *value* in health care and eliminate waste. When you make a health-care purchase today, you typically don't know exactly what you are getting or how much it costs. No wonder markets in health care are not working and prices are going sky-high. Making accurate, understandable information about outcomes achieved by particular physicians, medical groups, clinics, and hospitals widely available will lead to improved quality. And let's keep walking down the path that our 2003 drug bill set us on—expanding the use of generic medicines, in place of more costly brand-name drugs.

We can eliminate billions of dollars now being spent on administrative costs. One way is to standardize and simplify the complex tangle of bureaucracy that characterizes our current insurance system. The existence of hundreds of private and public insurance plans means that health-care providers must navigate an incredibly complex and confusing ocean of paperwork, regulations, and restrictions, while patients and families find it almost impossible to intelligently compare plans, choose among them, and control the cost burdens borne by them (and their employers).

Forget the single-payer system—that is, a single government-run insurance program like those in Canada or Britain. Recall my personal experience with Britain's National Health Service, where blunt rationing by a few government officials and politicians at the top sharply limits access to the latest developments in health science. Today, you frequently hear practicing physicians speak positively about single-payer systems, mainly out of frustration with the paperwork and myriad regulations that they have to put up with every day as they care for patients. And although systems like that in England do a much better job of guaranteeing basic levels of care for everyone, including the poor, over time a single-payer system that relies on the monopsonistic purchasing power of government discourages innovation, new medical discoveries, revolutionary research, and medical progress. In the long run, the quality of treatment enjoyed by Americans would irreparably suffer under a single-payer program.

Standardizing paperwork and making various health-care plans easier to compare would reduce the hours spent by providers in managing red tape and enhance the ability of families to find the right kind of coverage for them. This requires government regulation. Consumers could then prudently shop, and their millions of daily decisions could shape the system toward value.

There is more to good health than good health care. For the first time, we are raising a generation of children who will live sicker and shorter lives than their parents. Where (and how) we live, learn, work, and play has a greater impact on how long and how well we live than medical care. We now know that brain, cognitive, and behavioral development early in life are strongly linked to health outcome later in life. Policy makers must approach health with the twin philosophies of encouraging individuals to make responsible personal choices and removing obstacles that prevent too many Americans from making healthy choices. Our nation must develop a culture of health.

It's also important to take a step back and ask the larger question, "What are the most important determinants of health in our society today?" Importantly, they are not the doctors, the hospitals, and the health services that might first come to mind. Instead, they are behavior and genetics. They are the so-called social determinants of health—things like diet, exercise, smoking and drinking, basic education, and socioeconomic status. The policy maker has a hand in affecting each of these; indeed, the most overlooked way to improve the health of our citizens is to focus on these social determinants. Improving K–12 education will improve health, which is why I've started a citizen-initiated statewide collaborative called Tennessee SCORE. SCORE is pulling together people from all around the state to address best practices in K–12 education in Tennessee. Improving K–12 education will improve health.

Today, health-care reform is at the top of the national agenda, both for the Obama administration and for Congress. Some in the media and on Capitol Hill express concerns that President Obama is being overly ambitious in trying to reform health care in the midst of the worst economic crisis since the Great Depression. They wonder whether our nation can really afford to fix the health-care system at a time when millions of people are out of work, the flow of credit has practically ceased, and the world economy is actually shrinking.

I would turn the question around and ask: Can we afford to do nothing about a wasteful and inefficient health-care system that drains billions from our economy, weakens the competitiveness of thousands of businesses through excess costs, and yet fails to deliver basic care to far too many of our citizens? We have a moral responsibility, I believe, to see that every single American has affordable access to health care. The need to improve the productivity, fairness, and consistent quality of American health care is deeply intertwined with our economic problems. Fixing health care will help the economy. Thus, I strongly support the administration's determination to act on both fronts simultaneously, great as the challenges will be.

In today's movement for health reform, most of which I strongly support with more egalitarian access and an intense and sharp focus on value (that is, outcomes and results for every dollar invested) and quality not just quantity, I do have one fundamental big red flag to wave: Government cannot run health care.

Although a case has been made that the government can run the automobile industry and banking industry (though I am not convinced), health care is too personal and the science and technology are moving way too fast for slow-moving, lumbering government control. Winston Churchill wisely mused: "It has been said that democracy is the worst form of government except all the others that have been tried." I'd say the same, having been a doctor in the British National Health Service, having worked for years in the federally-run Veterans Administration hospital system here at home (both socialized systems), and having served at the highest level of our government, when it comes to whether government should trump competition, markets, and a business approach in health-care discovery and delivery.

Why?

First, politicians run government. My colleagues in the Senate aren't businessmen; they are politicians. That is who they are and that is how they will behave. They think short-term: Washington is a two-year town and not a twenty-year town. Remember, Medicare is going bankrupt in just eight years! But the politician is always focused on that next election—the one in two years. And politicians, since the rare exception is the one who comes to town as a self term-limited citizen legislator, will be loyal first and foremost to the immediate whims of those citizens who will elect him in the next election. As the senator from Tennessee, I, of course, will look first and foremost to the interest to the almost 7 million people from Tennessee. And that is what a politician should do, but that is not necessarily what one running the enterprise of health care should do.

Second, government is inefficient. Thirty percent of the health-care dollar is wasted through overuse, underuse, and misuse. The only way to root out the waste is achieving efficiency. And the federal government is not good at efficiency. In fact, the body I led, the Senate, was specifically designed by our Founding Fathers to be inefficient, slow, and deliberate and removed from the passions of the people. The Senate's proverbial role, as defined by Thomas Jefferson and George Washington, was to be the saucer into which the hot tea is poured to be safely cooled. And that is why we have unlimited debate and why any single senator can bring the body's progress to a halt. That's good for government but not good for the entity running health-care delivery.

This same inefficiency is engrained in our three branches of government. The president of the United States is our nation's leader, but his hands are tied without action by the coequal branch of the U.S. Congress. Such slowness and inefficiency is not consistent with the breathtaking speed at which proteomics and genomics are being introduced daily to save lives of those with cancer.

Third, government spends too much too irresponsibly and, from a former lawmaker's perspective, this is because the government is not spending its money, it's spending someone else's (your) money. "Let's start a new program that will do some good; we can use someone else's money to do it." And the government too often "cooks the books." Government tells us there is a trust fund for Social Security and for Medicare. Is there really? Not by the generally accepted accounting standards. Have we really been running trust fund surpluses for years, or are these just IOUs and government borrowing?

I encourage my colleagues in Washington who seem to be embracing hugely increased government spending and heightened government regulation not to go too far in ignoring the powerful, transforming forces of competition and the profit motive. Unfortunately, government tends to have a strong bias against competition; it does not tolerate having some entities win and some lose based on value. Can government compete on a level playing field in health care? Some believe so, but there is no historical evidence to support this.

So let's have government define the playing field and set the rules. But then let's have individuals and private enterprise, with all their innovation and transforming potential, be the players who lead us to a more equitable, efficient, and effective health-care sector.

Now that I am out of politics and public office, I am free to engage fully. I will continue to make my voice heard as the health-care reform is discussed. The heavy lifting will not come with passing a reform bill, but rather with how the legislation is implemented by the private sector. I will continue to speak out on the lecture circuit, on TV and radio, and through articles and interviews in the print media. In addition, we must train a whole new cadre of leaders who can look at the challenges from a new perspective, in a much more integrated and even out-of-the-box way. With this in mind, I taught two health economics courses last year at Princeton, and this year I am breaking new ground by teaching a truly multidisciplinary course that includes fifteen second-year business students and fifteen fourth-year medical students at Vanderbilt University. I am downloading everything I know about medicine, policy, economics, and politics to this class of bright and committed students; they are the generation who can bring fresh ideas and cross-cultural business/medical solutions to the problems that plague us. In time, I hope to bring students from the law and nursing programs into the same course. I believe it is in settings like this that we can cultivate the cross-disciplinary conversations that will be essential to building a health-care system where the incentives for all participants are aligned on value for the patient. The students of today are our salvation for tomorrow.

Over the past three decades, health care has been a black hole of American politics—a seemingly insoluble, incredibly complex set of problems that most in government would rather ignore, or tinker with around the edges, rather than risk their political capital in tackling head-on. But I'm optimistic that we will soon make real progress in collectively developing meaningful solutions. Health care is such a basic necessity—and the economic and human costs of the existing system are so enormous and painful—that Americans of every political persuasion are finally ready, I believe, to coalesce around commonsense approaches.

THE SECOND OF MY THREE BUCKETS OF CURRENT ACTIVITY IS AN extension of the first: the use of private capital and markets to supplement what the government is investing in health services. Government must set the ground rules and establish the broad regulatory framework, but the delivery of health care should remain within the province of the private sector (with the exception of the Veterans Administration system). The private sector brings resources, innovation, efficiencies, and dynamism to the field, which is why my own instincts lean heavily toward creative entrepreneurial ventures. I'm not only a firm believer in the robust value of private enterprise, I've also been a practitioner of it. I'm convinced that the ethical pursuit of profit can be a powerful force for good in the world—a driver of economic growth, innovation, and enhanced quality of life for everyone from the very poor to the affluent. I'm fascinated by the managerial challenges involved in designing, building, and running a successful enterprise. And my brother's experience in founding and developing HCA has demonstrated that for-profit organizations have a vital, constructive role to play in bringing improved health care to millions of people in America and around the world.

Working as a partner with Cressey & Company LP, a private equity firm specializing in middle-market health service investing, I help guide investors' funds neither into brand-new start-up companies nor into large, successful firms, but rather into established midsized organizations that we feel are poised for growth. The businesses that have attracted our interest are involved in a wide range of health-care services, from hospice and home care to behavioral health and laboratory testing. The common thread: All are designed, in one way or another, to improve quality of care for the patient, to broaden access to treatment, or to deliver higher value for the patient through better outcomes and lower costs. Lasting health reform will require true public-private partnerships, and through Cressey & Company, I am focusing today on the private side of this collaboration.

MY FINAL BUCKET CONSISTS OF MY ACTIVITIES IN THE GLOBAL health and poverty arena. This is an outgrowth of that first trip to Lui, Sudan, where I saw with my own eyes the terrible human cost of poverty as well as the potential good that caring citizens with a heart to serve can do. Over the past thirty years, 5 billion people in the world have progressed by most socioeconomic measures; but a billion have gotten progressively poorer. I'm focusing on the "bottom billion," those living on the equivalent of one dollar or less a day, who lack access not only to basic health care but to many of the fundamental conditions that make good health possible: clean water, sanitation, nutritious food, decent shelter.

The good news is that today we know the many things that can work to reverse the plight of those in need around the world. Of the more than 9 million children under the age of five who die every year, two-thirds of those deaths are preventable by inexpensive, proven methods—like simple oral rehydration for treatment of diarrhea, cheap antibiotics, malaria bed-nets, and vaccines. Thus today I work closely with non-profit organizations: recently traveling to Bangladesh with Save the Children to study the use of vitamins to save the lives of newborns, and visiting Mozambique where I performed surgery for later-stage tuberculosis and visited an innovative housing project run jointly by Africare and Habitat for Humanity. These programs work, and are making remarkable, sustainable progress.

Along with my colleague Jenny Dyer, with whom I had worked previously when she was working with Bono on faith-based initiatives, I oversee a remarkable young foundation called Hope Through Healing Hands (see Hopethroughhealinghands.org), which serves as the umbrella organization for all our global health activities. To date we have supported HIV initiatives for over thirty thousand of the poor in Middle Tennessee through Project CORE; provided resources to Save the Children to support five thousand community health workers in the poorest communities around the world; established health education resources for more than one hundred thousand Latino churches around the world; invested in the faith-based international HIV/AIDS relief program of Franklin Graham's Samaritan's Purse; and contributed half a million dollars to the building of an education center for HIV-affected families with the remarkably successful TASO program in Uganda. In 2010, we are sending eight student-scholars to Africa and Central and South America to gain experience and understanding as they serve the neediest of the world. We started this organization from scratch just five years ago. It is non-profit, built on the shoulders of thousands of volunteers, and a powerful example of how something that starts as a small idea can rapidly grow to have major global reach.

I still keep one foot in Washington through my board participation with the Millennium Challenge Corporation (MCC). It's a fairly new, U.S. government–funded global development organization whose goal is to reduce poverty by promoting long-term economic growth in some of the world's poorest nations. The MCC demands absolute accountability for the taxpayer money we invest. We do so by using seventeen objective indicators of good governance, economic freedom, and wise investment in human resources to determine those countries where substantial U.S. taxpayer assistance through public-private partnerships will have the greatest impact in reducing poverty in a sustainable way. MCC investments focus on infrastructure, agricultural productivity, health care, water, sanitation, education, and private-sector development. This is one development program where I know taxpayer dollars are being used wisely for sustainable impact in the developing world.

And finally in this third bucket of global health, I continue my medical mission trips overseas. Over my years in the Senate, I visited or worked as a physician in thirteen African countries, including conflict areas such as Darfur, southern Sudan, and the Congo. Now I can stay a little longer and do a little more. In July 2008, I led a small delegation to Rwanda with Tom Daschle for the ONE Campaign, to study the effectiveness of current U.S. initiatives such as PEPFAR, the MCC, and antimalarial programs. Though I have spent much time decrying the lack of civility and partisanship in Washington, D.C., I also wish Americans could witness the inspirationally positive occasions like our recent trip to Rwanda. It was a motley crew that spent four days together in a tiny bus traveling the countryside of the most densely populated country in Africa: Tom Daschle; Cindy McCain (wife of then presidential candidate John McCain); John Podesta (president and CEO of the Center for American Progress, former chief of staff to President Clinton, and head of President Obama's transition team); Mike Huckabee (former Arkansas governor and 2008 Republican candidate for president); and me. Did you see coverage of our journey on the news? I bet not. It's a side of Washington that is rarely featured in today's hyperpartisan media. Let's build on trips like this.

These trips have a huge personal impact. Not only do they remind me of how lucky I am to be an American, with the opportunity to live a rewarding life in which I can develop my skills and interests to their fullest potential, they also keep me grounded in the nitty-gritty realities of life, including the oppressive challenges with which hundreds of millions of people have to grapple every day. Too often, well-intentioned policy makers and academic experts develop programs in isolation from the people they're intended to serve. The result is wasted resources, problems that remain unsolved, and deepening cynicism about the inability of government or nonprofit organizations to make any real headway in coping with such issues as global poverty. Perhaps it would help matters if those charged with devising solutions had to spend a week or two every year working in a concrete-walled clinic in a remote region of Africa, without electricity, running water, or basic medical supplies. It helped give me perspective. At the very least, it would reinforce the urgency of the challenges we have to meet. It might also inject a much-needed note of realism into the plans and programs they create.

My medical missions have helped me to see that a commitment to meeting the health-care needs of the world can be a vital part of American foreign diplomacy in the twenty-first century—for reasons both altruistic and selfish. We know all about hard power when it comes to international relations; it's time we spend a lot more time and focus on soft power, including health diplomacy. Here's a bit of what I wrote about the subject of health diplomacy in a 2008 article in the *Yale Law and Policy Review*:

Why is health such a powerful and universal message of peace and goodwill? The answer lies in large part with the intimacy of one's health, which touches everyone in a personal way.

Health is a basic need, and the desire for good health is universal. Health holds a unique place in human relationships. The most important and powerful times in family relationships are those of failing health. And the most moving and seminal moments are those of healing and relief from affliction and pain. Healthcare delivery, whether vaccination or treatment for tuberculosis, is closely associated with trust.

Health is the source of the most potent of forces in each human: the fear of death and the desire to preserve our own lives and the lives of those we love. Because health is so fundamental to all humans—of all nations, religions, races, and situations—healthcare communicates a remarkable message of understanding and human connection across all boundaries and thus provides a unique, heretofore under-applied, tool of diplomacy.

Healing is an unmistakable and universal message of goodwill. It is the direct opposite of aggression and harm. The message and gestures of health and healing do not require explanation. The message is not encumbered by differences in language. And it does not rely on an abstract political concept of educated people to touch the lives of the poor and oppressed.

Healing a sick person typically does not take years. I am reminded of the simple hernia repairs I completed at Lui Hospital in Sudan, procedures that take only an hour but are lifesaving in that particular region because of the high risk of fatal obstruction. The simple act builds trust.

Moreover, sickness can be prevented. Twenty-eight thousand children die every day in the world, but two-thirds of those deaths are preventable with tools that today are proven and inexpensive. And that is fundamentally why public health diplomacy is today, more so than anytime in the past, ripe for use as a currency for peace. Curing the diseases of the world is not just about charity, it is about increasing cooperation and harmony in a global society.

Using healthcare enlivens the diplomacy of inspiration rather than simply intimidation. You do not go to war with someone who has saved the life of your child. What a difference it would make if more people in the world found themselves saying, "The Americans helped heal our children."

The trust established through healing and the delivery of medicine and the understanding that comes from the one-to-one connections and person-to-person intimacy of medicine set the backdrop for peace and understanding. If we remove disease from our neighbor's struggles, then our own security is bolstered. And through medicine, health, and saving lives, we secure a future with potentially fewer enemies with whom to struggle.

Health diplomacy—built upon the compassion and generosity of those who employ it—helps undermine the support of the extremism and radicalism that is spreading so insidiously around the world. Medicine is a currency that overpowers division and hatred. It can foster peace and, as a by-product, radically change America's position, credibility, and respect throughout the world.

Yes, health can be a currency for peace. In the years to come, whatever else I do in my life, continuing to participate in and promote health diplomacy will certainly be high on my personal agenda. Even as it provides hope and comfort to others, it enriches my life and the lives of Karyn and the boys in ways that are difficult to quantify or explain—but that I know my own father with his simple and basic values would have understood and appreciated.

So as I turn the page on medicine and politics, I do so with a few final reflections. I continue to believe that our country needs citizen legislators, people who will come out of the private sector to serve for a season, bringing their particular expertise to bear on our problems, and then returning to everyday life to serve as ordinary citizens. I believe our government could be greatly strengthened by more citizen legislators and fewer career politicians, more people who understand what it takes to earn a dollar in the real world, and less who have lived off the public payroll for most of their careers. I believe we need more people who will refuse to accept the status quo as normative, whether it is in health care or K-12 education, and will aspirationally seek innovative solutions.

My communications director Amy Call came into my Capitol office one day, upset and fretting over a computer problem we were experiencing in our communications office. The computer tech said that what we wanted to do was impossible. When Amy relayed his message to me, I replied, "Amy, don't tell me it can't be done. It *can* be done. Go tell them to figure out how."

Amy looked at me for a moment, turned on her heel, and went to find the computer guy. She relayed the message forcefully and with assurance: "Don't say it can't be done. It *can* be done. Figure out how." And he did!

That is a message for our nation. In every field, barriers exist where experts say, "It can't be done." It's what I heard when I wanted to do heart transplants in Boston, and when I first decided to run as a doctor for the Senate. But from what I've witnessed, I've come to believe that in America almost anything can be done. We just need to figure out how to do it. We all need to find our Shumways, our Tommy Frists, our Howard Bakers, to inspire us to take on the next challenge.

Holding office in America is not an end in itself—or at least it shouldn't be. But it is one means of helping, an opportunity to serve. Helping people and giving hope, finding solutions to seemingly insurmountable problems, and making a real difference in the world brings an incredible amount of significance and value. It can be by working in a lab, donating a kidney, volunteering with the poor in Southeast Washington, or spending time reading to your daughter. It's the passion to serve that counts. I'm so glad that I don't *need* the U.S. Senate or any other office to bring meaning to my life. I've found an inexhaustible source of meaning in my love for Karyn, that woman I fell in love with the moment I first saw her in a clinics building at the MGH, my three boys who leave me proud each and every day, my faith in God, my friends, and hopefully in some of the things I've been able to accomplish along the way that makes others' lives a little more fulfilling.

For twelve years, I was defined by Washington standards, and during the last two years of my term, I was defined by some of my fellow senators and the press as a potential candidate for president. They tried to analyze everything I did by how that might play as a candidate. It was beyond the pale of their imaginations that anyone could do something in Washington without political calculations.

I understand that, but I choose to have a different formula. One of the unwritten rules of being majority leader is that you never take a piece of legislation to the Senate floor that you can't pass, that you don't know that you have the votes to win. But to me, it was worth it to bring certain issues to the floor whether we could win or not. I preferred to push something out there and bring some attention to the issue, even if we lost the vote. We did that with medical tort reform, which we lost time and time again, but it set the stage for state reform around the country. We did it with expanded school choice for children living in the District of Columbia. It pays to lead on principle even if you don't always win.

I'm often asked these days if a good man or woman can actually make a difference in government. While acknowledging the difficulties and all the negatives of public life, I always respond affirmatively. Good men and women must get involved with government; they must risk the humiliation and insults of running for public office, they must risk the potential of baseless investigations that strike at their integrity, they must risk public ridicule when they act to protect those with disability. It is vital that they do so.

John Adams expressed it so well when his son showed an interest in seeking public office:

Public business, my son, must always be done by somebody. It will be done by somebody or other. If wise men decline it, others will not; if honest men refuse it, others will not. A young man should weigh well his plans. Integrity should be preserved in all events, as essential to his happiness, through every stage of his existence. His first maxim then should be to place his honor out of reach of all men. In order to do this he must make it a rule never to become dependent on public employments for subsistence. Let him have a trade, a profession, a farm, a shop, something where he can honestly live, and then he may engage in public affairs, if invited, upon independent principles. My advice to my children is to maintain an independent character.[1]

I'd say something similar to Jonathan or Bryan or Harrison, my own sons, if they chose to enter public service. No, it is not easy; it is not lucrative—or at least, it should not be. But it is essential that good people get involved. As Dad so often said, "Good people beget good people."

Yes, of course, some men and women in American politics are more self-serving than they are public servants, but their isolated, poor examples should not denigrate all, nor impugn the entire system. Certainly these abominably selfish people bring disgrace on a noble and honorable means of serving our country, and demoralize many young men and women from wanting to become involved in pursuing public office, but we must not allow the improprieties or insincerities of some to tarnish the many truly great men and women who have given themselves tirelessly, often at great cost to themselves and to their families, to help improve our nation. And you mustn't shirk the responsibility or shy away from the opportunity to serve your country in whatever way you can. Kid Rock shows you don't have to be a politician to serve and celebrate the greatness of America. As Dr. Martin Luther King, Jr., put it: "Everyone can be great . . . because anyone can serve. You only need a heart full of grace, a soul generated by love." America is worth working hard to maintain; our nation has always been and will always be a risky venture; but it is worth it.

America desperately needs innovative solutions to seemingly insurmountable problems; we can find them and we can implement them. In my life and yours, let's commit to serve others—in healing, in politics, in faith, in education, and in charitable work. We all have a duty to do so. God will help us, as we each manifest a heart to serve.

ACKNOWLEDGMENTS

A Heart to Serve has been a long time in the making. The initial concept was to tell a story of service. It evolved into a call to action for each of us to discover our own passions and channel them toward service. The one constant from the outset has been fellow Nashvillian, writer and friend, Ken Abraham, who has traveled with our family literally around the world and interviewed hundreds of individuals to accurately capture and depict the nuances of serving others. To him I am deeply indebted.

"I promise this is the last draft." The words ring hollow to Karyn who lovingly tolerated not only my time spent writing this work but the thousands of nights away doing transplants, doing surgery in Africa, or addressing the interests of Tennesseans while in the Senate.

Many people gave generously of their time, energy, and advice to make this volume possible. Dad's "good people beget good people" philosophy leads me to begin with my selfless Senate and political staff, whose interviews and conversations enriched this work: Emily Reynolds, Mark Tipps, Linus Catignani, Bart VerHulst, Amy Call, Dean Rosen, Mitch Bainwol, Dawn Perkerson, Liz Hall, David Schiappa, Sue Ramthun, Marty Gold, Allen Hicks, Brandi White, Alex Vogel, Lee Rawls, Eric Ueland, Gus Puryear, Ken Bernard, Nick Smith, Mark Esper, Michael Miller, Andy Olson, Allen Moore, Meredith (Medley) and David Broome, Graham Wells, Ginny Wolfe, Rob Hoppin, and Kate Linkous, and so many more to whom I will be eternally grateful.

Special heartfelt thanks goes to Matt Lehigh, my former press aid then executive assistant as we transitioned from Senate life back to Nashville. And, of course, not a day went by in the Senate that I wasn't given marching orders by my right-hand assistant and longest serving staffer Ramona Lessen, the glue to the Senate Frist team. To all the other staff who made it all happen, thank you for your service to America.

The Sudan chapter and all of my subsequent work in HIV globally rests principally on the shoulders of my African traveling companions: the remarkable surgeon whose Christian faith and commitment to healing continues to inspire me daily, Dr. Dick Furman; his best friend and leader of Samaritans Purse, Franklin Graham; and on the ground and in the bush, Kenny Isaacs and Scott Hughett, who taught me safety and survival—and how to give anonymously. And I thank, for her contributions to the book but also for her commitment to the underserved around the world, Jenny Dyer, who brings hope around the world by overseeing our foundation, Hope Through Healing Hands.

The book would not have been possible without the indirect participation of my brothers and sisters who indelibly colored the pages on family and values. Cole and Corinne Barfield both traveled to Lui, Sudan, and both today dedicate their professional lives to service through healing; Dad would be proud.

I remain deeply grateful for the support over the years by Tom Nesbitt and John Gibson, both of whom I have known since the first grade, both of whom are doctors, and both of whom provided fond recollections that I had long forgotten. I want to thank Dr. Karl VanDevender and Dr. David Charles for their input and joining me on medical trips to Africa and Russia, and my former collaborator Charlie Phillips for his notes from the transplant years. To jog my memory along the way were Jean Ann and Barry Banker, Denise and Steve Smith., Ed O'Lear, and Tracy Frazier.

I owe a deep debt of gratitude to photographer Farris Poole who shot the cover transplant shot; over a five-year period Farris dramatically documented my seemingly whimsical journey from transplant surgeon to Senator. Photographers John Howser from Vanderbilt and Steve Starr with Samaritans Purse dramatically captured the emotions of the moment of transplantation and humanitarian work in Africa.

It all began with the incomparable advisor, agent, and friend to all, attorney Bob Barnett, who introduced me to the dynamic publishing team at the Hachette Book Group's Center Street imprint, led by Rolf Zettersten. I have deep appreciation for the diligence and enthusiasm of his colleagues, including Whitney Luken, Katie Schaber, David Palmer, Shanon Stowe, Chris Murphy, and Pamela Clements. To the entire team at Center Street/ Hachette Book Group, your professionalism is deeply appreciated. I owe a deep debt of gratitude for preparation of the manuscript to Chris Walker, Christi Gibbs, Ellen Williams, and Lee Barfield, and to Karl Weber who made valuable editorial contributions that helped shape the final draft. And especially to Jane Lynch Crain, who has done it all for me: policy, politics, fundraising, charity work, expert writing—and now masterful assistance in editing a manuscript that had to be artistically shaped and condensed from a work originally four times longer in length.

That's the tip of the iceberg. To all the others I have not mentioned but who have participated invaluably with your stories, your experiences, and your generosity, a big thanks from me.

And most importantly, Karyn and the boys. My family has been the inspiration for service; they have given me unwavering support for all of the days away in medicine, in politics, and in humanitarian work. To Karyn, Bryan, Jonathan, and Harrison, I dedicate this book.

NOTES

11. Unexpected Storm

1. *Washington Week with Gwen Ifill* & *National Journal*, December 6, 2002; http://www.pbs.org/weta/washingtonweek/transcripts/transcript021206.html.

2. *National Journal* magazine; www.nationaljournal.com/pubs/almanac/2006/people/tn/tns1.htm.

3. Transcripts, The White House, Office of the Press Secretary, December 12, 2002; www.whitehouse.gov/new/releases/2002/12/20021212-3.html.

4. Ibid.

5. Senator John Warner, interviewed by Margaret Warner, *News Hour Special Report*: Weekly Political Wrap Archive; December 20, 2002. Online News Hour: Stepping Aside; December 20, 2002; www.pbs.org/newshour/bb/politics/j.

12. Getting It Done

1. Reported by Jonathan Karl, CNN, *Inside Politics*, January 7, 2002, reported at 4:00 P.M. EST. Cable News Network; CNN.com; http://Transcripts.CNN.com/TRANSCRIPTS/0301/07/ip.00.html.

13. When Push Comes to Shove

1. Jonathan M. Katz, "Senator Sold Stock Before Price Dropped; Shares Fell Two Weeks Later," Associated Press, September 21, 2005, p. A 03.

2. Floyd Norris, "What did Bill Frist Know and How?" *New York Times*, September 29, 2005, p. 3.

3. Gethan Ward and Keith Russell, "Insider Trading notoriously hard to prove, lawyers say," *The Tennessean*, September 24, 2005, p. 4.

4. Jeffrey H. Birnbaum and R. Jeffrey Smith, "SEC, Justice Investigate Frist's Sale of Stock," *Washington Post*, September 25, 2005, p. A 01.

5. Ibid.

6. Editorial, "Trusting Mr. Frist," *Wall Street Journal*, September 30, 2005, p. A 10.

7. Ibid.

8. Carrie Johnson, "Frist Sale of Stock Launched in April, Senator and Advisers Discussed It in E-Mail," *Washington Post*, October 1, 2005, p. A 09.

9. Carrie Johnson, *Washington Post; The Tennessean*, April 27, 2007, p. B 1.

14. A Promise Kept

1. David McCullough, *John Adams* (New York, NY: Simon & Schuster, 2001, paperback edition, 2004) p. 415.

INDEX

353